RETHINKING THE U.S.
STRATEGIC POSTURE

An Aspen Institute Book

RETHINKING THE U.S. STRATEGIC POSTURE:
A Report from the Aspen Consortium on Arms Control and Security Issues

Edited by Barry M. Blechman

BALLINGER PUBLISHING COMPANY
Cambridge, Massachusetts
A Subsidiary of Harper & Row, Publishers, Inc.

International Standard Book Number: 0-88410-870-0 (CL)
0-88410-910-0 (PB)

Library of Congress Catalog Card Number: 82-11436

Printed in the United States of America

Library of Congress Cataloging in Publication Data

Main entry under title:

Rethinking the U.S. strategic posture.

Includes bibliographical references and index.
1. United States—Military policy—Addresses, essays, lectures.
2. United States—National security—Addresses, essays, lectures.
3. Disarmament—Addresses, essays, lectures. I. Blechman, Barry M.
II. Aspen Arms Control Consortium.
UA23.R46 1982   355'.033073   82-11436
ISBN 0-88410-874-0
ISBN 0-88410-910-0 (pbk.)

CONTENTS

FOREWORD

In recent years, many of the fundamental assumptions governing decisions on strategic nuclear forces and strategic arms control have come increasingly into question. Popular concerns about the dangers of nuclear war reached new heights during the spring of 1982—both in Europe and North America. The Soviet occupation of Afghanistan and its coercive role in the Polish repression capped a long period of deteriorating U.S.-Soviet relations and raised serious questions as to whether existing defense strategies and postures are appropriate for a mid-term future in which confrontation, rather than cooperation, is likely to dominate. Technology continued to advance, providing both opportunities to exploit new capabilities in the interest of the nation's security and risks that long-standing principles may no longer be valid. Perhaps the most important changes have occurred within the United States itself, where a series of setbacks abroad and continuing political and economic difficulties at home brought about fundamental revisions in American perceptions of the utility of military power, the challenges posed to the nation's security, and the risks and benefits of nuclear arms control.

In recognition of these trends, the Aspen Consortium on Arms Control and Security Issues organized in 1980 a study group on the U.S. strategic posture. The Consortium's intent was two-fold. It sought first to reconsider the basic factors that contribute to decisions about U.S. strategic forces, reexamining and evaluating each assumption to determine if it could withstand the light of present and prospective international reality. The study group's first meeting, in Aspen during the summer of 1980, was devoted to this reappraisal. On the basis of that review, the Consortium then sought through the study group to devise an integrated policy for strategic nuclear forces— one that embraced not only the weapon programs necessary to maintain an adequate military and political balance but that also considered whether and, if so, how negotiations could enhance U.S. security. This was the focus of the study group's second meeting, again in Aspen, during the summer of 1981. A special working group was organized to prepare these recommendations; this group met in Washington on four occasions during 1981 and 1982.

The report reflects this duality of purpose. The first ten chapters— each of which addresses specific aspects of the military, political, and technological context in which decisions about strategic forces must be made—represent the individual efforts of their authors. Although each of these chapters has been reviewed and discussed by many other members of the study group, in the end, each remains solely the responsibility of the individual who prepared it. The final chapter, which contains the study group's recommendations, is the collective effort of the working group and is the collective responsibility of its members.

Decisions concerning strategic forces are complicated by the diversity of factors that affect them. Obviously, past and prospective changes in the threat posed to this country's security and interests by hostile powers, notably the Soviet Union, must be an overriding concern. But these military considerations form only a part of the environment in which decisions about strategic forces must be taken. The first seven chapters of the report discuss several of these basic factors, each of which will have a profound effect on the U.S. strategic posture, just as they have strongly influenced the study group's deliberations.

In the first chapter, Barry Blechman introduces the report by discussing the ways that U.S. strategic forces serve American interests and the dangers that those purposes necessarily imply. In the second chapter, Walter Slocombe looks more closely at American views of the utility of strategic forces, focusing particularly on changing perceptions of appropriate strategic doctrines and weapons capabilities. In the third chapter, William Hyland takes a comparable look from the Soviet perspective, seeking particularly to explain the relationships between Soviet perceptions of the utility of nuclear forces and changes in the size and character of their force posture. In the fourth chapter, Marshall Shulman examines the confluence of these two perspectives, discussing the role of strategic forces and strategic arms control in U.S.-Soviet relations—both in the recent past and the likely future.

The next few chapters deal with three additional influences on strategic weapons and arms control decisions. In the fifth chapter, Christoph Bertram describes how the balance of U.S. and Soviet nuclear capabilities influences European politics and relations between each of the great powers and Europe, illustrating these phenomena with NATO's December 1979 double-track decision to deploy additional intermediate-range nuclear forces and to seek to negotiate limits on these types of weapons. The sixth chapter departs from broad foreign policy considerations. In it, William Perry highlights the major technological developments that will determine both the threats posed to U.S. strategic capabilities and the opportunities to enhance those capabilities through the end of the century. In the seventh chapter, Alan Platt addresses the domestic political considerations that also strongly influence decisions about strategic forces—using the history of the SALT II Treaty to illustrate his points.

Chapters eight through ten are devoted specifically to arms control. In the eighth chapter, Michael Nacht discusses an issue that has remained prominent on the nation's agenda because of both technological developments and political trends: Should the United States seek to amend or terminate the 1972 treaty limiting the deployment of antiballistic missile systems? In the ninth chapter, Michael May discusses an issue that may be fading in prominence but remains important: Should the United States continue to adhere to the terms of the SALT I agreement and SALT II treaty? We move beyond these mid-term issues in the tenth and penultimate chapter. Here, Joseph Nye looks to the longer-term future of arms control, seeking to identify the ways and forums in which arms negotiations may be able to make significant contributions to U.S. security in the years ahead.

The final chapter of the report contains the study group's recommendations. They are not unanimous, since the group was selected deliberately to represent diverse points of view and to be balanced; even so, there was a surprising degree of agreement on many controversial topics. When a consensus could be reached, it is reported as such; when it was not possible to reach agreement, both majority and minority views are presented. Separate statements by four members of the working group are appended to Chapter 11.

The members of the study group represented the variety of substantive considerations that must go into decisions about strategic forces and strategic arms control. Among others, its membership included scientists and engineers, military officers, attorneys, foreign policy and defense specialists, and political analysts. Many of the group's members have served in official government positions, in both Democratic and Republican administrations. Indeed, the study group's members also represented a diverse number of political viewpoints and were balanced between what we may in shorthand refer to as hawks and doves.

The study group was chaired by Barry Blechman, who also edited its report. The working group that prepared Chapter 11 included Edwin Deagle, Sidney Drell, Sidney Graybeal, William Hyland, Spurgeon Keeny, Jan Lodal, Michael Nacht, Joseph Nye, George Rathjens, Brent Scowcroft, Marshall Shulman, Leon Sloss, John Steinbruner, James Woolsey, and myself.

The study's design and report benefited from the comments of individuals who served on its advisory committee including: McGeorge Bundy, Robert Ellsworth, Richard Garwin, Thomas Hughes, Philip Odeen, Wolfgang Panofsky, William Perry, George Quester, George Seignious, Helmut Sonnenfeldt, and Robert Wertheim.

In addition to chapter authors and members of the working group and advisory committee, the following people attended one or both of the Aspen summer meetings: E.C. Aldridge, Richard Burt, Jean-Louis Gergorin, Jean-Marie Guehenno, Michael Getler, Arnold Horelick, Robert Jervis, James Johnson, David Jones, Jan Kalicki, Robert Legvold, Walter Mondale, Jack Ruina, Dmitri Simes, Larry Smith, Strobe Talbott, James Wade, Charles Wolf, Casimir Yost, and Charles Zraket. Robert Soule served as rapporteur for the 1980 meeting; Steven Miller was rapporteur in 1981 and also helped to draft Chapter 11. Participation in the study group's meetings, of course, does not necessarily imply endorsement of its recommendations.

No study in such a dynamic arena as this can separate itself very far from real politik and changing strategic and domestic environments. However, in part because we sought a broader, longer-term perspective and in part because much of this work took place during the transition between administrations, we have sought to eschew concern with specific tactics and detailed prescriptions for near-term actions. Moreover, the field on which the East-West strategic contest is played is much too large to allow a comprehensive approach. For this reason, the study group focused on those issues that seemed most important in the long run and in which it felt it had some competence. The result is imperfect but, we hope, a stimulating and possibly illuminating look at the increasingly labyrinthic problems that face the nation as it strives to survive with peace and freedom.

The Aspen Institute has organized conferences and workshops on various aspects of arms control and international security for more than a decade. This activity has grown from an annual one-week summer workshop in Aspen to several meetings per year at various sites, including an annual conference on European security each June at the Institute's offices in Berlin.

In 1976, the Institute joined with other academic organizations to form the Consortium on Arms Control and Security Issues. Through such a joint effort, each of the participants hoped to make possible an expansion of their own activities concerning these issues and also to provide a basis for a more intensive exchange of information. Three years later it was decided to increase the outreach from the meetings sponsored by the Consortium by issuing publications such as this one, which extend well beyond previous reporting. In addition to the Aspen Institute, the Consortium as presently constituted includes the Foreign Policy Program of the Brookings Institution, the Center for International Studies of Cornell University, the Center for Science and International Affairs of Harvard University, the Center for International Studies of the Massachusetts Institute of Technology, the Graduate Institute of the RAND Corporation, the Arms Control and Disarmament Program of Stanford University, and the Center for International and Strategic Affairs of the University of California at Los Angeles.

The Consortium is grateful to Georgina Hernandez and Erika Stork, who arranged the many meetings of the study group and managed the massive flow of paper generated by the project, and to Carol Franco and Steven Cramer of the Ballinger Publishing Company for their support and encouragement. The unfailing efforts of Nancy Horton for making the arrangements that made the two summer conferences in Aspen both pleasant and effective are also much appreciated. Most of all, I believe all those involved share a sense of gratitude and respect for the long, demanding effort that Barry Blechman has devoted to the seemingly intractable job of clarifying what so many disparate individuals thought. Finally, we are indebted to the Carnegie Endowment for International Peace, which assisted the study in several ways, and to the Rockefeller Foundation, whose support of the Consortium made this study possible.

Paul Doty
March 11, 1982
Cambridge, Massachusetts

1 PERSPECTIVES ON STRATEGIC FORCES

Barry M. Blechman

Questions about nuclear weapons dominate debate on U.S. defense policy within the upper reaches of the executive branch and the Congress and nearly monopolize public discussions of defense issues. This is not surprising; not only are the stakes associated with these weapons extraordinary, but their implications for the nation's security are inherently ambivalent. On the one hand, it is widely accepted that the possession of a large nuclear arsenal is essential to the nation's security and in large part sustains the U.S. role in world affairs. On the other hand, it also is widely understood that when deployed in the arsenals of hostile nations, particularly the Soviet Union, nuclear weapon systems with intercontinental reach pose the ultimate threat to the continued existence of American society.

Despite repeated attempts to bridge this apparent contradiction, no theory defining a coherent role for nuclear weapons in national security policy has successfully withstood the test of time. No one has yet suggested convincingly how to obtain the putative benefits of nuclear strength and yet be shielded from the dangers of nuclear war; the problem remains unresolved intellectually and politically. As a result, whenever the country must decide how many and which nuclear weapon systems to acquire or retire, or how to think about their possible use in wartime, or whether, and if so how, to negotiate their

1

limitation with other nations, it inevitably confronts grave dilemmas and contradictions on fundamental points.

This is not to say that everything about nuclear weapons is contentious; obviously, there is a great deal with which much of the American public would agree. An overwhelming majority, for example, believes that in light of the character of the present and prospective international system nuclear weapons are an unfortunate necessity for American security; few support proposals for the unilateral abandonment of all nuclear weapons. An overwhelming majority also feels that the primary purpose of strategic nuclear weapons is to prevent war—to deter attacks on this nation and its allies; few believe that a full-scale nuclear war between the United States and the Soviet Union would be less than catastrophic. The need for redundancy and diversity in American strategic forces and for maintaining procurement and research and development programs sufficient to avoid falling significantly behind the nuclear force levels and technological state-of-the-art in other nations also passes largely unquestioned. And, finally, opinion polls have shown repeatedly that most Americans want nuclear arms control, accepting the proposition that the nation's security can be enhanced by negotiating equitable and verifiable limits on U.S. and Soviet nuclear forces.

Beyond these basic propositions, however, opinion about the most appropriate U.S. nuclear posture tends to be fragmented. How many strategic nuclear weapons should be deployed? Of what types? For what purposes? How can the United States most effectively deter attacks on itself and its allies? How rapidly should research programs be funded, and what types of new weapons should receive the greatest emphasis? How should resources be allocated between strategic and other types of nuclear weapons and between nuclear and conventional forces? What goals should be pursued in arms control negotiations? What specifically constitutes an equitable and verifiable arms control agreement? These and similar questions permeate debate on American defense policy today, just as they have for the past thirty-five years.

PURPOSES OF STRATEGIC WEAPONS

Perhaps the most fundamental issue concerning strategic weapons is the question of their purpose: Why does the United States acquire and maintain strategic forces? In what ways is the strategic force posture expected to protect the nation's security and support its foreign policies? This is not the sort of question for which the nation's position can be spelled out in one exhaustive document. Rather, the roles that the United States ascribes to nuclear weapons are made evident by a plethora of actions taken or not taken in various situations and by the general impression created by statements of political leaders on numerous occasions. Even so, the positions generally taken set the basic atmosphere for consideration of more specific issues, like the preferred size and structure of strategic forces and the priority to be accorded to arms control negotiations. More importantly, the positions generally taken have significant effects on U.S. foreign relations since at issue, really, is the prominence accorded to the risk of nuclear war.

In a sense, the most pervasive and therefore most important purposes of nuclear forces are served best when no extraordinary actions or statements have to be made to draw attention either to the forces or to their capabilities. The United States' extensive nuclear arsenal—like its huge economic output, dynamic technological infrastructure, dominant financial position, and large standing conventional military forces—is a manifestation of its status as a great power; it needs no advertisements to influence world politics. The nuclear arsenal, indeed, places the United States in an even more special status, defining it as one of the two greatest world powers. Implicitly, all these factors (including the size and capabilities of the strategic nuclear aresenal) condition decisionmakers in other nations to pay attention to expressions of this nation's policies and objectives. Because the United States is both a great conventional military power and one of two nuclear superpowers, it is conceded a certain degree of respect, assuring—all else being equal—that others prefer to avoid challenging its interests.

Unfortunately, all else is frequently not equal; not uncommonly, the United States' willingness to make use of its great economic and military resources to defend its interests or to secure its objectives comes into question. Questions arise not infrequently about the pertinence of the nuclear arsenal and the willingness of U.S. policymakers to risk nuclear war to counter threats to the nation's interests. These are the central issues regarding the role of nuclear weapons in U.S. foreign policy: What is the range of contingencies that U.S. policymakers should seek to deter by recourse to the threat of nuclear war, and in what form and to what degree must those threats be made prominent to attain the desired effect? In short, what types of challenges to U.S. security interests can be blunted by the risks that can be implied by the strategic nuclear arsenal, and what kinds are impervious to them?

These questions are made difficult by the interrelationships among the effects of different instruments of policy, particularly among the effects of different types of military forces. Attempting to analyze the effects of strategic nuclear forces in isolation is necessarily artificial. When the United States takes a position concerning a world event, actors in the situation perceive and are affected by the full range of political, economic, and military levers of policy that the United States—in fact or potentially—can bring to bear. Whether or not U.S. decisionmakers choose to draw attention to the potential role of strategic forces, they are a factor to be considered, remaining in the background as possibly relevant if the situation deteriorates and thus to a degree conditioning the responses of foreign decisionmakers. Nonetheless, for analytic purposes and to facilitate consideration of requirements for strategic forces, it is necessary to attempt to isolate their most important purposes.

At a minimum, of course, we rely on the threat of nuclear war to deter both overt aggression against U.S. territory and also any attempt to coerce this nation by posing the threat of nuclear or conventional attack. The ability of U.S. strategic forces and U.S. conventional military strength to achieve these objectives is not in question under normal circumstances. Our stake in the nation's own territorial and political survival is evident enough to make nuclear threats regarding this objective inherently credible, to a large extent independent of actual capabilities.

But much more is asked of the strategic force posture. Specifically, it is asked to be capable of inducing other nations, particularly the Soviet Union, to avoid lesser challenges to the security interests of the United States and its allies, challenges that could lead to situations in which attacks against them could become possible. Here we enter more controversial territory.

In the first instance, extention of the role of nuclear weapons beyond the basic guarantee of U.S. territorial integrity entails a commitment to make first use of nuclear weapons, if necessary, to defend allies and other vital interests. Such a guarantee, for example, has for years been a central element in U.S. policies concerning defense commitments to the members of the North Atlantic Treaty Organization

(NATO) and to such other close allies as Japan, Australia, and New Zealand. Less overtly, the possibility of nuclear use is a usually unspoken part of the background conditioning U.S. policies regarding certain nations that it has long protected; Israel, South Korea, and Taiwan presumably would fall in this category. In these contexts, strategic forces support foreign policy not only by deterring nuclear attacks against these nations but by contributing to an atmosphere in which cooperation is facilitated between them and the United States and in which potential adversaries are more inclined to seek peaceful means of resolving disputes or, at least, of putting their hostile designs aside for a time.

By contributing to the credibility of U.S. security guarantees to nations like these, U.S. nuclear forces help limit the spread of nuclear weapons to other countries. Nuclear weapon programs in several nations have yielded to U.S. blandishments that such programs threatened continued American willingness to backstop that nation's security, at times only after prolonged diplomatic interactions. Similarly, U.S. nuclear forces and the security guarantees they support can be understood as one of several background factors that have induced some nations, for example, in the Middle East to accept American efforts to mediate local conflicts. In both these roles, U.S. strategic forces quietly serve important foreign policy interests.

Beyond commitments to specific nations, the possibility that nuclear weapons might be used in defense of important interests could be an important implicit or explicit sanction in a variety of situations. A stance that suggests a willingness to risk nuclear war could be a means of defining a vital stake in a situation by making clear the importance attached to particular actions. Steps taken to draw attention to the risk of nuclear war could be a way of lending weight to other expressions of the seriousness of the nation's demands. This has been done in the past. In 1973, for example, the Soviet Union threatened to intervene militarily in the Middle East unless Israel ceased actions that threatened the encircled Egyptian Third Army. The United States responded with a variety of military and diplomatic actions, including moves involving strategic nuclear forces and statements intended to draw attention to the risk that any direct U.S. and Soviet military involvement in the situation could escalate with incalculable consequences. Similarly, when in January 1980 the United States became concerned that the Soviet Union was preparing to intervene militarily into a deteriorating situation in Iran, U.S. government officials also drew attention to the risk that such an action would lead to U.S.-Soviet military conflict that could escalate unpredictably. The actual consequences of the warnings issued in these specific illustrations are controversial; they are clearly valid examples, however, of the ways in which strategic forces—or, more precisely, the risks that those forces can be made to imply—can be used to support diplomacy.[1]

Such, then, are the main purposes of U.S. strategic nuclear forces. Among their credits are the likelihood that these forces have played a major role in preventing large-scale, and particularly nuclear, war for nearly forty years and specifically that they have provided Europe its longest period of peace in modern times. Against these purposes and credits must be set the enormous destruction that would occur if the threats that secure these objectives should materialize and the relationships that are based on nuclear deterrence fail. The balance sheet is uncertain; but, increasingly, Americans have become more aware of the consequences of a failure of deterrence.

THE CREDIBILITY OF
EXTENDED DETERRENCE

For many years, when the United States had a clearly dominant intercontinental nuclear position, nuclear warnings in defense of allies or as deterrents to other threats against U.S. interests could be issued with relatively little risk. Most importantly, when the United States was in a position to attack Soviet strategic forces and be reasonably confident that very few Soviet weapons capable of striking U.S. territory in retaliation would survive, such positions could be adopted with virtually unquestioned credibility. In the mid-1960s, however, when the USSR deployed for the first time strategic forces capable of withstanding a U.S. surprise first strike and retaliating with great effect on American territory, the credibility of positions that depended on a willingness to risk nuclear war became more questionable. Throughout the 1970s, as Soviet strategic capabilities continued to improve relative to those of the United States, increasingly serious questions arose about the prudence of relying on nuclear warnings to support U.S. policy and, conversely, about which, if any, U.S. strategic force posture would make such positions more credible.

Answering these questions depends most importantly on judgments about how nations—most specifically the Soviet Union—make decisions. Such judgments tend to rely on personal assessments that are based on interpretation of the fragmentary information known about Soviet decisionmaking and on such personal qualities as experience and risk-taking propensities.

What, for example, is the effect of uncertainty on Soviet decisions? Some would argue that the effectiveness of nuclear deterrence lies mainly in the awareness of Soviet leaders of the ultimate dangers posed by any extreme crises. In such situations, the use of nuclear weapons might be initiated not because of a conscious decision by central political authorities to do so but rather because of miscalculations about the opponent's reaction to a prospective event; for that matter, events simply could get out of hand. Among other factors, breakdowns in command and control procedures, independent actions by political or military officials, pressures of the battlefield and domestic politics, and the catalytic effects of smaller nuclear powers all could result in the breaking of the nuclear threshold and the unplanned and purposeless escalation of nuclear war once it began. The nuclear arsenals of the two sides are now so large that the ultimate consequences of such an uncontrolled escalatory process are virtually unimaginable. To the degree that these uncertainties are emphasized, it would suggest that all political leaders—including Soviet officials—are likely to be reluctant to enter situations in which nuclear war may become a serious possibility.

The implications of such a perspective are paradoxical, however. On the one hand, it implies that emphasizing the risk of nuclear war may be a means of protecting American interests in many situations, that this would be the case regardless of relative nuclear capabilities, and that the decisive element in making such threats credible (and effective) is an evident willingness to run risks. In short, stress on the uncertainty in nuclear scenarios suggests that U.S. nuclear warnings may be effective because Soviet leaders would fear that nuclear war might result regardless of the seriousness or lack of seriousness with which the threat was made initially. On the other hand, the uncertainties of behavior in nuclear crises suggest that a catastrophic war will not be avoided over the long term so long as the great powers rely on nuclear weapons for deterrence; in other words, policies emphasizing the role of nuclear weapons in foreign policy are imprudent because they tend to aggravate implicit dangers.

A second factor generally believed to influence the behavior of national decisionmakers and thus the credibility of nuclear threats is the evident importance of the interests at stake in the situation. For example, in the case of the U.S. commitment to use nuclear weapons, if necessary, to defeat aggression against the NATO nations, it can be argued that the inherent ethnic, cultural, economic, and political affinities between U.S. and European societies—to say nothing of the location of U.S. troops and their families in Europe—are sufficient to convey a great degree of credibility. This can be enhanced by steps to facilitate the initial use of nuclear weapons and the escalation of nuclear war if that became necessary, such as the development of appropriate doctrine, plans, and the emplacement of nuclear weapons in the potential theater of operations. The basic kernel of credibility, however, would be assessed as deriving not so much from these preparations to fight nuclear wars as from the presumed Soviet perception of the consequences to the United States if its interests in Europe were challenged successfully.

Some would apply this logic to other situations, such as contingencies envisioning Soviet threats to the oil resources of the Persian Gulf, but extension of nuclear deterrence to areas outside those traditionally defined as vital to American security quickly runs into difficult questions about the military capabilities necessary to make nuclear warnings credible. Indeed, given recent trends in relative U.S. and Soviet nuclear capabilities, many now raise such questions concerning the basic extension of the U.S. nuclear umbrella to Europe and Japan. Some of the recent implications of these questions are discussed by Christoph Bertram in Chapter 5.

To argue that the potential deterrent benefits of U.S nuclear forces *should* be extended beyond protection of the United States' own territorial integrity, particularly to counter threats of conventional aggression against U.S. allies, is to suggest that alternative means of securing whatever interest is at stake—means that would permit avoidance of the risk of nuclear war—would be infeasible for political or economic reasons. In particular, it is to suggest that the United States and its allies cannot compete effectively with the Soviet Union in conventional military capabilities or that a shift toward reliance on a purely conventional defense would not be an effective deterrent or would pose other political problems. If these potential problems were not considered valid, the use of conventional military forces could be the primary sanction behind the U.S. commitment, with U.S. nuclear capabilities serving only the presumably less demanding and less risky role of deterring Soviet nuclear aggression.

To argue further that the potential deterrent benefits of U.S. nuclear forces *can* be extended beyond the deterrence of attacks against the United States itself is to suggest that Soviet officials can be made to believe that the United States would be willing to accept grave risks in situations in which its stakes may not be clearly of the highest order. Furthermore, it is to suggest that a U.S. threat to initiate nuclear war—and, if necessary, to escalate such a conflict even to the point of an all-out exchange between the two sides' homelands—can be made believable to Soviet leaders despite their achievement of what is generally described as "rough parity" in overall strategic capabilities with specific advantages in certain types of nuclear forces.

Propositions like these, of course, are quite controversial. They raise the central tangible manifestation of questions about what does and what does not deter: How many and what types of nuclear weapons are necessary to make the strategic force posture credible in whatever ways it is expected to support U.S. foreign policy?

THE REQUIREMENTS OF EXTENDED DETERRENCE

It clearly would be preferable to have strategic forces that were superior to those of the Soviet Union in all respects. Competing demands on U.S. resources, however, to say nothing of the potential of the USSR to match increments in U.S. strategic capabilities, make the attainment of such across-the-board superiority unlikely or at most transitory. Even if superiority is not feasible, however, many suggest that improvements are necessary in the U.S. force posture to make even minimal extensions of the U.S. nuclear umbrella credible.

Politically, it is often suggested that the U.S. force posture must not be seen to be inferior to that of the Soviet Union in any significant aspect. The appearance of such a U.S. disadvantage, it is maintained, may raise questions about the credibility of U.S nuclear guarantees by suggesting that in the event of a confrontation unilateral options would be available to Soviet leaders. As a result, U.S. officials could be placed in the position of having to choose between complying with Soviet demands and threatening to escalate to even higher levels of conflict, a threat that might not be credible because of projections of expected levels of destruction in the United States itself.

Of course, as Marshall Shulman points out in Chapter 4, comparing the U.S. and Soviet force postures is no mean task. The strategic balance is dynamic, and the two sides do not have identical deployment cycles. As a result, the situation can look better or worse depending upon which past year is taken as a benchmark and whether present or prospective future capabilities are selected as the basis for comparison. This phasing problem is compounded by the fact that although U.S. decisions are most often made in public view, and therefore future U.S. capabilities are fairly certain, new Soviet weapons do not become evident publicly until there are tangible signs of their imminent appearance, such as missile flight tests. To hedge our uncertainty about Soviet intentions, we properly base forecasts of their future capabilities on the most conservative assumptions.

The primary difficulty in assessing the strategic balance, however, is caused by the many differences between the two sides' force postures. The United States and the USSR emphasize different kinds of forces: Long-range bombers for the United States and air defenses for the USSR; sea-based missiles for the United States, land-based missiles for the USSR; forces for antisubmarine warfare for the United States, and programs for civil defense for the USSR. The asymmetries between U.S. and Soviet force postures are stark and numerous. Thus, when single components or capabilities are compared in isolation there often appears to be an imbalance—an asymmetry that is then alleged to have adverse political implications. At the same time, insofar as different components have differing advantages and disadvantages, it also is misleading merely to add capabilities together to reach judgments about the overall balance.

The long debate about the consequences of the asymmetrical theoretical vulnerability of U.S. intercontinental ballistic missiles (ICBMs) is the best case in point. Not only is this vulnerability said to make a Soviet first strike more likely in a crisis, but, many maintain, knowledge of this unilateral capability causes Soviet leaders to perceive greater freedom of action well short of such crises and induces leaders in third nations, particularly those dependent on U.S. nuclear guarantees for their security, to pay more careful attention to Soviet demands. A few would take the logic one step further, arguing not only that the United States must do something about the vulnerability of its ICBMs, but that ICBMs must be retained in the force posture in order to avoid appearing as though we had been driven from the land by Soviet weapon developments, a perception predicted to have adverse political consequences of its own.

To many others, this line of reasoning demonstrates the pitfalls of imputing excessive political significance to mechanical comparisons of specific types of nuclear capabilities. The putative adverse political effects just described all hinge on the judgment that in the face of the enormous destructiveness of the two sides' nuclear arsenals, a marginal advantage in a single type of capability could have a significant effect on behavior. It ignores, of course, an enormous array of factors. Most importantly, it does not take account of the basic uncertainty and therefore reluctance to act that would attend any step toward the initiation of war or continued escalation after a war had begun. From this perspective, the potentially incalculable consequences of an all-out nuclear exchange means that caution and prudence are likely to be the rule, as has been the case in those few instances when the great powers have confronted one another in situations that conceivably could have escalated to nuclear war. To believe that a sane Soviet leader would initiate nuclear war, or even doggedly pursue a position implying a risk of nuclear confrontation, on the basis of the kinds of calculations that go into a determination that the U.S. ICBM force may be vulnerable does not square with the past behavior of the nuclear powers. Yet concern about the political effects of ICBM vulnerability hinges on just such a belief.

Militarily, U.S. policy states that the credibility of extended nuclear deterrence must be maintained by a strategic force posture with greater endurance (i.e., an ability to survive repeated enemy attacks), counterforce capabilities (i.e., capabilities to attack opposing military forces and installations), and sufficient flexibility to wage nuclear war in a variety of scenarios and in rapidly changing circumstances. Such a posture, it is believed, would convince Soviet leaders that they could not emerge victorious from a conflict at whatever level it was raised to, thereby providing military incentives to Soviet leaders to end a confrontation before the nuclear threshold had been crossed. From this perspective, even if the Soviets found U.S. threats to make use of nuclear weapons credible, they might be deterred by such threats only if they calculated that they could not stymie the United States by escalating to an even more intense level of warfare. To fulfill these military requirements, as well as to satisfy the political criteria previously described, important changes have been taking place in U.S. strategic doctrine and in the capabilities of U.S. strategic forces. These are discussed at length by Walter Slocombe in Chapter 2.

During most of the late 1960s and early 1970s, U.S. doctrine stressed that to maintain a credible deterrent, U.S. forces should be capable of withstanding a first strike and of retaliating with devastating impact against Soviet economic targets and population centers. In the face of continuing improvements in Soviet strategic forces, however, American planners have come increasingly to embrace the same concept that, as Bill Hyland points out in Chapter 3, seems to lie behind Soviet force planning: To deter nuclear war, strategic capabilities should be adequate to fight such a war and survive. Thus, beginning seriously during the Ford administration and continuing during the Carter and Reagan years, U.S. policymakers have sought to develop targeting plans—and the command and control systems necessary to implement them—that would permit the flexible use of strategic forces against military targets and the defense industries that would sustain a prolonged military effort. At the same time, greater attention has been paid to measures to improve the potential of strategic forces—by strengthening the communications systems connecting them to military and political decisionmakers, and by assuring the invulnerability of the command authorities themselves—to survive repeated nuclear strikes, even if they were carried out over a considerable period of time.

This change in emphasis in U.S. strategic planning also has led to pressures for larger numbers of weapons in the U.S. strategic arsenal, as well as for improving their lethality against hardened point targets such as missile silos. All sorts of nuclear war scenarios can and have been described, most of which envision limited exchanges directed at different types of targets in support of diplomatic bargaining during crises. To determine force requirements, however, the most stressing scenarios must be considered. These typically assume the direct engagement of U.S. and Soviet military forces in Europe or the Middle East, the use of tactical nuclear weapons on the battlefield, and the exchange of nuclear volleys between the two homelands to disrupt the industrial base sustaining the war effort, coerce the opponent into surrender, or achieve some other strategic objective. Not surprisingly, such scenarios require many strategic weapons. Not only would inventories have to be large enough to compensate for those forces that might be destroyed by the opponent's nuclear strikes, but weapon stocks would have to be sufficient to permit attacks on the many potential military and industrial targets while still holding sizable forces in reserve to influence bargaining over the terms of the conflict's resolution.

Many are incredulous at the thought of such a war actually being fought. The assumptions involved about the rationality of decisionmakers under incredible pressures, about social coherence in the face of unprecedented devastation and suffering, about the continuance of effective governmental operations, about the strength of military discipline, and about the effective operation of thousands of machines and millions of people strain the imagination. From this perspective, requirements for strategic forces whose primary purpose is to prevent nuclear war are being determined by calculations that depict an inconceivable war—a sort of nonfulfilling but extraordinarily costly fantasy.

Important technical questions also are raised about the realism of protracted nuclear war scenarios, particularly about the technical feasibility of developing command and control systems capable of functioning effectively during intense or prolonged nuclear exchanges. But even setting aside these reservations about the realism of nuclear war planning scenarios, important questions have been raised about the wisdom of structuring a force posture that aims to deter war on the basis of the requirements for fighting such a war should it occur.

The general concern in this regard is that such planning could actually increase the risk that nuclear would one day occur. By planning to fight nuclear wars, even if the purpose is to strengthen deterrence, the argument runs, the United States and the Soviet Union are developing ways of thinking and patterns of behavior that make nuclear options less extraordinary. In other words, by planning to fight nuclear wars in order to strengthen deterrence and thereby make nuclear war less likely, the two great nuclear powers are in fact making such wars thinkable and therefore more likely.

Particular concern is directed both at programs designed to improve the capabilities of strategic forces to attack opposing strategic assets and at the targeting plans and command and control systems that aim to make flexible use of strategic forces feasible. These steps, some argue, create incentives for the opposing side to attack preemptively in the event of an extreme crisis. These incentives would decline to the extent that each side improved the ability of its forces to survive an attack. If significant components remained vulnerable, the argument runs, once one or the other of the great powers judged that war was unavoidable, it would perceive rising incentives to shoot first, hoping to limit the damage it would suffer in retaliation.

This argument results from a true dilemma. On the one hand, most people can agree that some degree of flexibility is desirable in the force posture. Almost no one advocates a force posture that would launch a massive retaliatory strike on an attacker's cities and industries as the only feasible response to the initiation of nuclear war, no matter what the reason and no matter how large or small were the initial attack. If nothing else, such an attack would invite a similar counterretaliation with similarly devastating results. Yet, on the other hand, it is also true that improving the flexibility with which nuclear forces can be used to some extent also increases the risk that in some future and undefinable extreme crisis the exercise of a limited nuclear option might appear to policymakers to be the best of a poor set of feasible choices; once the nuclear threshold were broken, nobody could be certain that any exchange, no matter how small initially, would remain limited, or of how it would end.

THE ROLE OF
ARMS CONTROL NEGOTIATIONS

A decision to deploy strategic nuclear forces implies acceptance of some risk of nuclear war. The degree of risk may fluctuate in response to international events, but so long as nuclear weapons exist there will be some danger of their use. This danger permits strategic forces to serve all the purposes previously described.

It is in helping to manage the danger of nuclear war that arms control negotiations can play their most important roles. This topic is addressed in several of the following chapters, most comprehensively in Chapter 10, which was prepared by Joseph Nye. A few summary thoughts may provide a conceptual framework for our readers.

First and foremost, the problem of avoiding nuclear war is the problem of establishing stable and mutually acceptable political relations between the United States and the Soviet Union. Such an accomplishment could go a long way toward ensuring international conditions that would not invite situations in which one side or the other might contemplate the use of nuclear weapons. The reestablishment of progress in U.S.-Soviet arms negotiations could help to foster a political climate in which such a rapprochment might become more feasible and sustainable. This is not to say that arms control can serve as the engine for the easing of U.S.-Soviet tensions; far from it. If anything, arms negotiations seem to be more a weathervane of political relations than their determinant. The interactions between the two are complex, however. It is clearly the case that an unbridled nuclear arms competition complicates and makes more difficult the establishment of close political relations. To some extent, progress in controlling the nuclear arms race may also make a positive contribution to better political ties.

Second, arms control negotiations can help to ease the danger that the spread of nuclear weapons to other nations will raise the risk of nuclear war. There is little question that as more nations obtain nuclear weapons the probability of their use will rise, if for no other reason than the multiplication of the dangers of inadvertent, unauthorized, or accidental use. Moreover, if nuclear weapons were to spread to nations with a history of prolonged and intense military conflict, the actual use of those weapons would seem to be likely. While the United States and the Soviet Union may be bitter ideological and political rivals, they have not fought one another directly for more than sixty years; indeed, they were military allies less than forty years ago. Their conflict therefore has a certain abstract quality to it, which makes the actual use of nuclear weapons somewhat less likely. Such is not the case for several pair of potential nuclear weapons states in Asia and elsewhere for whom, one would expect, the possession of nuclear weapons might seem to be of more tangible benefit.

Arms control negotiations can help to limit the spread of nuclear weapons in two ways. Directly, the negotiation of agreements like the 1968 Non-Proliferation Treaty and arrangements to help implement and monitor the undertakings contained in that agreement can make it more difficult for states without nuclear capabilities to obtain them. Indirectly, to the degree that the nuclear powers manage through negotiations to contain the role of nuclear weapons in their foreign policies and to reduce the size of their nuclear arsenals, they would strengthen the ethical and political basis of their efforts to persuade others not to develop nuclear weapons capabilities.

Third, the danger of nuclear war also depends to some extent on the character of the two sides' force postures. The previous discussion of the possible adverse effect of building greater flexibility into strategic forces illustrates this phenomenon. Arms negotiations potentially could permit the United States and the Soviet Union to adjust their force postures in tandem in order to correct (or avoid) the most dangerous instabilities in the military balance. By reaching agreements specifying mutual limitations on their strategic forces, the two great powers could move together to contain and reduce whatever incentives may have been provided by the characteristics of their strategic weapons for one or the other to initiate a nuclear strike. Such agreements also could reduce planning uncertainties and therefore pressures for larger and more unstable deployments. Over the long term, agreements could help to channel weapons research away from areas that could raise questions about the stability of the strategic balance, as suggested by William Perry in Chapter 6.

Finally, arms negotiations could contribute to a political atmosphere in which mutual suspicions and extreme interpretations of events—both of which, under certain circumstances, could lead to a greater risk of war—find it more difficult to flourish. Informal discussions between representatives of the two side could help answer troubling questions about certain activities observed by national means of intelligence; conversely, such a forum could be used to make clear to the other side what types of activities, statements, or doctrines on its part raised suspicions. It also might be possible to negotiate specific measures that could build confidence on the two sides that the other did not have hostile intent. Such things as prior warning of weapon tests, the facilitation of the monitoring of such tests by national technical means of intelligence, the placement of unmanned sensors on the territory of the other state to warn of missile launches, and the prohibition of certain deployment areas or activities by strategic forces have all been suggested as potentially valuable means of building confidence between the two great nuclear powers and thus reducing the danger of nuclear war.

Arms control negotiations could serve other important purposes as well. Among other things, for example, they help relieve the strain that prospective weapon programs are likely to place on both nations' economic situations. But the primary purpose of arms control talks is to reduce the risk of nuclear war. In contemplating how best, if at all, these negotiations might be revived and promoted, it is important not to lose sight of this overarching goal.

NOTES

1. See, for the Iranian incident, Barry Blechman and Douglas Hart, "Dangerous Shortcut," *The New Republic* (July 26, 1980), 13–15; for the 1973 crisis, Barry M. Blechman and Douglas M. Hart, "Nuclear Threats as Instruments of Foreign Policy," *International Security* (Summer 1982).

2 THE UNITED STATES AND NUCLEAR WAR

Walter Slocombe

This chapter examines changing U.S. views of how nuclear weapons can contribute to the protection of U.S. international interests. Since U.S. views of the utility of nuclear weapons are inextricably bound up in the history of the development of the nuclear forces themselves, it begins with a review of that history.

Historically, the role of strategic nuclear forces in American doctrine has been an amalgam of three issues: First, and by far the most debated as an approach to strategic nuclear policy, has been the problem of how best to deter a Soviet attack on the United States itself. This discussion, shaped perhaps by memories of Pearl Harbor, has focused on a complete surprise attack as supposedly the most difficult defense problem. It has directed markedly less analysis to the problems of maintaining deterrence in the midst of a deep crisis, of mobilizing after strategic warning (the true failure in 1941), and of maintaining limitations on warfare and control over forces after a nuclear exchange had begun.

The second issue, and the most important diplomatically and politically, has been the effort to maximize the degree to which U.S. nuclear forces contribute to deterring an attack on American allies. This concern reflects the single fundamental fact about postwar international security issues: The United States, unlike the USSR, has real allies whose protection, in its own interest, it is deeply concerned to assure and yet who are distinct and genuinely independent states with different and sometimes conflicting perspectives. In this context, political factors of choice, decision processes, and potential divergences of interest have a prominence unmatched as concerns the first issue. At the same time, more technical issues of weapons characteristics are less prominent.

The third issue, and least discussed, has been the shaping of U.S. operational doctrine—how the weapons would be used if war came, for whatever reason. One particular problem is the balance between the ultimate deterrent of a retaliatory threat to destroy cities and industry—the concept that has dominated public debate—and the targeting of intercontinental strategic nuclear forces on military installations—where in fact the main operational effort has long been directed. Similarly, a continuing but little discussed operational issue has been limitations on the decisionmakers' ability to command the forces, should it ever be necessary to use them.

This chapter reviews briefly the historical development of these issues and outlines how they can be addressed, if not resolved, successfully in the coming decade. The fundamental thesis of the argument is that more attention should be given in the future to the less discussed issues of deterrence in grave crisis and the role of nuclear weapons in deterring attacks on or coercion of U.S. allies.

THE HISTORICAL BACKGROUND: HIROSHIMA TO CUBA

Until around 1950, the United States had very few deliverable weapons even though it had a monopoly on nuclear weapons technology. At the beginning of the postwar era, this perceived shortage dominated thinking about the strategic significance of nuclear weapons. Indeed, the controversy over building the hydrogen bomb was in part cast as a choice between a few large fusion weapons and larger numbers of fission bombs to improve target coverage.

In numbers and capabilities, delivery systems were not far ahead of the bombs themselves. As a part of the general reorientation of the United States toward a historically unaccustomed world role, the early Cold War years saw the gradual deployment of aircraft capable of carrying nuclear weapons. In 1948, B-29s were sent to Britain: Nuclear weapons were not sent with them, but as the carrier of the bombs that destroyed Hiroshima and Nagasaki, the B-29 was in the immediate postwar years a symbol of American nuclear potential. Later, the giant part-jet B-36, deployed in the United States, was relied on as the principal U.S. delivery system for nuclear weapons. The early 1950s saw not only the deployment of the medium-range, all-jet B-47 aircraft at a number of bases around the world, but also the initial decisions that led to the later deployment of the all-jet intercontinental B-52 bomber and, building on captured German efforts, the first U.S. work on ballistic missiles.

During the 1950s—that is, during the very height of the Cold War— the United States relied on what by today's standards seems a numerically limited and highly vulnerable force—B-47s at a variety of peripheral bases, B-36s and later B-52s in the United States itself, and, toward the end of the period, medium-range ballistic missiles deployed overseas as a stopgap. Not until the early 1960s did the United States begin to deploy large numbers of highly survivable forces designed explicitly for the purpose of attacking the Soviet homeland—B-52s, Polaris submarines, and Minuteman intercontinental ballistic missiles.

From the beginning, however, the U.S. government recognized that nuclear weapons—both because of their destructiveness and because of their potential, in the hands of others, to make the United States directly vulnerable to unprecedented destruction—had changed the historic role of military force. The Soviet Union's initial atomic bomb test in 1949 came sooner than U.S. scientific intelligence anticipated, but that test only accelerated, perhaps exaggeratedly, perceptions of new American vulnerability. The image of what nuclear weapons could do had been shaped by the devastation of Hiroshima and Nagasaki and reinforced by the postwar experiments at Bikini. In a sense, the widespread (whether or not historically accurate) view that the two atomic bomb attacks on Japan had forced Japan's prompt surrender and avoided a bloody amphibious invasion by what would subsequently be called conventional forces probably created high public and official expectations of the politically critical role of nuclear weapons. The history of U.S. nuclear doctrine—as reflected both publicly in weapons debates and declaratory policy and also internally in generally still-secret details of operational plans—has been one of efforts to realize in practice these expectations of the crucial role of nuclear weapons in U.S. security policy.

The basic issue of the utility of nuclear forces for the United States has been twofold. First has been the issue of extended deterrence: How can nuclear weapons contribute to the prevention or defeat of Soviet efforts to attack U.S. interests and friends in distant areas? Soon after 1945, the United States perceived itself as needing a military defense at the perimeter of Soviet power under conditions in which the Soviet Union would be likely to have a substantial conventional military advantage. In relation to this issue, there has been continual tension between two views. On the one hand, there are those who urge trying directly to offset the Soviet conventional advantage and, on the other, those who suggest compensating for it by a willingness to employ nuclear weapons quickly. In that debate, the offsetters are challenged to show how the United States and its allies can possibly hope to match the size of Soviet forces, while the compensators have to explain not only how threats to use nuclear weapons could be made credible enough to deter the USSR but also how their use would produce a militarily decisive result against a determined—and also nuclear-armed—adversary.

The second issue is also longstanding: What is required to deter a direct Soviet attack on the United States? Though it is a thesis of this chapter that the issue of extended deterrence is both more critical and more difficult to solve, it has been this latter issue that has received primary attention in the public and, indeed, in much of the official debate on nuclear issues.

Throughout the nuclear era, the impact of Soviet nuclear capabilities and doctrine on American forces and plans has been far more a product of the general view of Soviet intentions and overall military capabilities, and of overall U.S.-Soviet relations, than of the specific characteristics of Soviet forces. For example, in the early era of forebodings of an imminent Soviet attack on Europe, the United States was virtually immune from a Soviet strike. Indeed, in the most tense years of the Cold War, the Soviet Union had only a limited capability to strike even Western Europe with nuclear weapons. Accordingly, U.S. and European military thinking was dominated by the problem of providing a credible deterrent against the perceived threat of massive Soviet conventional military capabilities. Doubts about the efficacy of relying chiefly on U.S. nuclear weapons for this mission were roused more by recognition in official military circles of the limits on U.S. nuclear capabilities than by concerns about Soviet nuclear forces—even though public opinion had an accurate (if slightly anticipated) sense of the potential of Soviet nuclear power. By the mid- to late 1950s, however, the Soviet Union's ability to attack Western Europe with nuclear weapons had become formidable in fact as well as in popular impression. Throughout the 1950s, this nuclear threat to Western Europe increasingly was joined by a potential to attack the United States as well. Concomitantly, the Atlantic alliance began to face more seriously the realities and costs of attempting to match Soviet conventional capabilities directly.

In an effort to resolve this dilemma, the United States, broadly supported by its European allies, sought to plan more explicitly how to exploit its nuclear potential for defense of the alliance. In part, this goal manifested itself in the deployment of medium-range and tactical weapons, initially because of their supposed ability to make a decisive difference in a conventional battle. More fundamentally, the United States—joined, at least formally, by its allies—adopted the doctrinal position that in the event of a Soviet attack threatening critical American interests, the United States would use nuclear weapons more or less automatically. To buttress the plausibility of this contention—merchandised by some of its enthusiasts as treating nuclear weapons as "just another weapon"—the United States pressed the development of nuclear weapons for tactical missions.

The logic of tactical nuclear weapons was—and remains—twofold: More flexible and usually smaller in yield than intercontinental weapons, they could be used on targets where destruction would directly affect, in theory at least, the military situation in the field. Still more important, because of their smaller size and direct military role—and, some would argue, their immediate deployment with battlefield forces—they would seem more likely to be used and thereby contribute to the credibility of deterrence. Indeed, one view was that the principal function of tactical nuclear weapons was not really tactical but strategic; they served as a link in the chain of escalation to a general nuclear exchange.

From the beginning and despite these technical innovations—which certainly did greatly increase U.S. flexibility and added a vast new range of risks to a Soviet attack—the effort to use nuclear superiority to deter conventional conflict in Europe faced questions on grounds of both credibility and military effectiveness. As Soviet nuclear forces became more capable—and particularly as Soviet theater nuclear forces began to be roughly equivalent to U.S. tactical forces—it was perceived to be unlikely that a decisive military result could be attained through use of tactical nuclear weapons. At the same time, realization that general escalation touched off by use of tactical nuclear weapons would likely result in massive destruction to Western Europe and eventually to the United States led to questioning whether the availability of these forces fully solved the credibility problem. As a result of these doubts, observers on both sides of the Atlantic, but particularly in the United States, began to challenge the adequacy for alliance purposes of an extended deterrence policy of relying on U.S. superiority in numbers and flexibility of nuclear forces.[1] This questioning was accelerated and exacerbated during the 1950s by exaggerated U.S. views of the rapidity of the Soviet nuclear buildup, first in respect to bombers and later and even more widely in respect to ballistic missiles.

Throughout the late 1950s and extending into the first half of the 1960s, the objective situation was that the United States had lost its nuclear monopoly. That is to say, because Soviet nuclear forces had become sufficiently numerous, even the most effective U.S. first strike against Soviet nuclear forces that could reasonably be expected could not be relied on to prevent vast destruction if the Soviets retaliated against Western Europe. Moreover, as Soviet intercontinental forces grew, it became impossible to deny the USSR the capacity to retaliate with considerable damage against the United States itself. Still, the United States maintained during this period a plausible claim to counterforce dominance. That is, U.S. strategic forces were far more numerous, and there was no question that the United States could by use of nuclear weapons do vastly more damage to Soviet military potential than the Soviet Union could to American military forces. Even with respect to civilian targets, damage to the Soviet Union would have been far greater than damage to the United States, though Soviet capability against Western Europe and other U.S. allies offset this advantage, at least partially. At the same time, the destructiveness of nuclear weapons was recognized to be such that the absolute levels of destruction—probable destruction in the United States and certain destruction in Western Europe—would have been beyond all historical experience, a perception that increasingly affected Western views of the significance of these differences.

In retrospect, the United States' nuclear superiority and counterforce dominance during this period was probably an important element—perhaps more important than U.S. leaders realized at the time—in counseling Soviet caution and in building U.S. confidence.

In two tense, potentially nuclear crises of that era—the prolonged Berlin confrontation and the brief but much more intense Cuban missile crisis of 1962—it seems in retrospect that Soviet consciousness of U.S. nuclear advantage was almost certainly one of the factors inhibiting their willingness to press initiatives to their logical conclusion. Particularly, such Soviet sense of relative nuclear disadvantage joined to other factors, including unquestioned American local conventional superiority, gave President Kennedy a psychological advantange in the Cuban missile crisis of 1962.

The effect of U.S. strategic advantages on American attitudes is less clear. Confidence in strategic capabilities could hardly have been without some effect on general behavior and public confidence. However, with loss of the U.S. nuclear monopoly and immunity also came realization that even if only a few Soviet weapons survived a U.S. attack, they could inflict terrible damage on the United States and even more on its allies. Accordingly, there was widespread uneasiness during this period about relying on U.S. threats of general nuclear escalation to respond to local crises.

EXTENDED DETERRENCE: FLEXIBLE RESPONSE

Continued U.S. nuclear superiority, and even counterforce dominance, postponed but did not prevent divergences between the United States' and its allies' views of the requirements of extended deterrence. For these reasons, the early 1960s was the era of U.S. pressure on the alliance to adopt the doctrine that came to be called flexible response. Initially advertised as a means of confining the worst destructiveness of a nuclear war to military targets and implicitly intended as a means of increasing the credibility of U.S. threats to use its nuclear counterforce dominance, the doctrine provoked great controversy within the alliance and was accepted only grudgingly.

Even today, "flexible response" as a catch phrase for alliance nuclear strategy has the not-inconsiderable advantages of generality and vagueness. Indeed, its central proposition advances uncertainty as a positive virtue: The alliance must—and will—be prepared to respond to a Soviet attack in whatever way is judged at the time most likely to defeat that attack if possible and in any event to punish and dissuade its continuation. To that end, NATO has proclaimed both an objective of being able to meet aggression successfully at any level and a readiness to increase the level of conflict if necessary to avoid defeat.

The concept implies NATO would have a long continuum of potential military operations, hopefully of increasing effectiveness and certainly of increasing violence and destructiveness. At one level of analysis, this range of choice is needed to permit selection of those actions most likely to be militarily successful. Still more important conceptually, the existence of such a continuum of responses increases the credibility of NATO's proclaimed willingness to escalate. There is indeed a sense in which the doctrine of flexible response is principally a matter of offering the alliance escalating steps that are individually smaller—and hence more easily decided upon and perceived by the Soviets as more likely to be chosen—than a single massive retaliation. Since all involved—the United States, Europe, and the USSR—maintain that any use of nuclear weapons is likely to escalate out of control, the existence of these smaller, more credible intermediate steps should reenforce the deterrent effect of all out nuclear retaliation.

Despite this policy—and prediction—of general escalation, the flexible response doctrine is also intended to provide the maximum possible prospect that a war could be terminated short of general destruction while still defending NATO interests. This aspect of flexible response—dubbed escalation control—recognizes the need to have a means of convincing an aggressor that, even if he could not be defeated directly, the costs of victory would still exceed his gain. By its readiness to escalate to greater—but still less than total—violence, NATO would hope to convince the Soviets to end the fighting on terms acceptable to NATO.

The doctrine suffers from the evils of those very ambiguities that are its strategic and political virtues. Continuing debates within the alliance and polemics from the USSR focus on the hard issues these ambiguities quite consciously seek to avoid. These issues include the adequacy of NATO conventional defense, the morality and realism of a doctrine that contemplates starting and then attempting to limit nuclear war, the speed and scale with which NATO would use nuclear weapons, the adequacy of NATO nuclear forces for a contest of escalation, the feasibility of controlling escalation once begun, and the acceptability to Europe—and the United States—of a doctrine that inherently contemplates, if it does not count on, first use of nuclear weapons in Europe.

Nonetheless, the doctrine—for all its ambiguities and for all its failure to resolve in neat explicit terms the fundamental divergences of U.S. and European interests—has both a political and a military logic. It offers a framework for NATO planning and defense that accommodates, as well as a doctrine can, the inherent tension between the attractiveness of massive nuclear retaliation as a deterrent and the incredibility of a NATO defense that posed no serious obstacles or risk to Soviet aggression short of an American initiation of general nuclear destruction. Politically, the doctrine—which proposes serious conventional defense and, however ambiguously, contemplates limited, and possibly first use of nuclear weapons as a step toward either a successfully negotiated peace or a further general escalation—meets both European and American needs for a doctrine that accommodates both their fears and their preferences. On the one hand, Europeans shy away from the idea of large-scale conventional defense—which is the obvious (probably the only) alternative to flexible response—not just because of its cost, but because they recognize that a modern conventional war between the superpowers, even if successful in avoiding permanent Soviet occupation, would destroy the heart of Europe only slightly less totally than a nuclear war. On the other hand, Europeans object equally to the idea of fighting a nuclear war only in Europe on similar and still stronger grounds and stress the need for U.S. central strategic forces to be available for European defense, whatever the risk to America. The United States has been willing to commit its central strategic forces and the existence of the United States as the ultimate NATO deterrent, following the failure of less total responses, but it has been unwilling to participate in an alliance strategy that would make that commitment the *only* serious element in NATO deterrence.

Flexible response thus provides a formula for both parts of the alliance to integrate commitments and fears and to obtain a basis for pointing to the presence within the NATO triad of those measures—conventional defense, flexibility in the use of tactical nuclear weapons, or ultimate resort to general nuclear war—that each regards as most important. The United States, in response to fear of overreliance on the credibility of a strategic or even a theater nuclear response to limited aggression, has with varying degrees of success pressed its allies to improve their conventional capabilities. The Europeans, for their part, have stressed the need to maintain a convincing ladder of nuclear escalation and to make the prospect of a war limited to Europe outside the USSR seem highly unlikely to both superpowers. Each part of the alliance has with different specific prescriptions called for a strong noncentral strategic element. The result may lack conceptual elegance, but it has provided an effective deterrent and, so far at least, a policy to which all concerned can, with whatever doubts, rally. Not many alliance arrangements have done as well.

The virtues of flexible response and the NATO triad, despite their faults, become apparent when a substitute is sought. Concurrent with the doctrinal change to flexible response was an effort to ease the problem of making European security so heavily dependent on a purely American decision to use (or not use) nuclear weapons. In the early 1960s, the search for an institutional answer to this problem crystallized in the concept of a multilateral force (MLF) that would add a distinctively European component to the forces comprising the alliance's ultimate strategic nuclear deterrent and would complement the solely U.S.-controlled intercontinental strategic nuclear forces.[2] Eventually, the MLF concept floundered on the alliance's inability to develop a politically workable multinational system to operate and control nuclear weapons: Singlehanded American decisionmaking, however undesirable, seemed better than agreement on a truly alliance-wide control system that was militarily realistic. Perhaps reflecting a judgment that this issue is more one of politics than of weapons, the formal burial of the MLF concept was accomplished by adoption of a system for increased U.S. consultation with its NATO allies on nuclear matters—the Nuclear Planning Group (NPG). While the resulting increased consultation and exchange of information has no doubt been useful and important, the NPG did nothing to resolve the fundamental question of credibility and made only a limited contribution to issues of political control of nuclear weapons.

Concomitantly, but by no means coincidentally, the early 1960s was also the era during which the French independent nuclear deterrent was developed and, more quietly but no less clearly, when the British renewed their commitment to maintain an independent national deterrent.

DETERRING ATTACKS ON THE UNITED STATES: ASSURED DESTRUCTION

In American public discussions of strategic nuclear forces, these issues of extended deterrence were greatly overshadowed by the question of the survivability and effectiveness of American strategic forces against a surprise attack on the United States itself. The fundamental problem of extended nuclear deterrence against Soviet conventional power has to do largely (if latently) with the credibility and effectiveness of a U.S. first use of nuclear weapons—either against Soviet battlefield forces or in retaliation against Soviet territory—as a means of responding to a Soviet attack in Europe that appeared to be on the verge of succeeding. In contrast, the basic debate at both technical and political levels about U.S. intercontinental strategic forces deals primarily with the problem of a Soviet surprise attack.

The strategic forces that were developed and deployed in the 1950s were extremely powerful but had the unfortunate characteristic of great vulnerability; their successors were designed to be very survivable. Ballistic missile submarines—which came into the force in the early 1960s—were (and remain) essentially invulnerable, and, until recently at least, the other strategic systems introduced in the late 1950s and early 1960s were also much more survivable than their predecessors. United States-based B-52s on air or ground alert avoided the vulnerability to surprise attack of B-47s at peripheral bases; solid fuel missiles in concrete silos were vastly more secure than their liquid-fueled, soft, land-based predecessors. The theory of assured destruction emerged from discussions about how many of these very survivable second generation forces should be acquired.

The assured destruction criterion specified that the United States should have forces sufficient, even in a day-to-day unalerted posture, to survive an all-out Soviet surprise attack and still retaliate with enough power to effectively destroy an arbitrarily defined but large percentage of Soviet cities and industry. The impression is widespread that this assured destruction doctrine was the dominant factor in determining American procurement and targeting policy in the 1960s. On balance this seems historically false, both in terms of what U.S. leaders thought and what they did to structure the force. It may well have been the private view of key U.S. civilian leaders that nuclear weapons could not prudently be relied on to do much more than deter a large-scale Soviet nuclear attack and thus could be designed accordingly. To some extent, for example, such a view was implicit in the emphasis on survivability that was critical in the design of the strategic weapons deployed in the 1960s. Even so, characteristics such as accuracy and target coverage—important to fight nuclear wars rather than merely to meet the requirements of assured destruction—were clearly important in the design and scale of such weapon systems as Minuteman I, II, and III.

The assured destruction concept, however, in the sense of planning to fight a nuclear war by concentrating on cities, was never the organizing factor in U.S. targeting doctrine. Industrial targets were certainly included in the target plan, but military targets were heavily covered as well. Even from the point of view of public declaratory policy, limiting the damage from subsequent attacks remained a major stated objective of U.S. forces should deterrence fail. The declining feasibility of attaining this objective during the 1960s reduced the prominence of so-called damage limitation in public statements; it did not produce any major change in actual U.S. nuclear war plans, which continued to provide for very large attacks on Soviet military forces, as well as against industrial targets and cities.

In fact, targeting decisions for nuclear weapons appear to have been surprisingly independent of both the public debate about the vulnerability of U.S. forces to a surprise attack and the intra-alliance political debate about extended deterrence. Initially, targeting had been largely the independent province of the U.S. Air Force, because it controlled the bombers that then were the only significant means of carrying nuclear weapons. With the development of substantial nuclear attack capabilities on aircraft carriers and submarines, and a resulting embarrassing lack of coordination beween the two services in planning for nuclear war, came creation of the Joint Strategic Targeting Planning Staff, an Air Force-Navy coalition within the headquarters of the Strategic Air Command at Omaha. The result was the Single Integrated Operations Plan (SIOP). As its name suggested the SIOP linked Navy and Air Force weapons into a series of coordinated plans for intercontinental nuclear strikes. The achievement of this coordination was a noteworthy technical and an even more striking bureaucratic accomplishment, given traditional military service conflicts. However, while the details of targeting during even the earliest years of nuclear forces remain largely classified, it is clear that the number of options available was very small. Increases in the number of nuclear weapons (and vast improvements in intelligence) brought changes in strategic targeting, of course, but in general, strategic (as contrasted to tactical) nuclear targeting remained focused on a few massive attacks on the largest feasible set of Soviet targets, with military targets dominant in terms of numbers. In short, if MAD were the right initials for the U.S. doctrine, the translation should have been massive, not mutual, assured destruction.

THE EMERGENCE OF PARITY: SALT AND STRATEGIC DOCTRINE

In hindsight, the United States is usually attributed with strategic superiority until about the early 1970s, but it was a superiority of only a limited kind. The United States had many more weapons, and after an exchange would have had a surviving nuclear capability that was much larger than the Soviet Union's. However, by the early 1960s U.S. leaders no longer believed (if they ever had) that any U.S. attack would be adequate to deny the USSR the ability to inflict vast damage to the cities and industry of the United States.

The debate over how to use the special sort of U.S. superiority lasted longer than the capability itself. Beginning before the Cuban missile crisis—but undoubtedly spurred after 1964 by the retreat forced on Nikita Khrushchev—Soviet strategic forces were transformed within a decade from the small, minimum deterrent (if that) force of the early 1960s to a survivable, diverse, and technically sophisticated force that has achieved, for the USSR, effective strategic parity with the United States. For a period in the 1960s, U.S. intelligence failed to recognize the extent to which the Soviet Union would build up its offensive strategic forces, while simultaneously overestimating the degree to which it would pursue ballistic missile defense programs. However, it was recognized early on that regardless of what the United States did, the Soviet Union would go beyond mutual assured destruction—preventing damage denial—to deny the U.S. confidence in holding an even narrowly defined military edge after a nuclear exchange.

During this same period, the United States was planning its third generation of intercontinental strategic forces. A fundamental decision was made to limit the number of intercontinental ballistic missiles (ICBMs) and submarine-launched ballistic missiles (SLBMs) deployed and instead to exploit U.S. technology to develop multiple independently targetable reentry vehicles (MIRVs) for both types of missile systems.[3] A major impetus behind the MIRV program was the desire of U.S. military planners to increase the number of targets that could be covered so as to be better able to carry out the operational targeting policy of a comprehensive attack on Soviet military, as well as economic power. The incongruity between that policy and the supposedly dominant doctrine of assured destruction may have been recognized, but it certainly did not lead to the conclusion that greater target coverage was unnecessary. In part, the issue was easily avoided because of a second rationale for MIRVs—that they were necessary to penetrate Soviet defenses. This argument's persuasiveness was aided by exaggerated projections of Soviet antiballistic missile (ABM) efforts; it helped civilian planners to sidestep the apparent inconsistency of approving larger numbers of weapons than any pure assured destruction theory could possibly require without squarely facing the underlying doctrinal questions.

In 1972 the first strategic arms limitation treaties (SALT) were signed. In many respects the principal political significance of the SALT agreement—and in an important sense the source of much of the later criticism of it—was its formalization of a state of strategic parity between the United States and the Soviet Union. In fact, however, that parity was the result, not of the SALT agreements, but of the Soviet buildup of strategic forces and of U.S. judgments that little could be done to offset it, at least on a long-term basis. Indeed, by the time the SALT talks began in 1969, the Soviet Union was—and was recognized by the United States to be—clearly on a course that would carry its strategic nuclear buildup to and even beyond parity with the United States in numbers of missile launchers. Moreover, the 1972 ABM Treaty marked the acknowledgment of the end of U.S. efforts to deploy active defenses to limit the damage it would suffer in a nuclear war; the treaty also closed off an active defense of ICBMs. This latter had been advertised as one of the principal purposes of the Safeguard ABM system under construction in 1972. In retrospect, it seems clear that even if fully deployed the system would have made virtually no contribution to the survival of U.S. ICBMs in the 1980s.

From the point of view of U.S. doctrine concerning the utility and role of strategic nuclear weapons, however, the most significant trend of the early 1970s was the increasingly explicit official questioning of a nuclear doctrine that featured large-scale retaliation against civilian and military targets and virtually nothing else. As early as his first State of the World message in 1970, President Richard M. Nixon had raised questions about the adequacy of a strategic targeting policy that would permit the American authorities no options in response to a major Soviet attack except a general assault. This questioning was reflected in a series of studies within the government—culminating in early 1974 in a classified presidential directive called NSDM 242. The conclusions of this analysis were articulated in 1975 by then Secretary of Defense James R. Schlesinger as the doctrine that came to be named for him—under which the United States would seek additional flexibility in its targeting plans. The policy was advocated on several grounds—as a means of strengthening deterrence by offering more credible options, as a means of controlling escalation by providing militarily significant limited strikes to show resolve to continue escalation if necessary, and as a means toward the long-sought goal of mobilizing strategic forces for theater warfare by making available very small strikes geared to specific military objectives. In addition and somewhat tangentially, it was argued that the new policy required not only new targeting but new capabilities, especially an ability to match Soviet potential to destroy American silos.

The campaign for greater flexibility in targeting and the quest for more effective ways to use nuclear weapons faced criticism from two quite different directions. Outside the government, the principal opposition came from those who believed—incorrectly, but often with fervent conviction—that U.S. doctrine had been, or in any event should be, based primarily on the threat to attack cities. That view argued that the mere contemplation of less than all-out attacks made nuclear war more "thinkable"—as indeed it was designed to make it more credible—and therefore more likely. Whatever the abstract validity of mutual assured destruction as a theory, however, criticism of Secretary Schlesinger for departing from it took on a quality of unreality, given the fact that U.S. nuclear weapons long had been directed against many military targets. The secretary's defenders argued, with some justice, that the issue was not whether military targets were to be included in U.S. nuclear war plans but the scale and flexibility with which they would be incorporated.

Far more private, and in many respects more difficult, was an argument over the degree of flexibility that was feasible and desirable to include in the SIOP. An important subsidiary element of Secretary Schlesinger's concept was pressure for more extensive preplanning of very limited options as a contribution to extended deterrence. It was argued that to maximize the contribution of nuclear weapons to the deterrence of limited aggression and to give reality to the concept of escalation control on which NATO placed such emphasis, it was necessary to expand the preplanning for use of strategic forces to include options envisioning very small attacks. This aspect of the new doctrine was also criticized sharply, partly on the ground that it would make nuclear war more likely by creating the impression that it could be limited, and partly on the familiar ground that the new theory lacked credibility. Technically, however, there was relatively little problem in adding very limited options to the SIOP and, in principle, at least, the availability of such options was entirely compatible with the long-standing U.S. emphasis on the potential use of strategic nuclear weapons in a war limited to one theater.

Partly due to the unexpectedly brief remaining terms of the president who signed NSDM 242 and the Secretary of Defense who announced it, and partly due to the sharply rising dispute within the Republican party over SALT, detente, and their personification in Henry Kissinger, these basic strategic policy issues remained unresolved in 1977 when President Carter took office. To a large degree, they remain unresolved at the end of the first year of President Reagan's tenure, but some new directions have emerged.

President Carter's four years were dominated publicly, so far as strategic force policy was concerned, by the same issues as had been debated previously:

1. Had the Soviet Union acquired a strategic edge that would give them political leverage first and perhaps a real military advantage later? To charges that the USSR had acquired a politically significant strategic edge over a United States lulled by SALT and detente and diverted by Vietnam, the Carter Administration argued that strategic parity existed, with Soviet leads in areas like ICBMs and throw-weight offset by U.S. leads in warhead numbers and submarines. The theme of the Carter strategic policy was to preserve parity, by arms control through SALT II and by measured U.S. programs like cruise missiles, Trident, and the MX mobile ICBM, rather than to close a general "window of vulnerability." President Reagan's rhetoric, both in the campaign and in office, has espoused the view that the United States is generally inferior to the USSR in nuclear weapons, but his program, in practice, eschewed the quick fixes and massive strategic force buildup that view implied and concentrated increased defense funds, instead, on conventional forces.

2. Was the U.S. nuclear guarantee to Europe still credible? The much debated strategic balance—at best in a state of parity, not U.S. advantage—coupled with a variety of U.S.-European political and economic tensions and a continuing Soviet buildup of tactical forces, brought new and more public debate over the place of U.S. nuclear weapons in NATO strategy. From misplaced reliance on U.S. strategic nuclear superiority as the answer to all NATO's defense problems, some European observers began to argue that parity and the

impending vulnerability of U.S. ICBMs utterly destroyed all credibility remaining in the U.S. nuclear guarantee and left Europe essentially defenseless, especially in light of improved Soviet tactical nuclear forces. Initially viewing European concerns about the Eurostrategic imbalance and the implication of parity as overblown, the Carter Administration saw European confidence in the United States shaken by the self-inflicted neutron bomb fiasco. Determined to show its own resolve and flexibility to maintain NATO deterrence within SALT limits and to restore allied confidence in U.S. nuclear leadership, the Carter Administration accepted the European challenge to fashion a response to Soviet tactical nuclear programs and European doubts that would buttress deterrence and NATO solidarity, by proposing to deploy additional U.S. long-range theater forces in Europe. However, no sooner had the United States shown its willingness to accede to apparent European desires than the European governments, under pressure from growing antinuclear sentiment at home, began to stress that an alliance program must not ignore arms control. Nor, added the Germans, who had led in calling for some effective U.S. actions, must any alliance response to Soviet programs put an excessive or, as they put it, "singular" burden on the Federal Republic. The upshot was the NATO decision of December 1979 to deploy a force of Pershing II ballistic missiles and ground-launched cruise missiles in five European countries while simultaneously seeking arms control measures that could reduce the scale of NATO's deployment or even eliminate it altogether by reducing Soviet SS-20s and other missile forces.

Stripped of its extraordinarily complex political context—East-West, U.S.-European, and domestic European—the basic rationale for the NATO decision was that NATO, in an age of parity in central strategic forces, needs to have a visibly European-connected but also clearly American-controlled nuclear force capable of striking the USSR, in order to avoid any question of the USSR being a sanctuary in a European war, even if central systems were not used. The USSR, recognizing the political tensions in the alliance—and, it seems likely, the significance of such a U.S. force if deployed—launched a major campaign to derail the NATO program, playing on the fears and concerns aroused in Western Europe by a debate that brought to the fore issues of security and risk that had long lain dormant.

The first year of the Reagan Administration was marked by worsening trans-Atlantic misunderstanding and confusion—about the new administration's seriousness about arms control and its attitude toward the possibility of a nuclear war limited to Europe, and about European commitment to collective security. President Reagan's proposal in November 1981 to forego the NATO long-range theater nuclear force deployment altogether in exchange for elimination of the Soviet missile forces to which it was designed to respond was both a return to the mainstream of allied thinking on arms control and a dramatic effort to undercut Soviet propaganda attacks and allay genuine European concerns that threatened to derail the alliance's deployment program. Whether it will preserve the program if no agreement is reached remains to be seen.

3. What overall doctrine should the United States adopt for strategic forces? President Carter gave an unusual degree of personal attention to nuclear issues, not only to the SALT talks and to nonproliferation—which were part of the ambitious arms control agenda that he saw as a clear moral imperative—but also to the details of the U.S. president's unique role as operational commander of U.S. strategic nuclear forces. The result of the comprehensive study of strategic targeting policy that he ordered was the promulgation of PD-59 in the last months of his administration, setting up as U.S. policy the goal of having sufficient forces and plans to convince the Soviets that no course of action leading to nuclear war could result in Soviet victory. The Reagan Administration seems to have accepted the basic premises of this countervailing strategy.

Underlying all the questions of strategic nuclear policy in the late 1970s, however, was the issue of SALT II. It was seen by its advocates as a means of managing a difficult and dangerous competition with the USSR and by its critics, on the one hand, as putting inadequate constraints on both sides and, on the other, as solidifying a Soviet advantage. The uncertain quest to ratify the agreement was fatally sidetracked by the Soviet invasion of Afghanistan, but even the Reagan Administration proclaimed its devotion to "real" arms control.

THE FUTURE OF DETERRENCE

The United States therefore entered the 1980s with the basic issues of strategic policy still unresolved. While recognizing the urgent need for programs to preserve parity against a continued Soviet buildup, the United States can reasonably claim at present a state of general parity with the USSR in strategic forces. Nevertheless, the disappearance of previous American numerical superiority in strategic forces has resulted in exaggerated notions of impending Soviet political advantages. Concurrently, more specific concerns about the vulnerability of U.S. ICBMs and the expansion of Soviet intermediate-range nuclear forces have focused attention on the need to modernize U.S. forces. For these reasons, as well as because of more general controversy over the U.S. world role, the late 1970s and early 1980s have seen a fundamental questioning of the place of strategic forces in American security policy. The debate about the SALT II Treaty focused attention on these questions—and probably exacerbated the questioning.

Much of the debate has concerned specific weapon programs and the role of SALT in a time of increased Soviet-U.S. tensions. However, as in earlier debates, there has also been an element of controversy over strategic doctrine and the purposes of U.S. nuclear forces. One product of an effort to focus on doctrine as well as force structure and to relate strategic policy more closely to current relative capabilities was the "countervailing strategy" developed during the Carter Administration. This was an evolutionary development of prior U.S. doctrine, not the fundamental departure sometimes advertised—and denounced. The analysis that preceded it and the impulse for a further statement of U.S. doctrine were clearly the products of pressures to consider the requirements of deterrence in conditions of strategic parity and to respond to perceptions that American strategic policy had been developed in isolation from any understanding of Soviet doctrine. The new policy retained the prior stress on deterrence as the principal purpose of U.S. strategic forces but sought to be more explicit than previously about what prospective U.S. actions would best deter various forms of Soviet aggression.

In order to deter the full range of threats to which strategic nuclear forces might be relevant, the countervailing strategy says, the United States must have not merely a capacity for destroying the full set of Soviet military, political, and industrial targets, but also a sufficiently flexible and enduring force capable of carrying out smaller attacks that would deny Soviet victory in such a war, even without further escalation. The countervailing strategy is based on the assumption that, faced with such U.S. capabilities and despite the dramatic increases in the size and capability of Soviet strategic forces, Soviet leaders would continue to recognize that no action of theirs that leads to the use of nuclear weapons could produce a meaningful Soviet victory.

In some circles, the countervailing strategy was denounced with the same vigor and most of the same arguments as its precursor, the Schlesinger doctrine. Like so much else in the Carter Administration, its merits were obscured by clumsy public presentation traceable to internal bickering within the administration. Nonetheless, the Reagan Administration has shown no real inclination to alter the policy. While the specific formulation will no doubt be changed, some concept similar to the countervailing strategy seems likely to continue to shape U.S. policy.

As a result, in the 1980s and beyond, nuclear weapons will continue to serve two general objectives: (1) to deter attacks on the United States and (2) to contribute to the deterrence of attacks on U.S. allies in Europe and, to some degree, elsewhere. Furthermore, it will be recognized that meeting these objectives requires more than a simple ability to destroy the full range of Soviet targets in a single, all-out attack. Determining what these objectives will require in terms of strategic doctrine, plans, and forces requires paying careful attention to how a war or crisis might occur and especially to its political and psychological context.

Deter Direct Attacks on the United States.   This core mission is the least disputed of the objectives of strategic nuclear forces. Indeed, some would contend that this mission constitutes the only significant role for strategic nuclear weapons. This argument implies that a force designed to meet the criterion of assured destruction in its crudest and least demanding form—a very survivable force large enough to destroy the major Soviet cities—would be a sufficient deterrent.

This approach often focuses primarily on the analytically simplest case of preventing a "bolt from the blue" attack. Despite the utility of the bolt-from-the-blue scenario as a testing case for certain technical analyses, it is wholly inadequate as a measure of strategic policy. It is highly unlikely that the Soviets would attack the United States (and still more implausible that the United States would attack the Soviet Union) as a deliberately calculated act divorced from an immediate and intense political and probably military confrontation. Indeed, in this century, very few wars, if any, have begun in such a way. Rather, major conflicts between great powers have begun because one side of a continuing political confrontation (not necessarily the initiator of the immediate crisis) decided that the long-term conflict was unresolvable, that eventually war was almost certain, and that it was better to act immediately than to wait, however uncertain the consequences of action. Indeed, many analyses of the causes of wars among great powers have rightly focused on the failure of military and political leaders to see the inevitable consequences of their immediate course and on their willingness to permit their countries to be swept along in a tide of events dominated by short-term reactions to immediate problems, leading to a destructive war they would never have chosen deliberately.

This historical experience suggests that, in fact, the most serious aspect of deterring direct attack on the United States is maintaining stability during crises, not deterring a surprise attack during normal times. That is to say, the United States must follow a policy—in acquiring strategic forces, in planning for their use, and even in presenting threats to the USSR—that insures that in a crisis there would be no significant Soviet incentive to attack the United States with nuclear weapons, even if, for example, it believed the United States was about to use nuclear weapons at a theater or battlefield level. Similarly, U.S. policy also should insure that in such a crisis, the United States itself would not be under pressure to initiate nuclear war to prevent the Soviets from gaining key advantage by preemption.

In short, the destructiveness of nuclear weapons is sufficiently widely recognized that it is only in the context of an intense and perhaps prolonged U.S.-Soviet crisis—probably involving the prior use of military forces of the two superpowers directly against each other—that there would be a serious risk that either side would use nuclear weapons against the other's homeland. Even in such conditions, resorting to intercontinental nuclear attack would likely be the result of a conviction that a nuclear exchange had become inevitable and that some advantage would obtain from going first.

Indeed, the United States might, for reasons of defense of Europe, be the one under greatest pressure to initiate nuclear attacks on Soviet territory. That fact in itself could prove an impetus to Soviet preemption. In short, it is chiefly in such a serious crisis that the objective of preventing direct attacks on the United States becomes both most serious and most difficult.

The countervailing strategy is directed precisely at this need to maintain deterrence even in grave crises where the Soviets might be prepared to take risks that would seem unthinkable in more normal times. The objective is to insure that the Soviets, even under such conditions, would conclude that no plausible course of action involving the use of military—not just nuclear—forces would produce a Soviet victory.

To meet this objective in such conditions, the requirement for U.S. targeting is relatively straightforward: Plans for massive attacks against Soviet military forces and economic targets are required as the ultimate deterrent, but they must be coupled to the maximum possible degree with an ability to strike large, but still limited, sets of military targets, using a variety of forces. The necessary characteristics of forces capable of serving these needs are much more complex. The most potent enemy of successful deterrence in such a grave crisis is likely to be the vulnerability of some particular element of the force, including the command and control system as importantly as any specific weapon system. Such a vulnerability would be triply dangerous: It would invite attack; it would drive enemy planning toward preemptive strategies; and it could make an immediate, all-out response the only viable form of retaliation. Ideally, the force structure and, especially, the command, control, communication, and intelligence (C^3I) system that would best meet the objective of deterring attacks during crises would present no target that would be advantageous to attack: That is to say, the objective would best be met if it were always clear that attacking the United States would be as certain to fail as waiting, however risky waiting might seem.

From the point of view of this first objective, therefore, the critical criterion for the design of new ICBMs and, indeed, for new bombers, submarines, and C^3I system elements is whether or not they reduce vulnerability. Mere increases in offensive capabilities, if unmatched by increases in survivability, would simply make the new missiles more attractive as targets, with perverse effects on the incentives of both sides to strike first or wait. Less widely recognized is the concomitant proposition that reduced vulnerability, particularly in a continuing crisis, ought also to be the touchstone for the design of theater nuclear forces in Europe and elsewhere. In a major crisis in Europe, a significant source of instability could be the existence of incentive to preempt against nuclear forces while they were still in a vulnerable position.

Force capabilities other than survivability and flexibility in targeting have secondary though still important roles in crisis stability. Inherent in any calculation of Soviet incentives to initiate a nuclear exchange or to start on a course of conventional attack that could lead to U.S. retaliation are likely Soviet predictions about the U.S. responses. A fundamental part of nuclear deterrence during crises will always be the possibility that a preemptive nuclear attack or a successful conventional one would trigger an all-out U.S. nuclear response that would substantially destroy the USSR as a communist regime and a world military power no less than as an industrial society. However, if in addition, the United States had forces and plans for their use permitting a choice of more limited responses that would prevent any enhancement of Soviet military power (or that would challenge Soviet power domestically or internationally), deterrence would be further strengthened.

In particular, during the coming period, prudence requires that the United States regard its ICBMs as vulnerable. Under these conditions, it is important that the United States make clear to the world and to the USSR what may have become obscured in domestic detente—namely, that a successful Soviet attack on U.S. ICBMs would not merely risk an all-out U.S. response but that the United States could choose to retaliate against Soviet military forces, including remaining strategic forces and Soviet conventional forces other than those immediately fighting the United States, in ways that would deny the Soviet Union any relative gain in the world military balance. The ability to carry out such attacks is increased not only by system accuracy but by flexibility, especially in terms of matching actions to current conditions. These elements must be part of the design of both our forces and the means of their direction and control.

These overall objectives are formidable and can never be attained entirely. However, there is clearly a need for continued focus on the survivability of strategic forces and on expanding available options for a militarily effective response to a Soviet strike against U.S. forces. Therefore, while attention still must be paid to the limiting case of deterring a bolt-from-the-blue attack, capabilities for mobilizing U.S. assets and sustaining high alert rates—i.e., for using to advantage the strategic warning a crisis would give—are even more critical.

In a context of an intense, ongoing crisis, the idea that decisions could be made rapidly enough to launch ICBMs out from under the attack (LUA) is more plausible than in a scenario envisioning a surprise attack under routine circumstances. It is in the U.S. interest to continue to make this possibility a factor that must be incorporated into Soviet calculations. However, the risks that the USSR could successfully preempt against U.S. ICBMs dependent upon launch-from-under-the-attack to survive—and, even more, the risks of mistaken response by such ICBMs—make it critical that vulnerabilities be reduced to the minimum feasible level and that the option of riding out an attack remain viable.

Finally, the importance of increasing the stability of international relations during crises gives rise to one of the major potential roles for arms control. In particular, the ABM Treaty of 1972 continues to play an important role in increasing stability during crises and, thus, in reducing the risk of nuclear war. No technical developments during the ten years in which the treaty has been in effect have in any way reduced the force of the initial argument: The existence of significant antiballistic missile forces on each side would be a destabilizing factor because they might create greater incentives for one side or the other to initiate a major attack, in the belief that the ABM system would be able to deal effectively with the inevitably less coordinated and smaller retaliation. Any analysis that argues for changing the current ABM regime on the ground that active defenses would enhance U.S. ICBM survivability would be seriously defective unless it also carefully evaluated the impact of Soviet active defenses against potential U.S. responses.

Contribute to the Deterrence of Large-Scale Attacks in Europe and Elsewhere. As has been noted, the problem of extended deterrence has been critical to the development of U.S. security policy since the late 1940s and remains so today. There are clear limitations on the nation's ability to use nuclear weapons to enhance its ability to deter war at less than the gravest levels. The very existence of nuclear weapons, however, contributes to some degree to deterring any type of Soviet aggression because of the inherent risk that any U.S.-Soviet confrontation could initiate an escalatory process eventually leading to the general use of nuclear weapons.

There also is a significant operational interplay between the potential use of nuclear forces in a regional conflict and the deterrence of conventional war. The existence of flexible and effective U.S. tactical nuclear forces compels the Soviet Union, in planning any military effort, to take into account the possibility that the United States would initiate use of nuclear weapons. This consideration constrains planning for purely conventional war because of the possibility that nuclear weapons could be used to exploit weaknesses in communications or logistical systems, or to destroy large concentrations of armed forces or critical operating bases. Perhaps even more important, declarations of readiness to use nuclear weapons, if necessary, to defend Europe have played a critical political role as a symbol of U.S. resolve and commitment.

Nonetheless, the problems of the credibility of nuclear threats are such that it is fatuous to rely on a rhetorical policy of purported readiness to employ nuclear weapons at an early stage to deter small attacks limited to particular regions. The overwhelming probability is that in anything less than a very large-scale conventional confrontation, the United States (and the Soviet Union) would be inhibited from using nuclear weapons; it seems likely that inhibition would exist even in such a major confrontation until it was clear how the conventional battle was developing. Each side's understanding of these possibilities, of course, diminishes the putative deterrent effect of the threat to use nuclear weapons.

Accordingly, a policy that seeks to substitute nuclear weapons for conventional forces as the principal means for resisting aggression on a local level contains within it the seeds of its own ineffectiveness. This is all the more true the less vital is the U.S. interest in the region and the smaller the Soviet conventional effort needed to prevail. To say that the U.S. and other nations cannot hope to resist Soviet aggression in a particular area "without quick use of nuclear weapons" is to risk saying, in effect, that no serious deterrent to such aggression exists. For unless the United States, with its allies and local supporters, can present a conventional capability that would require a truly major Soviet conventional military effort to overcome it, deterrence would be gravely undermined. Even if the United States were resolved to use nuclear weapons without first mounting a major conventional defense—an unlikely situation in political terms—the USSR is unlikely to expect that such is the case. Furthermore, in all but the most unusual situations, limited tactical nuclear strikes, though immensely destructive and bearing a high general political cost, would be themselves unlikely to defeat decisively a determined Soviet conventional attack. In these situations, the threat of nuclear weapons is useful only to complicate Soviet conventional planning, to deter Soviet use of nuclear capabilities, and, conceivably, to threaten a widening of the conflict to avoid defeat.

These observations concerning the limited credibility of the threatened use of nuclear weapons in marginal conflicts apply to some degree even for very large military confrontations, such as a Soviet attack on NATO's central front. However, on that front—and to some degree also in northeast and southwest Asia—the availability of limited but still militarily significant nuclear options backing a serious conventional defense can add significantly to U.S. ability to deter Soviet aggression. The chain of argument is familiar: If conventional defenses are sufficient to require a major effort to overcome them, then vast costs already would have been incurred by the United States, and significant U.S. interests would clearly have been in jeopardy before the question of using nuclear weapons would arise. In such conditions, a resort to nuclear escalation, while still perhaps irrational on some abstract calculus, would be a far more plausible prospect. If, in addition to threatening general nuclear war, the United States could use nuclear weapons in ways that would deny the USSR the fruits of victory (e.g., by destroying large parts of its conventional military capability), an important further contribution would be made to deterrence. To the extent such options were available, the U.S. threat would not be one of merely desperate but dangerous general escalation. Instead, the prospect of nuclear attacks that would be militarily effective to deny or offset the benefits of conventional successes for the Soviet Union would in Soviet contemplation combine both high probability with an unproductive result for Soviet objectives and interests.

Operationally, confronting the Soviet Union with this highly effective deterrent package entails, besides improved conventional capability and a continued assured destruction capability, the continued deployment of nuclear forces and the design of plans for their effective use in operations against opposing military forces. Initially, such attacks would be directed at destroying Soviet military units actually engaged in the attack, presumably using battlefield nuclear forces. But plans and capabilities (including C^3I) are also required for larger but still less-than-total attacks with a high potential to make victory, as viewed through Soviet eyes in advance of (or during) a war, seem a remote prospect. Logically, of course, it is not inevitable that such attacks be aimed at Soviet military forces to deny victory. In principle, selective attacks on economic or governmental targets could be sufficiently damaging to deny any Soviet gain from regional military successes. However, it would appear that attacks aimed at Soviet military forces or facilities—even if they were not the forces directly engaged in the attack—would be most likely to maximize Soviet perceptions that their chances of gaining an overall victory were not promising, because such attacks would threaten to leave Soviet post-war military potential unacceptably weakened. The threat of such offsetting, if not defeating, countermilitary attacks would be a powerful deterrent in advance and, if carried out, would offer whatever hope there might be of limiting the conflict.

Broadly, the case for making plans and acquiring forces capable of carrying out less than all-out attacks against military targets is that probably the most credible, and therefore the most effective, threat to the Soviet regime, short of the total destruction of the Soviet state, would be damage to Soviet military and political power out of all proportion to the potential gains of Soviet aggression. It is certainly *not* necessary that these U.S. options be focused principally on the parts of the Soviet military establishment that would be most difficult to attack (e.g., ICBMs or deployed army divisions). Rather, the objective should be to destroy Soviet military power as a system by, for example, striking at key command centers, logistical bottlenecks, or fixed combat support facilities. At the same time, it is clear that the requirement to be able to respond effectively at all levels is a tall order and that the possibility of limited Soviet counterresponses must be considered. The United States and its NATO allies, for example, would be quite vulnerable in military terms to limited nuclear strikes.

The effort to design credible and limited countermilitary options is hampered by the tendency of some of their more enthusiastic advocates to imagine that nuclear war can be given a precision that has eluded the capacity of man in the past with far less horrible weapons and that ignores the immense qualitative differences between nuclear and conventional weapons. No one should overestimate the possibility that a nuclear war—or even a major conventional war between the United States and the USSR—could be kept from escalating irrationally. Quite apart from inevitable psychological and political pressures to expand the conflict rather than accept defeat (or even unequal losses), the command and control systems on both sides are suffi-ciently vulnerable, and the uncertainties of nuclear war are so great, that the greatest probability is that an effort to contain escalation would fail. Once war had begun, the pressures would be immense on each side to launch attacks larger than might be judged strictly neces-sary in order to guard against further loss of control of the forces that would make further attacks impossible. Nonetheless, both sides would have a continuing interest in holding down the scale of losses—at least so long as destruction had not yet reached a level where even more could seem meaningless.

Therefore, for military and political reasons—and as a moral im-perative—it is in the United States' interest not to ignore any possi-bility that a nuclear war could be kept limited. It is particularly crit-ical to convince Soviet leaders that, whether or not aggression led to uncontrolled escalation, the USSR would still not gain by aggression. The United States and its allies cannot afford to rely solely on the Soviet leadership recognizing—or, rather, predicting—that aggression by them would unleash a process that would leave the USSR a ruin.[4] The utility of planning for limited and flexible options and having those plans taken seriously by the Soviet Union—in which effort im-provements in command and control arrangements for crises would pay higher dividends than most improvements in weapon systems—is not that such a policy offers a hope of winning a nuclear war or that it is a substitute for deterrence. Rather, the recognized existence of such plans and the ability to carry them out if need be presents a strong reason for Soviet leaders to conclude that aggression is not likely to succeed, even if total destruction is avoided, and for them to be deterred by that conclusion from the aggression that would test the adequacy of the plans and the accuracy of their predictions.

The objective of this approach is to make the Soviets conclude that *some* unacceptable U.S. counterblow is certain, even though what form it would take could not be predicted with confidence. Indeed, the evidence is that Soviet doctrine itself contemplates less than all-out exchanges focused on military targets, at least in the initial stages of conflict. To this extent, a U.S. policy that seeks to deny the Soviets victory by some means short of general mutual devastation has the advantage of addressing the problem in Soviet terms. In particular, by confronting Soviet leaders with the prospect that the U.S. will re-spond to the changing military situation and not merely make a pre-programmed spasm, this U.S. approach tends to work upon Soviet realization that war is an uncertain matter in which risks and opportunities are hard to calculate.

Implementing such a policy requires far more than simply directing planners to develop a variety of increasingly sophisticated and differentiated target packages, although this in itself would be a substantial task. From a program point of view, the clearest need is for more survivable and enduring command and control systems and for more effective and realistic plans for maintaining constitutionally legitimate and strategically coherent control of U.S. forces in war. The United States (and its allies) also must face the issue of the kinds of forces that would be required and the implications of such forces for broader political and military concerns. For example, the question has been raised as to whether the availability of such options might be compatible with accepting an overall equivalent force relationship. The argument is that either because of Soviet superiority in conventional forces or because of the supposed need for U.S. nuclear superiority in order to obtain flexibility, a successfully implemented countervailing strategy would require that the United States have more than equality. However, superiority in the sense of greater numbers appears to be neither sufficient nor even invariably helpful—and therefore clearly not a necessary requirement. The destructiveness of nuclear weapons is such that the effectiveness of their targeting for limited purposes is far more a function of the quality of the forces and system used to control them than it is of their size. Indeed, it seems likely that the chief material deficiency of current U.S. nuclear capabilities from the point of view of such a strategy lies in the command and control system, not in the forces themselves.

CONCLUSION

Despite all the proclamations of fundamental change in the strategic relationship, the basic tasks of U.S. strategic forces in the 1980s remain as before—to deter Soviet aggression, not just massive nuclear attacks on the U.S. but also Soviet use of its conventional military capabilities, that the West has been unwilling to match directly. What is needed—and what, if attained, would provide the best framework for arms control agreements to limit the scale and danger of the nuclear confrontation—is a strategic doctrine that recognizes more clearly than in the past the political and strategic context in which nuclear deterrence must work. This implies, first, greater attention to the problem of deterrence at times of crisis—the times at which it would be both most urgent and most difficult—including the immensely difficult problem of how to maintain control of such forces after they have begun to be used. Second, it requires continued focus on how nuclear weapons, and more flexible and more credible plans for their use, can contribute to deterrence of attacks on our allies—without permitting inherent differences of perspective on these issues to tear the alliance apart.

NOTES

1. It is in many respects a misnomer to describe the nuclear weapons policy of the 1950s as that of "massive retaliation." That term is better applied to the declaration by the Eisenhower Administration that the United States would not let the USSR set the limits of a local aggression, as the Truman Administration was charged with doing in Korea. A determination to exploit U.S. nuclear power was certainly part of the policy, but because the risks of large-scale nuclear war were recognized, it is a caricature of the doctrine to say that it contemplated that the United States would level Moscow at the first sign of Soviet aggression.

2. As a result of arrangements worked out in the 1950s and 1960s, many European NATO nations shared (and share) in the tactical nuclear forces of NATO through so-called dual key arrangements. These provide a significant element of joint decisional responsibility but only for weapons of relatively limited range. Moreover, their operational effectiveness under wartime conditions is debatable.

3. Concomitantly, important decisions concerning the bomber program were made in the adoption of the short-range attack missile (SRAM) program, which substantially eased the problem of attacking heavily defended targets with bombers.

4. Indeed, if it were certain that such an escalating process would result from a major U.S.-Soviet military clash, there is little need for nuclear planning more refined than massive attacks (and, indeed, not much requirement for serious conventional planning). The case for planning for more limited options maintains that such escalation, though likely, is not certain—and is only in the most dubious sense desirable—and that what deters is not what would happen but what the Soviet leadership expects could happen.

3 THE USSR AND NUCLEAR WAR

William G. Hyland

The 1980s promise to be a new era for the USSR. The strategic superiority of the United States has clearly ended. Strategic parity has been achieved, and in important respects the USSR has or soon will have some strategic advantages. In terms of the major strategic weapons, the period ahead is likely to unfold along lines already determined: Long-range bombers, sea- and land-based ballistic missiles, and a variety of cruise missiles will constitute the backbone of strategic offensive forces on both sides.

Both sides, however, have the technical capacity for a major expansion in these categories, and potential restraints against such an expansion have been weakened. Arms control agreements and the incentives to maintain a general political equilibrium are weaker. Strategic advantages, especially in capabilities to destroy hardened targets and to attack opposing military forces, beckon both sides. Outside factors—the role of Chinese weapons, regional imbalances in Europe and the Persian Gulf—also add to instabilities. In addition, for the USSR there are the difficult problems created by an increasingly stringent economic situation and by the disruptions that are sure to be generated by the inevitable changes in the top political leadership. Against this background, the Soviets will have to make a number of critical choices over the next few years concerning their strategic objectives and the resources devoted to the military sector. In doing

47

so, of course, they must evaluate how their choices may affect similar decisions being taken in Washington. On the whole, both the strategic and the geopolitical relationship between the two superpowers seems more fluid than at any time since the Cuban missile crisis. Two questions create the greatest uncertainties: whether the USSR can and will continue with the broadly based buildup of its military forces that it has pursued for nearly 20 years and, if so, what this may portend for Soviet foreign policy.

THE BUILDUP OF SOVIET STRATEGIC FORCES

Shortly after the end of the Cuban missile crisis, when American and Soviet negotiators were tying up some loose ends, a prominent Soviet official, the deputy foreign minister, V.V. Kutznetsov, commented to the effect that never again would the USSR allow itself to be put in the same position. The implication was that the Soviet Union would make every effort to redress the balance of military power. The subsequent buildup of Soviet military power has indeed been a conscious, deliberate policy aimed, in part, at reversing the verdict of October 1962 rather than reacting to U.S. programs and policies. The most dramatic and visible element has been the buildup in strategic weapons, but the scope of the effort embraced virtually every aspect of Soviet military power and, of course, has been quite costly.

Khruschev's Legacy[1]

The Soviet Union owes Nikita Khrushchev more than it is willing to acknowledge. He is scarcely mentioned in the USSR, but nevertheless, it was Khrushchev who laid the foundations for the buildup of Soviet strategic power. He also raised critical questions about the nature of nuclear war and its utility as a political instrument. He forced the party to confront the very notion of the inevitability of war in the nuclear era and its compatibility with Marxism-Leninism. He appreciated, almost instinctively, the far-reaching political ramifications for the USSR of acquiring long-range nuclear rockets. He perceived the opportunities for coercive diplomacy and psychological warfare. He recognized that strategic missiles symbolized the opening of a new era of East-West competition on a global scale. He created the strategic rocket forces as a separate entity and enunciated a Soviet version of the doctrine of mutual assured destruction. And he encouraged the development and production of new military hardware: The first three generations of Soviet ICBMs and of ballistic missile launching submarines were developed during his regime.

But Khrushchev did these things in a style and from a vantage point that has tended to obscure and confuse his contribution, perhaps because he learned the lessons of the nuclear era too well. He became obsessed with nuclear weapons as the only feasible means of conducting modern warfare. From this conclusion he made frequent quantum leaps: dismissing or denigrating the role of conventional weapons and the traditional armed services, brushing aside the Russian tradition of large standing armies, and ridiculing large warships as obsolete. But his brashness also enabled him to overcome the awe that modern military technology seemed to hold for Stalin's political successors. Above all, he tried desperately to translate the perception of a new nuclear balance into significant Soviet political gains.

The tight linkage Khrushchev drew between the new strategic balance and its political results led him into miscalculations: His imprudent attempt to exploit the "missile gap" in 1957 led to the Berlin crisis and, eventually, to the effort to redress the real strategic balance by the Cuban adventure. Both incidents stand in some contrast to Khrushchev's more prudent approach to actual military programs. Contrary to the widespread impression in the West that the Soviet Union would maximize its strategic military potential in the late 1950s, Khrushchev chose to forego a large deployment of the Soviet Union's first ICBM, the SS-6. Instead, he waited for the more advanced and more reliable SS-7s and SS-8s. Even then, actual deployment levels were not massive; only 200 or so of these second generation ICBMs eventually were deployed. Moreover, Khrushchev chose to place most of these missiles in secure underground silos, even though a more rapid buildup could have been achieved through continued proliferation of the more vulnerable above-ground launchers.

Similarly, early Soviet deployments of missile launching submarines seem moderate. The first version, the diesel-powered G-class, was crude and minimally effective: Its missiles had limited range (about 350 nautical miles) and the submarines had to rise to the surface in order to fire. Only about seventy launchers were deployed. Only a few submarines were deployed of the follow-on version, also the first nuclear-powered missile launcher, the H-class; eight submarines became operational with about 30 missiles of a slightly longer range, 700 nautical miles. The same pattern pertained in heavy bombers: the Bison (MYA-2) and Bear (TU-95) were never produced in large numbers and until this day have yet to be replaced.

An important political aspect of Khrushchev's strategic view was an enthusiastic agitation of the entire range of arms control issues. More than any of the postwar leaders, Khrushchev was responsible for making arms control and disarmament a perpetual aspect of the East-West debate. Indeed, he virtually bludgeoned the reluctant Western powers into various test-ban negotiations, only to threaten them crudely with the largest nuclear explosion in history in 1961. He started the wretched practice of submitting a potpourri of proposals in the annual Soviet disarmament memorandum to the United Nations. In the third world he succeeded in identifying the USSR with arms control. It should be emphasized, however, that his style was largely propagandistic; only one major agreement was concluded, the limited nuclear test ban treaty of 1963, which, by then, was only a recognition of the political impossibility of continued testing in the atmosphere. This treaty, of course, was Khrushchev's tactical device to soften the impact of his disastrous defeat in Cuba. Ironically, creating the impression of progress in arms control may well have cost him much needed support in the Soviet military in the crisis that led to his downfall in October 1964.

Khrushchev also broke new political ground by drawing the professional military more directly into politics. He enlisted Marshal Zhukov's support in the showdown with Malenkov and Molotov in June 1957. He reasserted the primacy of party control when he unceremoniously dismisssed Marshal Zhukov from office on relatively vague grounds only a few months later in October 1957. Nevertheless, a precedent had been established of promoting a senior marshal to Minister of Defense (e.g., Marshal Rodion Malinovsky succeeded Zhukov and Grechko succeeded Malinovsky). The lingering wartime disputes and animosities among the top military officers probably saved Khrushchev from a more severe showdown over Zhukov's dismissal and the issue of party control over military affairs. In any event, the military submitted not only to Zhukov's dismissal but to Khrushchev's nearly nonstop attacks on the size and the mission of the military forces, until they finally joined, or encouraged, the decision to remove him in 1964.

The Brezhnev Buildup[2]

The unprecedented removal of the First Secretary of the Communist Party of the Soviet Union in 1964 was in itself enough to introduce massive confusion. It soon became apparent that military policy, along with all other major positions, was due for revision.

The new policy direction was to restore more balance among Soviet military components and to begin a laborious buildup across a broad front. At the end of 1965 there was a symbolic increase in the official defense budget, an innovation that was continued every subsequent year until 1970 (an official increase of almost 40 percent in five years). The new approach included not only a buildup of strategic missiles but also the strengthening of conventional ground forces, including substantial increases along the Chinese frontier in the Far East. The Chinese aspect alone eventually amounted to an increase of roughly 10 to 15 percent in the overall total of Soviet defense spending. In addition, plans were expanded for a new, ocean-going navy, for reequipping the Soviet army, especially in European Russia and Central Europe, and for creating a new tactical air force. Little wonder that the magnitude of such an effort would consume considerably more than 10 percent of the Soviet Union's economic resources each year.

It is misleading, however, to read into the strategic buildup more than is justified by the evidence. The Brezhnev effort in strategic weaponry was constructed on the basis of technology that was already developed. The new ICBMs, the SS-9 (and SS-10, which later foundered), the SS-11, and the Y-class submarine were clearly already in a stage of advanced development in late 1964. Brezhnev's contribution was to decide on the final size of the force. In the earlier ICBM deployment, from 1959 through 1965, and in the second phase, from 1966 through 1971, the pace of deployment conformed very closely to a pattern that could be found in U.S. rates of deployment.[3] In other words, the buildup of ICBMs was not a rapid one because it proceeded more or less along lines that matched the production curve for U.S. ICBMs. Indeed, this similarity with U.S. experience is so striking as to suggest that the production and deployment of some major weapon systems in the USSR is influenced as much by technical and production factors as by political plans.

This has been obscured by the fact that the actual deployment of new Soviet ICBMs greatly exceeded U.S. intelligence projections.

The actual number of ICBMs deployed is nevertheless instructive. The gross number of Soviet ICBMs typically is compared with the U.S. level in order to demonstrate that the Soviets have been determined to achieve superiority. A comparison of separate ICBM systems, however, raises some questions about this interpretation. The SS-11, for example, was roughly comparable in capability to the U.S. Minuteman ICBM, which reached the final deployment level of 1,000 (this, too, was an arbitrary decision rather than a reflection of any strategic design). The SS-11 program by 1971 had reached 850 ICBM silo-launchers plus an additional 120 launchers located in former MR/IRBM fields. Another 60 silos were added in 1971-72. Thus, the final total, 1,030, only slightly exceeded the U.S. program.[4]

The truly unique aspect of the Soviet ICBM buildup, of course, is the large ICBM, the SS-9, and its replacement, the SS-18. It is this system that Western analysts invariably emphasize as evidence of the Soviet drive for a clear strategic advantage. As the number of SS-9s increased in the late 1960s, there was intensive speculation in the United States that the objective was to gain a capability to attack U.S. Minuteman silos. This may indeed have been the ultimate Soviet objective, but the favored scenario for doing so turned out to be wrong. In this scenario, the SS-9 was singled out as early as 1967 in the United States as the candidate to be the first Soviet missile to be equipped with multiple independently targetable re-entry vehicles (MIRVs). Such a MIRV capability was predicted to be operational by 1971-72. Confirmation seemed to have been provided by the testing of a multiple warhead (but not a true MIRV) that began in the USSR in August 1968. In 1969 American officials were predicting a Soviet objective of at least 400 SS-9s, each probably armed with three warheads, which would be the required combination in order to attack U.S. silos with one warhead per silo. By 1970, some officials even claimed the Soviets had already acquired a true MIRV capability.

In fact, the SS-9 program had been a logical progression from the previous generation (SS-7) and was probably designed by the same team. Its size and throw-weight was larger than its predecessor, but not because of its MIRV potential, because the SS-9 was never developed to be equipped with MIRVs. The first Soviet MIRVed missile, the SS-18, was still another generation of technology. Testing of this missile with MIRVs did not begin until 1974, and deployments of the SS-18 were not completed until 1980-81, about ten years later than the initial U.S. projection.

As in the case of the SS-11, there seems to have been hesitation and confusion in the final phase of deployments, a hesitation introduced not by strategic doctrine or military strategy but by politics—the strategic arms limitation talks (SALT).[5] As the SALT negotiations continued, it became obvious that the minimum U.S. price for an agreement constraining antiballistic missiles (ABMs) would be a freeze on all ICBMs. This was initially agreed in May 1971, but it had been a central proposition in the American position since the Spring of 1970. The Soviets, having already agreed to a low level of ABMs, which probably was their main SALT objective, began to adjust their ICBM deployments in anticipation of a final SALT agreement. The original SS-9 deployment was nearing completion at 306 silos; this included eighteen silos that were abandoned in 1970-1971. Foreseeing a freeze on the total number of ICBM silos, the Soviets added twenty completely new and different silos that turned out to be for the SS-18 ICBM. The final total, therefore, was 288 SS-9 silos and 20 new SS-18 silos. Why the Soviets made these last-minute additions in such marginal quantities rather than finishing the original program is not clear, especially since they subsequently retrofitted all SS-9 silos to SS-18 silos. Presumably, they wanted to establish a precedent for the new ICBM launchers for MIRVed missiles, that Moscow knew would be deployed during the period of the five-year interim SALT agreement.

In sum, all of the Soviet ICBM building programs were halted in 1971, short of the level anticipated by the United States in the late 1960s. Moreover, as a result of further bargaining in SALT, the Soviets also conceded that eventually they would dismantle their older SS-7 and SS-8 ICBMs (a total of 209) in order to trade them in for new launchers on submarines, as provided for in the SALT agreement. Thus, the final Soviet ICBM program has been frozen for several years at 1,398 ICBM launchers (including sixty light SS-13 silos, a solid-fuel missile that apparently never found favor).

It is instructive to compare the total of 1,398 ICBM launchers (i.e., minus the SS-13) with the programmed U.S. missile forces as of 1965-66, when the Soviets were making decisions for the five-year plan. At that time there were 1,000 Minuteman silos and about 200 Atlas and Titan launchers. It may well be that the Soviets planned the original 850 SS-11s and 306 SS-9s, for a total of 1,156 ICBMs, as a match for a potential U.S. total of about 1,200. The irony is that the SALT negotiations pushed the Soviets beyond this very crude numerical parity in order to add 120 silos for dual purpose missiles targeted against both Europe and the United States, and to add eighty SS-19 and SS-18 silos for the next generation of ICBMs.

It is not at all certain that the Soviets sought numerical superiority in ICBMs as part of a clear strategic design. It is the uniqueness of the very large throw-weight of the SS-18 plus the inexorable improvement in missile accuracy, rather than the total numbers of Soviet ICBMs or the rate of their buildup, that support the contention of an objective of superiority.

The buildup of submarine-launched ballistic missiles (SLBMs) offers a roughly similar story, though of course there are some important differences. Introduction of the modern, nuclear powered, Y-class submarine, comparable to the U.S. Polaris, lagged far behind the Soviet ICBM programs. Construction of the first Y-class submarine did not begin until early 1965. By 1967, as two submarines of the new class became operational (with thirty-two launch tubes), the United States had already completed its buildup of 656 SLBMs in forty-one submarines. In contrast to the Soviet ICBM program, Moscow's SLBM program could not be brought to a neat terminal point to coincide with SALT. To reach a force comparable to the United States, calculated in terms of the number of submarines that routinely could be kept on station, meant a force of about sixty Soviet nuclear submarines. After resisting the placement of any limits whatsoever on SLBMs in SALT, in early 1972 the Soviets made it clear to U.S. officials that the submarine total for SALT-counting purposes could be sixty-two modern submarines with 950 missile launchers.

Only in 1981 did the Soviets reach this goal, which, incidentally, suggests that a ten-year projection for purposes of force planning is well within Soviet capacity. Indeed, the final size of the SLBM program provides additional evidence that the Soviets do deal in long lead times: The SALT ceiling of 2,400 launchers, agreed in principle at Vladivostok in November 1974 and intended to last through 1985, was implied in the Soviet SALT position as early as 1970-71. Thus, freezing ICBM launchers in 1971-72 in effect at no more than 1,400 and adding 950 SLBMs yields a total 2,350 Soviet strategic missile delivery vehicles. If one includes the 160 obsolete bombers, the overall total of 2,500 is well within the bargaining area finally confirmed in the 1979 SALT II Treaty. Indeed, both the U.S. and USSR have been content with plans for missile forces through 1985 not significantly different from the numbers envisaged in 1969-70.

SALT I was nevertheless a watershed. It ended deployments of ballistic missile defenses, for all practical purposes, but ushered in a new phase of the Soviet buildup, precisely in those areas that were not constrained by the agreement: qualitative improvements of both ICBMs and SLBMs and the introduction of MIRVs. The history of subsequent negotiations for SALT II and the parallel history of the continuing Soviet buildup once again suggest that the rough guidelines of the previous period remained valid. Essentially, the buildup of weapons proceeded along predetermined technical lines, but some adjustments were made in the SALT bargaining process.[6]

The switch to the new fourth generation of ICBMs (SS-18s, SS-19s, and SS-17s) to replace the older SS-9s and SS-11s was completed at about the same rate as the earlier U.S. conversion to MIRVed missiles. From 1974 through 1980, the Soviets converted 288 SS-9 silos to SS-18 launchers and converted about 440 SS-11 silos to SS-19 silos (excluding sixty silos for the SS-19 already constructed in 1971), a conversion average of about 120 per year (compared to a U.S. MIRV conversion rate of about 130 per year).

This rate was probably envisaged in 1974 when the Soviet Union first proposed a MIRV ceiling of 1,000 to last through 1980. Later, at the Vladivostok summit meeting in 1974, they agreed to a ceiling of 1,320 MIRVs through 1985, presumably reflecting a decision to split their MIRVed forces between 900 ICBMs and 420 SLBMs. As the SALT bargaining became more intense in 1977-78, however, the Soviets were willing to adjust to a ceiling of 820 for land-based MIRVed ICBM launchers (against their own proposal for 850) and a total of 1,250 MIRVs altogether (as the Soviets had proposed in late 1977). All of these variants were well within rough limits suggested by the earlier (1973-74) phase of post-SALT I negotiations. This fact in itself, of course, may be an indictment of SALT, since it could be argued that the Soviet MIRV program is not essentially different under SALT than it would have been without any limits. Of course, such a judgment begs the question of what the political environment might have been without any SALT restraints and what changes this would have caused in Soviet force planning.

What the foregoing suggests is that: (1) Soviet force planning tends to be shaped by their five-year economic planning increments; (2) the actual implementation of strategic weapon programs is a rather mechanical and almost routine process; (3) force goals may well be dictated as much by technical considerations as by firm political objectives; and (4) SALT has had an impact, but the actual changes in Soviet forces it has brought about have been marginal.

This leaves the question of what the next phase will bring. Unlike past periods, the problem of pure numbers of weapons has receded: Much will now depend on new qualitative advances. Unlike the past twelve years, SALT has become a highly uncertain factor. The possibility of a complete breakdown in arms control cannot be ignored by either side, nor can the impact of a major acceleration of American strategic programs.

SOVIET STRATEGIC GOALS

What are the strategic goals for Soviet forces in the 1980s? Will Moscow be content with rough parity as Soviet political leaders constantly claim? Or do the Soviets harbor designs for superiority as many Western analysts insist? Two factors seem to have propelled Soviet leaders toward seeking potential strategic superiority: the influence of their military doctrines and the presumed political utility of a distinctly favorable strategic balance. On the other hand, two factors must suggest that there are real limits: the overall resource requirements of the Soviet economy and the politics of an inevitable succession period. One final factor, Soviet foreign policy objectives, could tend in either direction.

The Influence of Doctrine[7]

Soviet military doctrine has reflected the shifting views of Soviet political leaders, adjusting first to Stalin's and then to Khrushchev's preoccupations. In the 1960s, however, strategic doctrine was probably significantly in advance of operational policy. This was because only a handful of military and political leaders were trying to think through the various aspects of the military buildup that was evolving in conventional and nuclear weaponry. Two propositions—on the decisive nature of nuclear war and the crucial importance of its initial phase—seem to have had an impact on the development of Soviet forces. By the mid-1970s, however, the foreign political reaction to Soviet discussions of the conduct of nuclear war and its "winnability" led to some muffling of the more strident viewpoints and perhaps a revision of some important ideas. As a consequence, pronouncements on doctrine have become a less reliable guide to future Soviet policy.

Still, many Western analysts consider military doctrine and military science the key to unlocking the enigma of Soviet intentions. Doctrine should explain broad policy, not just the Soviet approach to the requisite numbers and characteristics of weapons; doctrine embraces the question of the purpose and character of war. An understanding of Soviet doctrine, then, is essential, and the evidential base for Western analyses of Soviet doctrine is found in the extensive public and semiprivate literature written by professional military officers and civilian strategists. In recent years a number of cohesive interpretations have been produced by Western analysts that tend to emphasize a broad Soviet consensus about nuclear war and strategic problems.

An interpretation of doctrines governing Soviet military policy in the 1970s includes the following major points:

1. War is not fatalistically inevitable, but the danger of war continues to exist; the imperialists, when driven to desperation, may well lash out with an attack on the USSR.
2. If a war does begin, it could remain a conventional war for "a certain time," but it probably would become a nuclear-rocket war. A limited nuclear war cannot exist for long, however, hence nuclear war would take on a worldwide character.
3. The first phase of a strategic nuclear exchange would be decisive. The strategic objectives (of the USSR) can be accomplished "from the very beginning." The war would be of "comparatively short duration" but could be protracted (a calculated ambiguity).
4. Soviet forces must be designed to fight a nuclear war.
5. Nuclear war, as every war, is a continuation of politics by other means.
6. Nuclear war—as any war—is "winnable."

There are many aspects of the foregoing that are by no means settled within the USSR and, most certainly, not agreed among outside experts. The problem of victory in nuclear war is the aspect that has drawn greatest attention in the West. What precisely is victory?

Victory is certainly alluded to in authoritative Soviet writing (including that of the current chief of staff, Marshal Ogarkov), and "victory" is defined in Soviet writings as "crushing" the enemy's forces and destroying the enemy's economic and political potential.[8] The military writings do not elaborate on how this is to be achieved and scarcely mention the concomitant destruction of the USSR or the cost of such a victory. Whether nuclear war is a usable policy instrument is left deliberately vague.

Indeed, a wide rhetorical gap on the question of the consequences of nuclear war has developed between Soviet military and political leaders. There is a large body of political statements that come perilously close to Malenkov's heresy of 1954, that nuclear war would mean the end of civilization. Brezhnev has said that " . . . the future of all mankind would be at stake" (June 23, 1981), and he has specifically denied the notion of winning a nuclear war: "It is a dangerous madness to try to defeat each other in the arms race and to count on victory in nuclear war." Brezhnev asserted that "anyone who starts a nuclear war in the hope of winning it has thereby decided to commit suicide." (*Pravda*, October 21, 1981). This rhetoric is intended, of course, for popular consumption, especially in Europe. It must be noted that the Soviets distinguish sharply between preparing to wage a nuclear war, which continues to be a legitimate enterprise—indeed, mandatory—and deciding in advance whether the outcome would meet some theoretical standard of victory. This is a crucial distinction.

Soviet commentators, including Brezhnev, can scarcely avoid acknowledging that the consequences of nuclear war would be significantly different from all previous war. It should follow that the destruction of nuclear war would drastically alter the traditional Clausewitzian proposition that war is a continuation of politics. But such a conclusion is consistently evaded. The Soviets cannot repudiate Clausewitz, given Lenin's approval of his dictum on war and politics, but Soviet theoreticians find it increasingly difficult to reconcile the well-advertised destructiveness of nuclear war with the concept that it would be merely a continuation of policy or politics by other means.

As one Soviet writer put it:[9]

If one subscribes to the thesis that war is a continuation of politics, then inflicting casualties cannot be an end in itself. To achieve a political goal through the use of armed force (and this is precisely what strategy is all about) is not tantamount to the killing of tens of millions of people on this or that side. What would be the political purpose of such a war?

The dichotomy between political rhetoric and military theory may account in some degree for the Soviet emphasis on survival measures, especially civil defenses. Soviet attempts to preserve the civilian leadership and major industries have received much more attention in the West than inside the USSR. Nevertheless, serious observers have concluded that in extreme cases the Soviets could, with sufficient warning, reduce casualties. The Soviets are inhibited from going too far in heralding civil defense because at the same time they must acknowledge that as a result of a political bargain they have given up one important means of defense—namely, antiballistic missile systems. It is probably significant that the new emphasis on civil defenses and other protective measures arose in the wake of the ABM Treaty of 1972; in part, civil defense efforts may have represented a psychological hedge against the open acknowledgment of massive vulnerability. In any case, neither the emphasis on civil defenses nor apparently the size of the program, have assumed the proportions of a truly nationwide effort to protect the population.

In sum, there is a basic Soviet dilemma about nuclear war: To minimize the consequences of nuclear war would be far too alarming, yet fear of war, however justified or profound, cannot be allowed to become a dominant factor lest the Soviet population lapse into a bourgeois pacificism. So war continues to be explained as a product of the last stages of capitalism, and therefore war as a continuation of politics cannot be disavowed, at least not at the Olympian level of the Politburo. To assert clearly that nuclear war remains an instrument of national policy would be so blood-curdling, however, that no Soviet leader could say so. A studied ambiguity is the result; it is probably the only acceptable course.

Yet there remain at the heart of Soviet doctrine two ominous propositions that are not as yet challenged or repudiated. First, the Soviets still maintain that the political and strategic objectives of the war would be decided in the initial phase of a general nuclear exchange; therefore, the side attacking first would have a decisive strategic advantage in determining the conduct and outcome of the war. Second, in considering the possible vulnerability of their own forces against such a decisive first-strike, the Soviets seem to have

adopted a strategy of launching-on-warning.[10] These two propositions are subsumed in the rubric of what Soviet propaganda usually
terms "a crushing rebuff." The operational effect of these points is
to move Soviet policy in the direction of large forces, capabilities to
destroy opposing forces, and operational planning that probably involves a Soviet first strike.

A critical gap in understanding the impact of Soviet military doctrine on strategy and planning is the virtual silence about China's role
in the next war. Indeed, the problem of China raises questions about
the broad concepts the Soviets have studiously defined as military
doctrine.

The Chinese factor poses the nightmare of a two-front war, yet virtually nothing has been published in the Soviet literature about the
consequences of fighting on both the Eastern and Western fronts.
Would a Sino-Soviet war include Japan and Korea? Would the
Soviets preempt against China, if faced with the near certainty of a
war in the West, and vice versa?

The lack of discussion in the public domain obviously reflects on
the subject's extreme political sensitivity. Brezhnev's Far Eastern
tour in 1978 and the attendant military maneuvers staged around
Khabarovsk were reminders that somewhere in the general staff the
Soviets are indeed making plans for this contingency. Nevertheless,
until there is greater clarity about the China factor, it is somewhat
misleading to talk about the Soviet military doctrine. The very existence of this large body of perceived truth, however, poses a barrier
to changes in Soviet policies in the 1980s.

The Utility of Nuclear Superiority

Since 1975 discussion of Soviet military theory and strategy has
gradually dried up.[11] The sources used in current Western analysis
are increasingly older ones and perhaps outmoded. This may reflect
the USSR's new strategic circumstances. In the 1950s and 1960s
strategic analysis was a new frontier; new ideas and thoughts were
given relatively free rein; the Soviet Union was rebuilding its armed
forces and thinking about the unthinkable. Extensive arming with
nuclear weapons required the reexamination of military theories. It is
not surprising that in this period the orthodox regime of Leonid
Brezhnev rejected the idea of mutual assured destruction as a

satisfactory political resolution of the problems of war and peace. Such a posture would have been too passive, if not pacifist. It would have implied a long-term, stable relationship between East and West. Something more dynamic had to be substituted. The result forged in the 1960s was a comprehensive, Clausewitzian doctrine that, in practice, turned out to be a justification to rebuild all the armed forces, to prepare these forces to fight in either a conventional or nuclear war, and to design them for a massive initial battle, all of which meant priority to creating extensive forces-in-being.

Once an improved state of military preparation was reached by the mid-1970s, new issues arose. Having acquired substantial intercontinental forces, could the USSR accept strategic parity with the United States as a permanent state of affairs? Was there a persuasive rationale for going further? Was there a real opportunity for achieving superiority? As the discussion of these issues proceeded in the USSR, there seems to have been a deliberate decision to accept what might be described as rhetorical parity by publicly denying any claim to superiority.

The advent of parity was evident in Brezhnev's major pronouncements in the early 1970s: "We have created strategic forces which constitute a reliable means of deterring aggressors." Even so, in the early 1970s this situation—a reliable Soviet deterrent—was considered precarious and subject to Western attempts to regain strategic superiority. This was implied in Brezhnev's warning that "We shall respond to any and all attempts from any quarter to obtain military superiority over the USSR. . . ."[12]

By 1975, however, the Soviet leaders apparently were convinced that the new strategic balance was firmly enough entrenched that a return to Western dominance was increasingly unlikely, hence the Western acceptance of detente:

International detente has become possible because a new relation of forces has been established in the world arena. Now the leaders of the bourgeoise world can *no longer entertain* serious intentions of resolving the historic dispute between socialism and capitalism, by force of arms. . . . (Brezhnev, June 14, 1975)

By 1977 the increase in the capacity of all Soviet forces had reached such a point that it was no longer effective politics (or policy) to trumpet the validity of a new balance of power. It was creating a backlash in the West, where Soviet statements about "superiority" or "victory" were cited in support of Western rearmament. A Soviet disclaimer was clearly needed. In January 1977, therefore, Brezhnev, in a speech at Tula, began not only to insist that the USSR did not seek strategic superiority but that the USSR was not intent on a first strike, an idea which he dismissed as "absurd and utterly unfounded." These denials, of course, were designed to counter the growing American apprehension that the new and more accurate Soviet ICBMs eventually would achieve a capability to neutralize the U.S. Minuteman ICBM force, thereby providing a strategic incentive for a Soviet preemptive first-strike.

By the end of 1977 Brezhnev had gone a step further and was insisting that the USSR "*will not* seek military superiority over the other side. We do not want to upset the approximate equilibrium of military strength existing at present . . . between the USSR and the United States." This new line was echoed rather consistently until, in late 1981, Brezhnev went even further: He denounced aspirations for victory in nuclear war as "dangerous madness" and ruled out the "concept" of a first strike.

The evolution of Soviet policy pronouncements is worth examining. The Soviets initially may have been intent on dampening potential Western reactions to changes in the actual strategic balance; they may also have wanted to solidify the status quo and preempt increases in U.S. and NATO defense programs, including NATO's December 1979 decision to deploy new intermediate-range nuclear weapons. The new, more moderate line in 1977–79 also coincided with the resumption and completion of SALT negotiations with the Carter Administration. Thus, there were sound, tactical reasons for Brezhnev's disclaimers. Nevertheless, there may have also been a deeper reappraisal of the risks of attempting to achieve a true superiority. A number of observers believe that along with the military doctrines that justified the Soviet strategic buildup there was a parallel stream of thought that held that in the end the Soviet Union could not expect to achieve a meaningful advantage in strategic weapons. This viewpoint maintained that the United States eventually would react and that the USSR could not sustain an indefinite strategic competition. Those who advocated this position in the USSR tended to be in the nonmilitary sectors but they may have included some military figures as well.

What may have happened is that this second viewpoint has gradually been given more of an airing at the Politburo level as the burden of defense has grown. Denouncing superiority might have been used as a tactical expediency, but the expediency created its own reality. Repeated disclaimers began to take on the aura of settled policy, no matter how insincere or cynical the initial motive. Inside the USSR, pronouncements such as Brezhnev's acquire a specific political weight when constantly repeated and echoed. Some evidence for this is found in further criticisms by Politburo members (e.g., Konstantine Chernenko) and in the sharp rebuttal written by the Soviet Chief of Staff, Marshal Ogarkov, who in 1981 argued rigorously for protecting defense expenditures. [13]

Since the invasion of Afghanistan in December 1979 and the collapse of SALT II, the Soviets also have had to consider the deterioration in Soviet-American relations and its implications for the strategic arms balance. Initially, the Soviets increased their rhetoric on the dangers of war and began to talk authoritatively about new risks. The Central Committee Plenum of June 1980 offered a reappraisal of the international situation and a revised course for Soviet defense policy. [14] At the meeting, Brezhnev claimed that imperialist circles were trying to "put pressure on" and isolate the Soviet Union. This effort would "misfire," Brezhnev asserted, because of the "immeasurable growth of the USSR's economic potential and *defense might*. . . ." The resolution of the Central Committee concluded, however, that there still existed "possibilities and socio-political force capable of preventing the slide down to a new cold war . . . ," but it called for an "all-around strengthening of the defense potential of our state in order to frustrate the plans of imperialism aimed at reaching military superiority. . . ." The Central Committee's deliberation implied that economic stringencies would not lead to a retrenchment in the defense effort. Indeed, there was no challenge to the overall economic balance between defense and civilian requirements, and, up to the party congress of February 1981, there was a campaign for a stronger defense.

Nevertheless, as international tensions grew in 1980, especially after the U.S. election and the promised increases in the American defense budget, the Soviets were forced to consider more soberly the consequences of a new long-term military competition. No definitive Soviet response emerged, at least not in the proceedings of the Twenty-Sixth Party Congress, which might have been the appropriate point of departure. A wait-and-see attitude seemed the dominant theme, but there was a growing sense that the USSR would be forced to match U.S. increases and, most important, that the United States was counting on Soviet economic weaknesses in a new competitive strategic round.[15]

The Economics of Defense[16]

An important reason for Soviet hesitation about a future strategic course must be the economic consequences of another phase in the military buildup. Western analyses of Soviet military spending indicate that in the post-Khrushchev period Soviet defense expenditures have grown more than 3 percent annually and now consume about 12 to 14 percent of the USSR's GNP. In a country where resource allocation is a perennial problem, the impact of such large peacetime demands by the defense establishment seems out of any reasonable proportion. A peacetime objective of preparing the country for war clearly falls within the broad definition of approved Soviet military doctrine, which in turn permits the military to make significant demands on the civilian economy. Moreover, the duration (at least fifteen years) of this substantial growth in Soviet defense spending suggests that the military sector has won a permanent position in Soviet economic planning. Soviet practice probably requires a doctrinal justification for such a major allocation. In this light, the argument that the initial phase of a nuclear war will determine its eventual outcome is not simply an interesting theory but a platform from which the military can insist on a continuing allocation of resources devoted to creating large forces-in-being. This, in turn, also implies a strong and continuing modernization program (some Soviet sources suggest a renewal period of about six to eight years for major weapons).[17]

Can the trend in Soviet military spending continue? Numerous studies point to a basic economic-political crisis in the USSR during the 1980s that could have a significant impact on defense spending. An early CIA study,[18] for example, claimed that the USSR had pursued three objectives: (1) to catch up with the United States militarily; (2) to expand its industrial base; and (3) to meet at least minimal consumer expectations. Reduced economic growth in the 1980s would make the simultaneous pursuit of these objectives far more difficult than it was in the past and pose hard choices for Soviet leaders. Thus, a Soviet political debate on future levels and patterns of military expenditures is increasingly likely. It may already have begun.

After signing the SALT II treaty in 1979, Brezhnev began to emphasize the production of consumer goods.[19] In his speech to the Central Committee in October 1979, he claimed that the situation in the output of consumer goods was "inexcusable," and he attacked the machine building industry, the traditional symbol of the heavy industrial-military complex. In fact, at the end of 1979 the official Soviet defense budget was slightly reduced, and CIA estimates included a slight decline in defense growth rates. Despite the rising tensions after Afghanistan and the emphasis on defense at the June 1980 Central Committee Plenum, Brezhnev in November 1980 was still needling the defense industries, claiming that while these branches had contributed to raising consumer goods production, these increased rates "must not be allowed to slow down in the next five-year period." The consumer goods orientation was also reflected in the first draft for the new five-year plan (1981–85) where the rates of growth for heavy industry were less than those projected for light industries.

By early 1981, however, when the five-year plan was officially announced, the difference between the two sectors was too narrow to be meaningful (i.e., growth rates of 26 to 28 percent for heavy industry versus 27 to 29 for light industry). In effect, political events in 1979–80 probably made any contemplated reduction in defense priorities impossible. At the party congress, Brezhnev simply noted that heavy industry would play a "big role" in producing consumer goods and that this sector already accounted for half of the consumer goods production (a rather startling statistic). In 1981 Group A, heavy industries, grew minutely slower (0.3 percent) than Group B, consumer goods. As Soviet-American relations continued to deteriorate, the Soviets emphasized that U.S. military superiority would not be tolerated and that U.S. efforts to achieve such superiority would be "matched" if necessary by increased Soviet military spending.

The Soviets cannot view another round of serious strategic competition with equanimity. On the one hand, U.S. rough intelligence projections for *increases* in Soviet spending for strategic forces total only about $10 billion (in constant 1979 dollars) by 1985, a target well within Soviet capacity. On the other hand, a five-year reduction in the rate of growth of overall defense spending, from 4 percent to 2 percent annually, would yield ruble savings of 28 billion, amounting to about 3 percent of the entire capital stock of the USSR. If such cuts were taken in military investment and not simply applied across the board, the effect obviously would be even more significant. A freeze on military spending would result in savings equal to 10 percent of *all* industrial investment in the Eleventh Five-Year Plan. This illustrates the magnitude of the Soviet dilemma.[20]

An additional factor is that the number of males reaching the age of military service in 1985 will be well short of the numbers needed for both the economy and for defense. This alone suggests the size of the armed forces may have to be reduced. In sum, economic and demographic factors impose limits on continuation of a Soviet military buildup. Savings in funds, in scarce resources, and in manpower could obviously result from a cutback in defense; but there are strong countervailing political and strategic factors against a reversal of twenty years of strategic policy. In any case, some major economic policy decisions are not merely required but will be mandatory.

The Politics of Defense[21]

Given the certainty of changes in the top Soviet political leadership, the internal politics of Soviet defense policy will become unusually significant. Will the Soviet armed forces and defense establishment continue to enjoy the privileged place in decision-making councils that it has occupied under Brezhnev?

Both the statistics on military spending and the actual growth of military hardware confirm the highly favorable attitude accorded to the military during the Brezhnev period. It is difficult to find any category in the military sector that has been denied. Brezhnev has permitted or encouraged an increasingly personal identification with military matters: He was awarded a marshal's baton and various victory medals; he is identified publicly as commander-in-chief and head of the defense council; and he has been the center of growing attention to all aspects of his military career. In addition to whatever personal bias he may have toward indulging the military sector, there are strong political factors involved in conciliating such a powerful vested interest group. An important point is that none of Brezhnev's probable successors have enjoyed this continuing involvement in military affairs. This could operate in different directions. In a succession crisis, the support of the military for an aspiring candidate could be quite potent. A commitment to continue a heavy defense program would presumably be the nominal price for military support. On the other hand, a successful domestic economic policy could require manpower cuts in the military and a significant reallocation of resources. Such a course would be a highly risky platform for a successor unless rationalized by a foreign policy that could demonstrate or promise to make major progress in weakening the coalitions opposing the USSR (East or West) and changing the "correlation of forces." This implies a conciliatory policy either toward China or, more likely, toward the West.

Predicting the likely course of succession politics is hazardous, but there are roughly four variants in the interaction between the political and military sectors in a succession period. At one end of the spectrum is the view that the Soviet state is inherently militaristic—that is, that militarism is deeply embedded in Communist theory and practice. The chances that this basic situation would change, therefore, depend not on tactical, internal shifts but on an array of external forces that, over an extended period, could consistently thwart the purposes of Soviet militarism. A second interpretation allows that military institutions and policies are influential in domestic policies but that this does not constitute militarism as such. Rather, the military establishment is included in a reigning coalition of conservative vested interests—heavy industry, military professionals, the secret police, and the leading party organs. If this view is correct, the Soviet military is a formidable force, not easily thwarted even by external setbacks. Still, it would be subject to Kremlin power politics and thus not an immutable force.

A third and quite different projection is that the Soviet system is destined for major internal change and that the succession period will produce this change by finally unleashing new reformist and somewhat more liberal forces. These forces, this view continues, will have to be responsive to the new realities of Soviet economic stringencies, which are powerful enough to force military reductions.

A fourth view is that succession periods do in fact produce new opportunities but that the practical results are likely to be tempered and that change will result only from a gradual accumulation of steps developing within a general strategic framework not radically dissimilar from the Brezhnev period. The effect on the military will thus also be cumulative, spread over many years.

Had the succession taken place a few years ago, it was likely that an evolutionary model would have been followed. Now, as the time passes, the shift from Brezhnev is likely to seem much more abrupt, if only because many of his contemporaries (Podgorny, Kosygin, Suslov) are also departing the scene.

THE OUTLOOK

In this early part of the 1980s the Soviets face a strategic choice: whether to treat the next several years as a period for a continuing geopolitical advance or to consolidate their position as a hedge against internal troubles later in the decade.

The Soviet Union has made some gains in expanding its sphere of influence since the 1975 intervention in Angola. Their specific adventures are well known—Angola, Ethiopia, South Yemen, Vietnam, Afghanistan. Moreover, a coalition of Soviet clients may be taking shape, as reflected in the friendship treaty of August 1981 between South Yemen, Libya, and Ethiopia. In the Middle East, the Soviets have a demonstrated ability to play several sides: retaining influence in Iraq while signing a new treaty with Syria; maintaining a neutral stance during the Iran-Iraq war despite the 1972 treaty with Iraq; and making some headway in Iran. To be sure, there have been setbacks—the Muslim condemnation of the intervention in Afghanistan, for example, and the final verdict in the Afghan war is still outstanding. On the whole, however, the past five to six years have been an advance in the Soviet position in the third world.

In Europe, the policy of detente seems to have survived the deterioration in U.S.-Soviet relations. The Soviets have succeeded to the point where European pressures on American diplomacy to resume East-West negotiations on arms control in 1981 posed a serious risk of a split in the Western front, which was reflected in another dispute over sanctions against Poland and the USSR. The Soviets have been determined to exploit the divisions between the United States and Western Europe through new economic arrangements with European countries—the natural gas pipeline—that have created vested interests in a continuing political tranquility.

In Sino-Soviet relations, Moscow made some gains by underwriting the Vietnamese attack on Cambodia in late 1978. The Chinese counterattack and Western countermoves, including the extension of American arms assistance to China, have offset the psychological impact of the Vietnamese-Soviet Treaty (November 1978). More recently, new overtures have emanated from Moscow to Peking.

This period, of course, has followed the achievement of strategic parity, and it would be reasonable for the Soviets themselves to attribute their forward movement in some part to the change in the strategic balance. The declining ability of the West to react vigorously or uniformly in Afghanistan or even in Poland may have encouraged the Soviets to believe that the risks of their foreign policy adventures have diminished significantly. This is never subject to conclusive proof, of course, but some correlation is probably made in the Kremlin between the strategic weapon balances and the overall correlation of forces. In any case, there must be strong arguments in Moscow (1) that the USSR has entered an optimal strategic period (or "window" as the jargon has it); (2) that the correlation of forces, including the military balance, will never again be as favorable as the early 1980s; and (3) that future opportunities may be constricted by a U.S. rearmament program.

Finally, there is the uncertain role for arms control. Soviet support for the SALT II treaty does not mean that they necessarily view the process as favorably as they did a decade earlier. In the 1970s the Soviets may have had an interest in stabilizing the strategic competition. Now they must contemplate that the American defense budget has been increasing almost every year since the first SALT agreement and increasing at a faster rate than inflation since 1975. Moreover, despite SALT, the United States has moved into a strategic modernization program—including the Trident submarine and missile, a revived B-1 bomber, the MX missile, development of cruise missiles in all environments (air, sea, and ground), new longer-range Pershing ballistic missiles, cruise missiles for surface ships and submarines—and has shown renewed interest in ballistic missile defense, which would require revision of the ABM treaty. On the face of it, the SALT process can (no longer) be inherently attractive to the USSR as a regulator of the strategic competition.

What remains attractive about SALT are its political implications. If SALT continues as an active negotiation, enough of the elements of detente with the United States may be maintained that (1) a clear Sino-American alliance would be slowed, if not forestalled; (2) a major NATO-European rearmament program would be inhibited; and (3) the U.S. defense buildup would be constrained. Matters are reaching a point, however, where these potential benefits of SALT may require concrete Soviet concessions. The Reagan Administration insists that a new SALT agreement would have to incorporate significant reductions, probably focusing on severe reductions in Soviet heavy missiles, and is pressing for a complete dismantling of the SS-20 force in the talks on intermediate-range forces in Geneva.

A new SALT negotiation would come at a time when the Soviets must rethink the strategic value of their heavy investment in fixed land-based ICBMs. If the United States does indeed move to acquire a capability to destroy Soviet missile silos, as would be the case with even 100 to 200 new MX missiles, the Soviet ICBM force would have to be considered in jeopardy by the end of this decade. Thus the Soviets would face a serious dilemma. There are some highly tentative signs that the Soviets may recognize the strategic implications of a mutual vulnerability to anti-ICBM attacks. Soviet criticism of the feasibility of limited nuclear strikes against ICBM silos is becoming more frequent. Without directly acknowledging it, there seems to be a greater emphasis on deterrence reflected in rising Soviet complaints about the threat of attacks on command and control functions by Pershing II missiles in Germany, which could disrupt any Soviet counterattack. If such preliminary signs are valid indicators, they could reflect some new pressures in the Politburo. In this case, the Soviet attitude toward SALT could change; they would have to seriously entertain concessions to head off or minimize American counterforce deployments, including a reduction of the comparable Soviet threat to U.S. ICBMs. A trade-off between SS-18s and MX may thus be possible.

Leaving aside the tactical adjustments for SALT negotiating purposes, there is little solid evidence on which to base a firm estimate of future Soviet strategic goals. There are simply too many uncertainties: economic complications, the political succession, doctrinal vagaries, and a highly fluid political relationship with the United States. Other less basic factors, such as the hazy future of SALT negotiations and the link between talks on intermediate-range missiles in Geneva and SALT, compound the sense of uncertainty.

Nevertheless, certain factors are more enduring and offer some insight. First of all, it seems likely that the pattern of modernizing strategic forces over a seven- to ten-year cycle will continue: By the mid-1980s the Soviets will be likely to deploy at least one new ICBM (if SALT constraints continue). The choice seems to be between a solid fuel missile that could be deployed as a mobile ICBM or yet another generation of the SS-17 or SS-18 type (i.e., a large missile using stable liquid fuels). In any case, a force of 10,000 missile warheads affords a wide variety of strategic options.

The same general pattern is likely to apply to the USSR's strategic submarine force, which has now reached the limits projected in April 1972: 62 modern submarines with about 950 launchers. Replacement of existing sea-based missiles with MIRVed varieties is well under way. The new Typhoon class will appear late in the 1980s and eventually make up the bulk of the force, replacing the older Yankee class. Eventually, the SLBM force will have sufficient missile range to operate close to Soviet shores—that is, in the Sea of Okhotsk and in the Bering Sea—although Soviet concerns about the vulnerability of a force deployed in such confined areas may result in more conventional deployment patterns. A new Soviet heavy bomber also is predicted by the United States.

These developments are not extraordinary; they follow lines implicit in previous deployments. What is not clear are possible Soviet responses to the emergence of new U.S. selective targeting options and counterforce capabilities. If the Soviet Union cannot accept the vulnerability of its land-based missile force, does this mean the Soviets will be committed to a launch-under-attack doctrine? Would it mean a higher level of alert forces on both sides? Would the Soviets choose to deploy a mobile ICBM?

The adoption of a mobile missile would be an effort to reduce Soviet vulnerability rather than to move toward hair-trigger responses. This, however, would run into a body of Soviet strategic doctrine that insists on seizing the initiatives in the first phase of a nuclear exchange. An alternative would be to accept the possibility of protracted nuclear war that was not decided in the crucial first phase. Conflicts of this nature, in fact, have been given greater attention and are reflected in a greater Soviet interest in strategic reserve forces, including an ability to reload and refire from missile silos. There are some signs of a Soviet shift to a concept of a prolonged war, reflected in the writings of the Chief of the General Staff, Marshal Ogarkov.[22] These are long-term decisions, however, that are more likely to be made in the late 1980s when the extent of U.S. programs is more clear.

A second new development might be in the direction of a Soviet cruise missile force; it would be prudent if the Soviets believe that their heavy investment in ICBMs may be in jeopardy from U.S. counterforce capabilities. The Soviets have a large enough submarine force to accommodate some strategic cruise missile deployments, and if, as predicted, a new Soviet bomber is coming along, it too could be a cruise missile carrier. In short, the Soviets are not likely to accept a significant disadvantage in cruise missiles, any more than they did in ICBMs or SLBMs. Nevertheless, growth in numbers of cruise missiles, if it occurred, could reflect a deeper trend away from first-strike capabilities.

Whatever the force developments, there will be the question of whether the Soviets continue to see the present period as a favorable one for extending geopolitical gains on the theory that the strategic balance is favorable if not optimal. Is there a new balance of power that could tempt a series of aggressive Soviet probes and adventures?

The answer must be inconclusive. There is certainly a greater new strategic confidence in the USSR today than a decade ago. This increased confidence has been growing gradually: Some observers date the beginning of the trend as far back as Soviet conduct in the 1967 Middle East war.[23] More assertive Soviet international behavior certainly was evident in the latter half of the 1970s, beginning with the 1975 intervention in Angola. This assertiveness, however, cannot be attributed merely to a judgment about the technical balance (e.g., numbers of missile warheads). It must represent a more basic calculation about the general correlation of forces, of which the new military balance is one important part.

If the Soviets do calculate their opportunities on the basis of a broad correlation of forces (and not simply on the narrow ratio of strategic weapons), they cannot ignore the geopolitical problems on their frontiers—Poland, Afghanistan, and China. They face situations that have potentially high political costs and risks, involve long-term political, military, and economic burdens, and threaten the security of their supply lines and flanks. Moreover, these situations challenge the presumption of a new strategic confidence: A superpower that is bogged down in efforts to shore up its immediate periphery and driven by fears of encirclement is not on a true ascendancy.

It is this latter judgment that requires a careful assessment. It has become ritual to proclaim that the Soviet system offers no ideological attraction, is politically and economically weak, and therefore relies only on military power. This is true but also somewhat misleading. Soviet weaknesses are not new, but it is yet to be demonstrated that they are truly significant in a broad historical sense. Although the Soviet economy may no longer be dynamic, it is still an enormously strong machine, capable of filling most of the USSR's needs and, incidentally, far less vulnerable to international currents and cyclical swings than its Western counterparts. Slow growth rates and declining productivity are not phenomena limited to the USSR. Even in its chronic problem of agriculture, the USSR has demonstrated an ability to buy its way out of repeated crises. In any case, the economy can continue to support a major military effort, even while trimming some resource commitments to defense.

The Soviet system lost its ideological appeal long ago. None of the developing countries are attracted by proletarian internationalism, but many leaders in the third world have been intrigued with the Leninist system for building centralized political power and authority. It has been the patronage of a great power—the political, military, and economic support that the USSR can supply—rather than ideology that has attracted Angola, Ethiopia, Yemen, and others to the Soviet sphere. The ideological struggle ended long ago, but the struggle for power and influence continues, and the USSR has some important assets.

The significance of Soviet military power is not that all else has failed. It is important precisely because Soviet leaders believe that military power is decisive in international affairs and is the prerequisite for advancing their political goals. Major turning points in their own history—the civil war and the German invasion—have been decided by military means. In the Cold War with the United States, an era of American nuclear monopoly, Stalin maintained huge conventional forces. In an era of U.S. missile preponderance, Khrushchev countered with massive medium-range forces targeted against Europe. In the era of strategic competition, the Soviets have again demonstrated their determination to build massive forces at least equal to those of their opponents and enemies. There is little reason for the next generation of Soviet leaders to regard military strength differently than did Lenin, Stalin, Krushchev, or Brezhnev.

NOTES

1. For a complete review of Khrushchev's military policies, see Thomas W. Wolfe, *Soviet Power and Europe, 1945-70* (Baltimore, Md.: Johns Hopkins Press, 1970), pp. 73-236, and *Soviet Strategy at the Crossroads* (Cambridge, Mass.: Harvard Press, 1964).

2. The early adjustments of Brezhnev's policies are also described in Wolfe, *op. cit.*, pp. 427–515.

3. Ian Bellany, "Strategic Arms Competition and the Logistic Curve," *Survival* (September–October 1974), 228ff.

4. Numerous sources contain figures for the Soviet missile buildup; the most authoritative are found in the annual Department of Defense *Reports*, which have been declassified for the years 1963–72. See also, David S. Sullivan, "Evaluating U.S. Intelligence Estimates," in Roy Godson, ed., *Intelligence Requirements for the 1980s: Analysis and Estimates*, (National Strategy Information Center, 1980), p. 57.

5. R. Garthoff, "Negotiating with the Russians: Some Lessons from SALT," *International Security* (Spring 1977); and R. Garthoff, "SALT and the Soviet Military," *Problems of Communism* (January-February 1975).

6. Garthoff, *Ibid.;* see also, Thomas Wolfe, *The SALT Experience* (Ballinger Publishing Company, 1979) and Gerard Smith, *Doubletalk* (Doubleday & Company, 1980).

7. There is a large body of literature on Soviet military doctrine. A general guide is William F. Scott, *Soviet Sources of Military Doctrine and Strategy* (National Strategy Information Center, 1975). I have relied on the analysis and synthesis by Joseph D. Douglass and Amoretta M. Hoeber, *Soviet Strategy for Nuclear War* (Hoover Institution, 1979). A recent survey is Derek Leebaert, ed., *Soviet Military Thinking* (George Allen and Unwin, 1981).

8. Douglass and Hoeber, *op. cit.*, pp. 14–15.

9. Henry Trofimenko, "The Theology of Strategy," *Orbis* (Fall 1977), 512.

10. Daniel O. Graham, *Shall America Be Defended* (Arlington House, 1979), p. 88, quoting Marshall Krylov; Douglass and Hoeber, *op cit.*, pp. 48, 77; Lawrence Freedman, *The Evolution of Nuclear Strategy* (St. Martin's Press, 1978), pp. 267–68.

11. For the more recent period see R. Garthoff, "Mutual Deterrence and Strategic Arms Limitation in Soviet Policy," *International Security* (Summer 1978), pp. 112–27; Dimitri K. Simes, "Deterrence and Coercion in Soviet Policy," *International Security* (Winter 1980-81), pp. 80–103; and Richard Pipes, "Why the Soviet Union Thinks It Could Fight and Win a Nuclear War," *Commentary* (July 1977), pp. 21–34

12. Brezhnev's quotations are contained in Garthoff, 1978, *op. cit.* See also, Mose L. Harvey, ed., *Soviet World Outlook* II, no. 2 (February 15, 1977). Of special importance are Brezhnev's interview with *Der Spiegel,* quoted in *The New York Times* (November 4, 1981); and the pamphlet "The Threat to Europe" (Progress Publishers, 1981).

13. Marshal Ogarkov, *Kommunist,* no. 10 (July 1981). The statements by Politburo member K. P. Chernenko in April 1981 suggest a Brezhnevite political attack on the feasibility of nuclear war; indeed, Chernenko's record of statements that are critical of a heavy defense orientation may be an interesting political indicator of disenchantment with the defense burden (see Foreign Broadcast Information Service, *Trends in Communist Media* (May 6, 1981), pp. 6–9.

14. *FBIS, Daily Report, Soviet Union* (June 24, 1980), p. R1.

15. "Soviet Defense Head Promises to Match U.S. Arms Spending," *Washington Post* (June 22, 1981).

16. The Central Intelligence Agency (CIA) has published a series of studies on Soviet defense spending, entitled "A Dollar Comparison of Soviet and U.S. Defense Activities." Data for 1965–75 were published in February 1976 and for the period 1971–80, the same publication is dated January 1981. An excellent analysis used in this section is Abraham S. Becker, *The Burden of Soviet Defense* (RAND, R-2752-A, October 1981).

17. Bellany, *op. cit.,* p. 230.

18. CIA, *Soviet Economic Problems and Prospects* (Government Printing Office, 1977).

19. William G. Hyland, "Kto Kogo in the Kremlin," *Problems of Communism* (January–February 1982), pp. 17–26.

20. Becker, *op. cit.,* p. 71.

21. On the role of the military in politics see Richard Pipes, "Militarism and the Soviet State," *Daedalus, U.S. Defense Policy in the 1980s* (Fall 1980); Dimitri Simes, "The Military and Militarism in Soviet Society," *International Security* (Winter 1981–82); Seweryn Bialer, *Stalin's Successors* (Cambridge University Press, 1980), 255ff.

22. Ogarkov, *op. cit.*

23. Stephen S. Kaplan, *Diplomacy of Power* (Brookings Institution, 1981), pp. 655–56.

4 U.S.-SOVIET RELATIONS AND THE CONTROL OF NUCLEAR WEAPONS

Marshall D. Shulman

The question of how best to assure the security of the United States in the age of nuclear weapons is at least as much a political problem as it is technical. "Political" refers not only to internal processes within the Soviet Union and the United States but also to the prevailing character of the relationship between them—the level of tension, suspicion, communication, cooperation, or conflict in the current state of their competition, which inevitably affects their respective nuclear and military policies. It is worth asking, therefore, what can be learned from a review of the recent and present Soviet-American relationship and its possible future course and how that lesson may bear on future prospects for the rational management of the strategic competition.

Predictions about any aspect of international relations are necessarily tentative given the large number of unpredictable variables involved, but several current developments point toward a continuation in the immediate future of the process of deterioration that has characterized Soviet-American relations in recent years. Some of these developments are both symptoms of the current deterioration and also probable causes of a further deterioration. Chief among them is the continuing intensification of the military competition between the two countries, both in nuclear and conventional weapons. A decade of effort to stabilize the nuclear competition through nego-

77

tiations has come to an unsuccessful end. While it is not possible at this writing to judge to what extent the constraints that had been under discussion will continue to be observed, it is apparent that both qualitative and quantitative improvements in the capabilities of both sides are continuing in ways that were not specifically constrained in the recent negotiations.

It is of particular significance that the new weapon systems planned by both sides likely to be less stable and less verifiable than present systems; future efforts to negotiate verifiable limits on the strategic competition thus may face difficulties even greater than those that confronted past negotiators. Because the new systems will be less stable (in the sense of their suitability for a first strike rather than retaliation) they will contribute to mounting apprehensions about the respective intentions of the two countries and therefore to a higher level of tension. Adding to this tension and to the potential for mutual miscalculation in crisis situations is the diminished effective diplomatic communication between the two countries.

There are also a number of factors external to the bilateral relationship that both are affected by the trend toward deterioration and seem likely to contribute to greater difficulties in the future. For example, constraints intended to inhibit further proliferation of nuclear weapons have been weakened as tensions between the superpowers have mounted. Another and more fundamental factor is the large and increasing number of potential conflict situations in various parts of the world involving the interests of the two countries: these add the exacerbation of East-West competition to local conditions leading to political upheavals. This is not limited to the developing areas, which can be illustrated by the increasing extent to which Europe has become a locus of the competition. The instabilities of Eastern Europe have raised questions concerning the extent of Western influence in areas of Soviet sensitivity and the renewed emphasis in Soviet political strategy on efforts to enlarge its influence in Western Europe both contain the elements of a complex gamble to change the political map of this vital area.

Finally, the domestic and international economic problems currently confronting the Soviet Union and the United States may have effects that could operate in either direction: toward a further heightening of tension in their relationship or toward an easement in the military competition as a result of budgetary constraints. Although the institutional causes of these problems in the two countries are not analogous, both are experiencing difficulties with productivity and overall growth rates, with consequent stress upon living conditions at home and upon economic relations with their respective allies. It is at this point a matter of conjecture whether the effect of these economic stresses will be to produce a higher level of tension internationally as an escape from intractable domestic problems or a more serious effort to reduce the flow of resources into the military sector.

THE RISE AND FALL OF DETENTE

Why have relations between the two countries deteriorated so precipitously during the past decade of mutually celebrated "detente," once heralded as the basis for a "structure of peace"? The question elicits an exchange of recriminations revealing that what was called detente was inherently flawed by the two countries' contradictory understanding of its meaning for both political and military aspects of the relationship.

The reasons for the breakdown become clearer when it is recognized that the detente emerging in 1972 did not spring full-bloom into existence at that moment but developed as the culminations of two decades' efforts toward moderation of U.S-Soviet relations. In each case, these efforts had proved abortive because they were intermixed with episodes of conflict. For example, the "spirit of Geneva" developed at the Geneva summit meeting and the signing of the Austrian peace treaty, both in 1955—intended to demonstrate "with deeds, not words" the Soviet interest in improving relations—were followed by the Soviet intervention in Hungary and renewed tensions over Berlin. The opening of academic and cultural relations in 1958 and Nikita Khrushchev's visit to the United States in 1959 were followed by the U-2 episode, the aborted summit meeting of 1960, and the Cuban missile crisis of 1962. The interest in detente reflected in the Harmel Report of 1967 and the initiation of the idea of strategic arms limitations talks at Glassboro in the same year were followed by the Soviet invasion of Czechoslovakia. Similarly, the detente of 1972, although more fully developed than these preceding efforts, proved short-lived (rather than "irreversible" as the Soviet leadership expected) because it was flawed by contradictions between Soviet and American understandings of what it implied for the conflictive elements of the relationship.

On the Soviet side, what came to be called detente in the West evolved from the political strategy of "peaceful coexistence." In its earliest forms, peaceful coexistence was justified by Lenin as a temporary, tactical expedient to protect the Soviet Union in periods of weakness. Under Khrushchev, peaceful coexistence became a long-term political strategy that reflected an increasing awareness of the danger of nuclear war and the political advantages of the peace issue in winning support in Europe and the third world. To Khrushchev and to Brezhnev peaceful coexistence meant competing with the "imperialist" West by means short of war. It implied businesslike relations and perhaps even cooperation in specific areas as two equal and preeminent powers. This was not seen, however, as contradicting continued active exploitation of opportunities for the advancement of Soviet influence. Specifically, the Soviet view of peaceful coexistence constrained neither Soviet aid to emerging forces defined as national liberation movements nor the ideological conflict with the West; in fact, Soviet theoreticians sometimes saw it as sharpening ideological differences. Although this argument was advanced to prove (to the Chinese, then in a militant revolutionary mode, and perhaps also to the ideologically-minded at home) continued fidelity to the original rhetoric of the Revolution, it also reflected the operational problems of the Soviet security apparatus in preventing an undermining of the official ideology during periods of reduced tension and increased contacts with the West.

For the United States, the notion of detente represented an evolution of the containment doctrine. In the early postwar years, containment in practice meant the defense of Western Europe, Greece, and Turkey from Soviet encroachment. After Europe was stabilized and attention shifted to the competition in the third world, containment was applied globally, and its application became more diffuse because of the difficulty of distinguishing among a variety of local radical nationalist movements whose degree of responsiveness to Soviet leadership was unclear. Meanwhile, successive American adminstrations, including Presidents Eisenhower, Kennedy, and Johnson, reflected a growing awareness of the costs and risks of nuclear weapons and sought ways to ease the competitive relationship. These efforts found their culmination during the administration of President Nixon in the summit meetings of 1972–74, the signing of the SALT I agreements, and the creation of eleven joint commissions for cooperative activities in such fields as health, science and technology, agriculture, and energy.

A trade agreement negotiated in 1972 looked toward a considerable expansion in economic relations.

To the extent that the notion of detente was given a theoretical underpinning in the United States, it was articulated as a form of containment. It was argued by the Nixon Administration that the Soviet interest in expanded economic relations would make it possible to create a "web of interdependence" that would draw the Soviet Union away from its autarchic tendencies into an involvement in and dependence upon the world economy. This would create interests and interest groups in the Soviet Union, it was argued, that would serve to constrain and modify Soviet behavior, resulting in what was called "a structure of peace." This meant that the incentive of a continued influx of grains, manufactured goods, capital, technology, and management experience would restrain Soviet expansionism and that the Soviet Union would be led in time toward acceptance of the Western international system in practice if not in rhetoric. (It should be noted that the validity of this expectation was not tested by events since the anticipated expansion of economic relations was not fully realized.)

It is apparent that although the Soviet Union and the United States, each for reasons of its own, saw advantages in a relationship of moderated tension and limited cooperation, their respective expectations of detente were different and in some respects contradictory. This contradiction was to lead within a short time to conflict in practice, both in the political and the military aspects of their competition.

THE COMPETITION FOR POLITICAL INFLUENCE

Soviet conduct of the political competition in the middle and late 1970s illustrated the contradictions implicit in detente and contributed heavily to its unraveling. In the Middle East, Angola, Ethiopia, Yemen, Vietnam, and Afghanistan, Soviet actions showed that the USSR did not feel bound by detente to exercise restraint in exploiting opportunities for the advancement of its influence or in responding to political turbulence on its borders. A widely accepted interpretation of Soviet behavior in this period is that emboldened by its military buildup the Soviet Union became more aggressive and sought to gain strategic advantage in Africa, the Middle East, and the Persian Gulf, in what came to be called in the West an "arc of crisis."

It is, however, more accurate to see the exacerbation of the political competition in this period as the result primarily of an increased frequency of political upheavals that reflected the turbulent state of international politics. It is no justification of Soviet lack of restraint but simply a matter of clarity in understanding to see these Soviet actions as a continuation of the long-standing Soviet policy of seeking to exploit opportunities, whatever their cause. The numerous upheavals in this period resulted not from a change in Soviet policy but from the underlying conditions of international politics. To attribute to the Soviet Union responsibility for creating conditions of instability in the third world—as distinguished from exploiting these conditions—serves to obscure the causes that create these situations and therefore to limit the effectiveness of Western responses. The point that is relevant for this analysis is that the Soviet view of peaceful coexistence imposed no inhibition and no restraint in the exploitation of these situations, whereas in the Western view it should have done so.

In the case of Angola, the decisive precipitating event was the collapse of the Portuguese colonial position in Africa. In the fluid and chaotic period that followed, the United States was handicapped in establishing a position of influence with the leading anticolonial nationalist force—the Popular Movement for the Liberation of Angola—by its last-minute association with its NATO ally Portugal and its perceived association with South Africa, while the Soviet Union suffered no such baggage. Although the United States, along with China and South Africa, gave aid to two other guerrilla groups, the National Union for the Total Independence of Angola and the National Front for the Liberation of Angola, it was further handicapped by the post-Vietnam inhibition in the U.S. Congress against foreign military intervention, overt or covert. To these two Soviet advantages was added a third: a large-scale South African intervention in the south of Angola, which was followed by the intervention of about 30,000 Cuban soldiers in November 1975. Although the Cuban intervention has been characterized as a "proxy" for the Russians, it would appear more accurate to see it as an independent expression of Fidel Castro's revolutionary mission in Africa, which in part paralleled Soviet interest and made possible the utilization by trained Cuban combat units of materiel supplied by the Russians.

The ascendancy of Mengistu in Ethiopia created another such opportunity for the Russians. For a time, the Soviet Union sought to maintain both its previously good position in Somalia and its newly gained influence in Ethiopia, but this straddle became impossible when the Somalis initiated the conflict in the Ogaden and, in the hope of support from the United States, evicted the Russians. The combination of Cuban combat troops with Soviet military advisors and materiel that had been successful in Angola was repeated in Ethiopia, this time with much greater coordination between the two. However, a divergence between Soviet and Cuban purposes developed over the Ethiopian campaign against the Eritrean rebellion. The Cubans, seeing the Eritrean efforts to regain their independence as a national liberation movement, withheld their support from this campaign while the Soviet Union resolved this ideological dilemma in favor of their national interest in supporting Ethiopia.

There were changes in practice that contributed to the perception of these events as a departure in Soviet policy: The scale and speed of the Soviet airlift of materiel, advisers, and Cuban soldiers reflected an increase in Soviet capabilities to project conventional forces, and the presence of East German technicians helping to run the Ethiopian government suggested preparation for a long-term position of advantage. Neither Angola nor Ethiopia, however, represented a significant shift in the policy followed by the Soviet Union earlier in Egypt, the Sudan, the Congo, Mali, Guinea, and elsewhere in Africa.

The conflict between North and South Yemen similarly provided the Russians with an opportunity, although a lower key one, to advance their influence. To counter the Marxist regime in South Yemen, the United States sent military assistance to North Yemen, both directly and through Saudi Arabia. Although the fighting stopped, the Soviet Union has continued its efforts to strengthen its influence in this strategically placed area. The effectiveness of both U.S. and Soviet efforts in the Yemens is not yet clear.

Iran was the most important example of a political upheaval resulting from internal instabilities that led to a sharpening of the Soviet-American competition. The overthrow of the Shah removed the main reliance of the United States in the containment of Soviet expansion toward the Persian Gulf and resulted in a radical change in the power relationships in the area. The militant Islamic movement that came to power in Iran was equally anti-Soviet and anti-Western, and so long as it remains in power it appears to represent serious problems for both powers without relative advantage to either. The loss of American influence did not result in an increase in Soviet influence and in fact complicated Soviet relations with Iraq; nevertheless, the traumatic effect of the United States' unanticipated loss of its position in Iran and its humiliating impotence in the face of the hostage issue had severe domestic and foreign policy repercussions that, rationally or not, contributed to a hardening of American policies toward the Soviet Union.

Although the Soviet invasion of Afghanistan is often lumped together with the preceding episodes in making the case for a Soviet turn to a more aggressive policy, it clearly belongs in a different category. If anything, Afghanistan illustrates Soviet political ineptitude and military miscalculation. The April 1978 takeover by a temporary alliance of the two communist factions—the Khalqs and the Parchamites—disturbed a workable Soviet relationship with a nonaligned Afghanistan and created a client dependency for the Soviet Union with a group that was incapable of governing and that inflamed many latent sources of opposition. Overreacting as it always does to a security problem on its border, the Soviet Union wrongly calculated that it could, with a force of five-and-a-half divisions, install a government of its own choosing, reconstruct the Afghan army, and gain control from the insurgents of major population centers and the lines of communication between them. The presence of these divisions is a dubious strategic or political advantage for the Soviet Union, so long as the insurgency continues to keep the Soviet installations insecure, and this appears likely to be the case for a long time. Although this flagrant Soviet violation of international norms of behavior had the most dramatic impact of the series of events, it should be remembered that there was not much left of the detente at the time of the invasion. Had the detente been in good health at the time, it is possible to conjecture that there would nevertheless have been some form of Soviet response to what it perceived as a border security crisis, complicated by the proximity of a militant Islamic movement, but that the mode of response might have been tempered by some consideration of its international effects.

From the Soviet point of view, it was apparent that U.S. conduct of the political competition in the same period contradicted its expectations of the detente. In particular, Soviet expectations of a large-scale increase of economic relations—including access to advanced technology, capital investment, loans, Western management, and manufactured goods—were unrealized, at least on the scale that had been anticipated. As a result of the 1974 Jackson-Vanik Amendment, the

Trade Agreement of 1972 did not enter into force, Export-Import Bank loans were not made available, and most-favored-nation status was granted to China but not to the Soviet Union.

In its relations with the Peoples Republic of China, the United States moved beyond normalization toward military cooperation. The agreement for joint Soviet-American diplomatic action in the Middle East was scrapped. The Carter Administration's emphasis upon human rights was perceived by the Soviet Union as part of a political offensive against the Soviet regime. The issue of the Soviet combat brigade in Cuba was seen as a deliberate and artificial effort by the United States to create a climate of confrontation. The rhetoric of confrontation in the United States rose as diplomatic contacts between the two countries diminished.

The military aspects of the relationship will be discussed in the following section, but part of this catalogue of Soviet recrimination would be that: SALT was not ratified; negotiations on a comprehensive test ban, military disengagement in the Indian Ocean, limits on conventional arms transfers, and a ban against antisatellite weapons flagged, largely because of a stiffening of American (and British, in the case of the test ban) positions; plans were announced for the deployment of American cruise missiles and advanced Pershing missiles in Europe; and the United States began a large expansion of its military forces. Needless to say, the Soviet leadership perceived these actions not as responses to Soviet behavior but as indications of a militant American intent.

THE FAILED EFFORT TO STABILIZE
THE MILITARY COMPETITION

Although the prospect of stabilizing and moderating the strategic military competition was a central aspect of the detente of 1972-74, in practice it proved no less vulnerable than the political competition to the differences in perception and expectation of the two countries. The two planes of competition interacted: The deterioration of the political climate made increasingly difficult the effort to stabilize the strategic military competition, and the continued military buildup contributed to the suspicion and hostility that returned to dominate political relations. These developments exacerbated a continuing factor: Because of the long lead-time involved between the weapon planning cycle and the entry of weapons into the inventory, and the consequent lag between stimulus and observable response, the two countries have been out of synchronization with each other, in both weapon programs and doctrine. This has tended to maximize the suspicion and apprehension with which each side evaluates the present and prospective state of the military balance between them.

It has been widely accepted in the West that the United States, bemused by detente, remained on a plateau of nuclear military effort in the 1970s while the Soviet Union continued to increase its military buildup beyond parity to superior advantage. This belief has been buttressed by the prevalent view that Soviet military doctrine rejects deterrence and accepts the possibility that it can derive at least relative advantage from a surprise attack or from some level of nuclear war. These beliefs have propelled the fear of a Soviet "window of opportunity" in the 1980s to attack American land-based missiles, skepticism regarding arms control agreements, the urgency for a sharp rise in military expenditures, and the acceptance of war-fighting doctrines for the United States.

In the prevailing political climate, these beliefs tend to be accepted without critical examination. Are they in fact valid characterizations of Soviet military policy? To what extent have they been influenced by internal factors in American politics? In this retrospective review of the process of deterioration of relations, it becomes apparent that it would be as misleading to accept these beliefs, however prevalent, as descriptions of objective fact as it would be to take at face value the Soviet characterizations of its military programs as purely defensive reactions to American programs.

Although monetary measures of the level of military effort are of limited significance (except for purposes of comparison of one period with another), it is reasonably well-established that the Soviet Union has been increasing its allocations to the military sector by between 3 and 4.5 percent a year since the early 1960s. It is not clear whether this increase was a response to the outcome of the Cuban missile crisis of 1962 or to the steep increases in the U.S. military budget for fiscal year 1961 (reflecting the "missile gap" controversy in the electoral campaign of 1960). In retrospect, it appears that Khrushchev's boast of a "shift in the balance of power" after the Soviet sputnik of 1957, although punctured, served only to stimulate American strategic programs. Whatever the cause, the Soviet Union made strenuous efforts from the early 1960s to overcome the strategic inferiority under which it labored from the end of World War II to about 1970. It is difficult to judge whether Soviet intentions were to achieve parity with the United States or to go beyond parity, since the Soviet planners were working against a moving target: rapidly changing strategic programs and debates in the United States.

It is not accurate to say that the American military programs were standing still in the 1970s. Although the total number of U.S. land-based intercontinental missile launchers remained at 1,054—reflecting the judgment that it was more efficient to put more warheads on each missile than to build more missiles and that, together with bombers and sea-based missiles, this constituted a more than adequate retaliatory capability—the U.S. strategic program continued to grow in other significant ways. During this period, the number of warheads on U.S. missiles trebled to more than 7,300, with another 3,400 projected; the accuracy and yield of U.S. missiles increased substantially; cruise missiles with extraordinary flexibility and accuracy were developed; new submarines and submarine missiles with greater range and accuracy were developed and deployed; and more powerful and accurate land-based missiles were in the course of research and development.

By dint of its intensified efforts, the Soviet Union after relatively short delays applied many of the U.S. military innovations (as well as some of its own) to its strategic forces, which in turn created new apprehensions in the United States. When multiple independently targetable reentry vehicles (MIRVs) and greater accuracy were incorporated in new generations of Soviet heavy missiles, many American analysts foresaw the theoretical possibility of a Soviet capability to attack U.S. land-based missiles with a relatively small portion of their own forces. This in turn was thought to call into question the adequacy of American strategic forces to deter selective attacks. Even those who remained skeptical about the plausibility of such a scenario expressed concern about the danger of political blackmail resulting from this theoretical Soviet capability.

It was difficult at the time to give a rational evaluation of these developments because the political climate in the United States during this period was particularly volatile and lacking in self-confidence. The succession of Soviet interventions and military buildup intensified a nationalist swing in American politics in reaction to the preceding period of post-Vietnam self-doubt and the perception of American weakness and setbacks. Perhaps enough time has now passed to make possible a more detached examination of some of the widely accepted beliefs then prevalent.

In particular, has there in fact been a shift in the balance of strategic power? Despite the increase in Soviet strategic capability in several important respects, it is doubtful that the Soviet Union has acquired any additional militarily usable strategic capabilities. Given the scale of destructiveness of nuclear weapons, the deterrent balance is certainly more stable than has recently been pictured. The projected vulnerability of U.S. land-based missiles rests upon calculations of risks for the attacker that strain plausibility, unless a total lack of rationality on the Soviet side is assumed. It also would require the assumption of irrationality on the part of Soviet leaders to imagine the use of Soviet medium- or intermediate-range nuclear missiles against Western Europe. Any sane Soviet leader contemplating such a step would understand that he would incur the risk of an American response with central strategic forces. This fundamental condition has been obscured by the debates over how the theater nuclear balance should be calculated.

The belief that Soviet doctrinal writings imply an acceptance of limited nuclear war as a possible advantage to the Soviet Union stems from a confused and superficial reading of that literature. In practice, Soviet military preparations have assumed that a credible deterrent must be underpinned by a capability to deal with various levels of possible conflict. In this respect, their practice does not differ appreciably from the American, and both countries have produced writings on the mission of the various services in the event of the outbreak of war. A careful reading of Soviet military and political writing gives no support for the belief that Soviet leaders accept the possibility that a limited nuclear exchange could reasonably be expected to remain limited. Neither Soviet nor American political leaders can harbor the illusion that the technical means exist for making the fine distinctions in time of war that theorists take for granted.

Whatever a future reexamination of the foregoing prevalent beliefs may show, they played an important role in aborting the effort from 1969 to 1979 to negotiate a stabilization of the nuclear aspects of the military competition. Although the United States took the initiative in drawing the Soviet Union into the strategic arms limitation negotiations, effective U.S. political support was lacking for the view that a stabilized balance of nuclear weapons would serve American security interests better than the traditional commitment to superiority. Support was further hindered by theories that superiority was required at each rung of a putative ladder of escalation. Successive American administrations were obliged to compromise with domestic groups fundamentally committed to a policy of superiority to such an extent that the area of negotiation excluded ongoing American programs; even so, there was not sufficient political support to ratify the agreements that had been reached. The often repeated and widely believed view that the Soviet Union had achieved a strategic advantage, that this advantage had made possible the Soviet interventions of the mid and late 1970s, and that the Soviet Union was preparing to fight or to threaten a nuclear war contributed to undermine public confidence in the SALT process. It would have required a strong and self-confident political leadership—fully committed to the proposition that American security would be better served by a stabilization of the nuclear military competition—to have developed a politically effective constituency in support of SALT.

Analogous suspicions and limitations impaired Soviet support of the SALT process. In the Soviet view, dilatory American negotiating behavior, the tactic of raising new issues at late stages of the negotiations, and the development of new systems with the justification that they were bargaining chips in the negotiating process contributed to Soviet uncertainty about the seriousness of the American intent in the negotiations. This uncertainty was perceptibly heightened by the trend in U.S. doctrinal thinking away from deterrence toward war-fighting theories, "flexible options," and capabilities for conducting limited nuclear war.

It seems probable that this uncertainty complicated the already difficult task of gaining and holding support within the Soviet system for the radical idea of using negotiations with an adversary to stabilize a military competition. The weight of traditional Soviet thinking about military matters and the relative strength of the Soviet military bureaucracy in determining its negotiating positions may have been responsible for the fact that the Soviet Union rarely initiated proposals during the negotiations; the course of the negotiations generally involved successive revisions of proposals initiated by the Western side. As a result of its habitual extreme secrecy about military as well as political matters, Soviet representatives have been unforthcoming about military data; the negotiations therefore took place for the most part on the basis of Western data without confirmation or denial from the Soviet side. Soviet secrecy also set narrow limits on the means by which adherence to the treaties could be verified.

Even after its acceptance of the American proposal for strategic arms limitation talks, it was doubtful whether the Soviet Union accepted the fundamental conceptual basis for SALT: parity, mutual deterrence, and strategic stability. Because of the ambiguity of Soviet military writings on nuclear warfare and of statements by its leaders and also because of its continuing deployments, the Soviet Union aroused apprehensions about its purposes in the negotiations and its military intentions. Even after it had attained approximate parity with the United States in the early 1970s, the Soviet Union showed no sign that it accepted the notion of a plateau at strategic parity. Whether it was because the Soviet Union felt itself engaged in defense requirements in several different directions, or because it was operating on the basis of an alarmist view of American technological capabilities, or because it was led by a strong military bureaucratic momentum, the nature and scale of Soviet strategic deployments in the 1970s inevitably raised questions abroad about whether its purpose was intimidation rather than deterrence. (In the Russian language, the two conceptions are indistinguishable.) Whatever may have motivated Soviet military programs, the Soviet Union clearly was not constrained by political sensitivity regarding the alarming effects of these programs on American or West European publics.

This was true not only of Soviet strategic programs but also of the continuing increase in Soviet conventional military capabilities. To the already large Soviet land army, enormously increased in firepower and mobility, was added a new maritime capability, which fueled Western suspicions of Soviet interventionist intentions.

It should be added that some modification of Soviet behavior was noted in the course of the negotiating process. Modest gains were made against the deeply rooted Soviet penchant for secrecy; the circle of Soviet officials with access to the relevant military data widened beyond the limited professional military staff; and concessions were made in the course of the negotiations that traditionally minded military officers found difficult to accept.

In 1980 the Soviet Union appeared to have leveled off its intercontinental missile modernization programs, but it is not clear whether in the absence of treaty obligations it will, for reasons of its own or in response to projected U.S. programs, begin to produce some or all of the new missile systems it has had under development. The Soviet weapon cycle is both more regular and more rigid than the American, and the two are not synchronous. Only after weapon systems now being funded and developed reach the testing stage will it be possible to judge the basis on which calculations of the present cycle of weapon planning were made.

Finally, in considering the decline of the effort to stabilize the strategic competition in the decade of the 1970s, some responsibility must be assigned to the inherent difficulty of comparing weapon systems with different characteristics. It would have required a more self-confident commitment to deterrence than either side possessed for the two nations to recognize the existence of a condition of gross parity. Given the heightened suspicions of the deteriorating political relationship and the rapidly changing military technology of the period, it is not surprising that each side saw the disparities in the two nuclear arsenals as conferring a possibly decisive advantage to the other. Each side continued to feel vulnerable, and the nuclear military competition continued.

THE FUTURE OF U.S.-SOVIET RELATIONS

Against this record of the deterioration of political and military relations between the Soviet Union and the United States since the mid-1970s, what factors may be expected to determine the course of this relationship in the 1980s? The preceding account suggests consideration of three categories of factors: Soviet, American, and international. Among the domestic developments within the Soviet Union, two can be expected to be major factors affecting Soviet relations with the United States: the succession and the economy.

We simply do not know enough to make reliable forecasts regarding which individuals will compose the future leadership of the Soviet Union and what their policy predilections will be, but it seems reasonable to expect that the period in which a new leadership is consolidating its power is less likely to permit accommodating agreements with the United States than one commanded by a confident leader. In the Soviet Union, as in any group situation, leadership contests tend to stimulate more aggressive behavior, or at least more militant posturing.

Whether the state of the Soviet economy can reasonably be expected to be a factor encouraging a policy of reduced tensions is a matter in dispute among Western writers. Recent performance of the Soviet economy continues to show low levels of productivity in both agriculture and industry and serious lags in the advanced technological sector. The heavy deflection of resources to the military sector clearly has impeded improvement both in these sectors of the civilian economy and in the overall rate of economic growth. Although there can be no doubt that any Soviet leadership would nevertheless increase military expenditures if the competitive level required it, the cost would be a further delay in mending the Soviet economy.

It can be argued, on an *a priori* basis, that if opportunities were to present themselves for a negotiated reduction of resources devoted to the military sector, Soviet economic problems could encourage responsiveness. Some writers have conjectured, however, that the combination of succession uncertainties, economic and nationality problems, and international tensions may lead to a period of tighter political controls in the Soviet Union and perhaps a greater militancy in foreign policy. The number of variables is so great that one cannot predict with confidence in which direction these factors will exert their influence.

Prospects do not appear favorable for the Soviet regime in its foreign policy. Political instabilities in Eastern Europe complicated by Soviet economic difficulties are likely to have widening and deepening consequences beyond those presently apparent. Relations with China involve current political competition, complications in Soviet military planning, and the prospect of more serious military apprehensions in the future. While Soviet ideology has clearly lost its appeal, opportunities for increased Soviet influence through military assistance to national liberation forces may continue to present themselves, subject to the vagaries of international politics and the effectiveness of Western responses. Although the current line of Soviet policy is to counter American rhetorical challenges vigorously, it seeks to maintain a pro-peace, nonthreatening posture, partly to underscore its effort to encourage a greater European independence from the United States and partly, perhaps, to keep open the possibility of changes it hopes for, but does not expect, in American policy.

As for the American side of the equation, economic problems are also among the principal domestic factors likely to have an influence on the future course of the relationship. The pressure of budgetary constraints on presently planned increases in military expenditures may work against the growing realization that even presently projected military appropriations are inadequate in an unregulated military competition. These conflicting considerations could generate either a more serious interest in earlier arms limitation negotiations or—if the presently ascendant political climate continues in force—a heightened emphasis upon the perceived Soviet military threat. The resurgence of nationalism, the clearest expression of which is to be found in the theme of anticommunism, seems unlikely to encourage movement toward any easement of tension with the Soviet Union or toward any resumption of substantive negotiations for the stabilization of the military competition (as distinguished from a purely public-relations approach to negotiations). While the present administration has not articulated its objectives in relations with the Soviet Union, the persistence of a reaction against the detente period seems more likely to encourage a policy of high confrontation on all fronts rather than any movement toward a moderation of tensions, despite some pressures in the business community for an increase in economic relations. Again, however, unpredictable variables on the international scene could influence this mood in either direction, and this cautions against extrapolating the present mood into the indefinite future.

Among the foreign policy factors, one uncertainty is the future relationship of the United States with its allies in Western Europe and Japan. The gulf is widening between the political mood in the United States and the growing dissatisfaction of unstable governing coalitions in many of the alliance countries. These sentiments represent a complex phenomenon, not well understood and not to be explained by any single factor. It is an amalgam of such domestic concerns as environmental issues, nuclear energy, and unemployment, together with concerns over interallied economic and political conflicts. At both leadership and popular levels, the impact upon European economies of U.S. economic policies is a source of concern, but more widely expressed at the popular level is a lack of confidence in the capacity of the United States to provide steady, measured, and responsible leadership for the West in its relations with the Soviet Union. This does not, however, appear to reflect any corresponding increase of sympathy for the Soviet Union. What finds increasing expression is the fear of not having control over their own fates in a conflict that may involve them in a direct and immediate sense. These sentiments tend to crystallize around such issues as military expenditures and defense policies, the implementation of the NATO decision to deploy American theater nuclear weapons in Europe, and the possible deployment in Europe of enhanced radiation weapons. Whether the United States will bring to bear sufficient resilience to contain these differences or whether it will react by moving toward a chauvinist isolation is not clear.

Nor is it clear what effect developing European sentiments may have on the prospect for negotiations on nuclear weapons. In the early 1970s the predominantly expressed European view was one of suspicion of SALT, which was seen as a symbol of superpower condominium and which, it was feared, would compromise European defense interests. It was only in the period of fading prospects for SALT that the weight of articulated opinion in Europe expressed a self-interest in a successful outcome, at least in part in deference to the growth of public concerns about the consequences of nuclear war in Europe. Although this shift in European sentiment came too late to gain effective support for ratification of SALT from those who were mainly preoccupied with the defense of the Atlantic alliance, it did serve to strengthen the case for at least the appearance of negotiations on the subsequent issue of theater nuclear forces. It is at least possible that these efforts to accommodate present allied popular sentiment may take on more significance in time.

A related uncertainty is the direction of future American policy toward the third world. The American administration's initial emphasis on anticommunism led to a Manichean approach to third world movements, in which the East-West competition tended to obscure local nationalism and other sources of conflict. If this were to continue, opportunities for the expansion of Soviet influence would continue to grow, and American collaboration with other noncommunist states would diminish. However, experience and the influence of Latin America and Western Europe may in time moderate this initial approach.

This is in turn related to the third category of factors that can be expected to influence the future course of Soviet-American relations: developments in international politics. Upheavals resulting from internal instabilities and the igniting of some of the many sources of conflict in the Middle East, Africa, Asia, and Latin America—including some evident candidates for conflict and some that may now be unpredictable—can and are likely to involve competitive American and Soviet interests and to raise the level of tension. In a period of diminished diplomatic contact between the two countries, the risks of miscalculation are increased, particularly in those situations in which there is Western reliance on tactical nuclear weapons to compensate for deficiencies in conventional capabilities. Iran is an obvious example of these potential sources of conflict. In a longer-term view, it seems probable that the interaction of North-South and East-West tensions will be mutually exacerbating.

Politically, the rising consciousness of the nations of the third world will be expressed in unstable and shifting alliances, beyond the capacity of either the Soviet Union or the United States to exercise a decisive influence. Trends toward nationalism and religious fundamentalism will be directed against the interests of both superpowers and other developed nations.

The economic issues preoccupying the third world—such as the food-population balance, fluctuations in raw material prices, and development assistance—will be less likely to elicit a common constructive response from the developed nations in a period of East-West confrontation. Competition among the great powers for influence in the third world has more often tended to express itself in arms sales than in development assistance.

The degree of cooperation required to respond constructively to issues of global concern and to contain and conciliate local conflict situations rather to exacerbate them grows ever more remote when the United States and the Soviet Union are locked into a relationship of confrontation. In turn, the relationship between the superpowers is invested with greater volatility as the turbulence of the third world increases.

LESSONS OF THE RECENT PAST

What follows from the foregoing characterization of recent relations between the Soviet Union and the United States and of the factors that may govern their future relations? In particular, what lessons may be drawn regarding future prospects for the regulation of the competition in strategic weapons?

In some quarters the end of the SALT process would be a matter for rejoicing and the collapse of what was called detente would be regarded as a blessing. It is argued that both SALT and detente are necessarily disadvantageous to the West, lulling its public into an acceptance of military inferiority and passive acquiescence to Soviet expansionism. It would follow from this argument that the appropriate Western policy would be one of confrontation and a forcing of the pace of the military competition, in the expectation that this would lead to the capitulation, collapse, or contraction of the Soviet Union. The more likely consequence of this policy, however, would be to bring about the disintegration of the Western alliance, an increased risk of nuclear war, the further strengthening of repressive aspects of the Soviet regime, the effects of higher mobilization upon our domestic society, and the greater intractability of every problem we face in international affairs.

Is there an alternative? Does the experience of the past decade suggest a more effective way of managing relations with the Soviet Union so as to protect our interests and our values and, in particular, to conduct the strategic nuclear competition with greater rationality?

No one can say whether it is too soon to pronounce an epitaph for the effort to negotiate a stabilization of the nuclear military competition. What can be said is that if history should afford us an opportunity to resume the process, we can learn from our recent experience how to use that opportunity more effectively.

If the resumption of strategic arms limitation negotiations is unduly postponed, the advance of military technology will make these negotiations increasingly difficult; they may in fact approach unmanageability. New systems soon to be deployed by both sides would be less stable and less verifiable than current systems. The widespread deployment of cruise missiles, for example, would make it difficult to know which missiles are conventionally armed and which ones nuclear, to judge the range of missiles from their external characteristics, or even, given their size, to know whether they can be counted with confidence. Only if new political or technological means become available to aid in the verification process can these problems be resolved.

If the resumption of strategic arms limitation negotiations is urgent, the linkage of these negotiations to other aspects of the Soviet-American competition is not in our interest, since it results only in the indefinite postponement of negotiations. Moreover, such linkage wrongly obscures our objective interest in stabilizing the nuclear military competition regardless of the vicissitudes of the political competition. To say that linkage must be accepted as a fact of life means that political leaders have failed to clarify the nation's real security interests. Although such negotiations are obviously easier during periods of low tension and when the political competition is relatively restrained, there is no necessary connection between SALT and detente; in fact, it may be argued that SALT is more necessary during times of tension.

One lesson that emerges from a review of the Soviet-American relationship is the importance of recognizing the process of interaction between the two countries, both in the political and the military spheres. Some analysts dispute this point; they argue that Soviet decisions on weapons procurement are entirely the product of internal factors—bureaucratic momentum, competition among design bureaus or between the services, and so forth. While these factors are certainly present, they are not adequate by themselves to explain past changes in direction and scale of Soviet weapons policy. What makes the process of interaction difficult to recognize at times is the delay before observable reactions appear and our own failure to appreciate how our widely publicized discussions of future plans are perceived abroad. It seems probable, for example, that U.S. plans for the production of the B-70 bomber had something to do with the subsequent intensification of Soviet air defenses, even though the United States produced only a few models of the bomber. It also seems probable that the acceleration of American strategic weapons funded by the fiscal year 1961 budget had some impact on subsequent increases in Soviet missile programs. Certainly, internal factors are significant, but the relative weight of competing internal pressures may be affected by perceptions of what the other side is doing or planning, just as is the case in this country.

A related point concerns a difference in judgment about how best to influence Soviet behavior in directions we favor. It is sometimes argued that the only language the Soviets understand is force and that therefore we must confront them with a tough policy in order to encourage restraint or a willingness to negotiate. This is to confuse firmness with bellicosity; a quiet and civil firmness, which is the mark of true strength, may be productive, but a bellicose challenge or ultimatum is more likely to evoke a belligerent response, as it would do with us. Political leaders in the Soviet Union, as elsewhere, cannot appear to be capitulating to humiliating demands from abroad. Similarly, threats of a military buildup for the sake of inducing Soviet concessions in negotiations are more likely to evoke intensified military programs on the Soviet side and have done so in the past. This is not an argument for inordinate unilateral restraint because evident weakness would also evoke Soviet aggressiveness. It does argue for the measured preservation of a military balance, with a clear indication that the option is open for operating at more measured levels through mutual accommodation.

This in turn leads to the critical importance of the acceptance by the political leaders of both sides that a stabilized and moderate nuclear military balance offers greater security than the pursuit of an illusory superiority that can lead only to an unregulated nuclear military competition. Perhaps more than acceptance, strong advocacy is required against inevitable domestic resistance. A concomitant point is the importance of confidence in the gross stability of the deterrent balance, instead of a febrile reaction to inevitable disparities in the weapons arsenals of the two sides.

It follows from the preceding point that greater rationality in the weapons decisionmaking process on both sides is an essential prerequisite for arms control agreements and may be even more important in the absence of arms control agreements. The present process permits random pressures from diverse sources to exercise more influence than an overarching political judgment. As often as not, doctrine tends to be an after-the-fact rationalization for systems procured for extraneous reasons. In a period of rapidly changing military technology, the importance of the technical stability of contemplated systems must be given weight as a matter of common interest. Consideration also must be given not just to the temporary advantages to be gained from deploying a contemplated weapon system but to whether security would be greater or less after the other side had applied the same technology. The point is well illustrated by the U.S. decision to deploy multiple independently targetable reentry vehicles (MIRVs) without thought of the adverse effects upon our own security of the subsequent deployment of MIRVs upon the heavier Soviet missiles.

It is evident that a reasonable balance of conventional forces is a necessary prerequisite for strategic arms control; in the absence of such a balance, there inevitably will be pressures for reliance on nuclear weapons to redress the balance in various theaters. This in turn not only requires a continued commitment to the first use of nuclear weapons and leaves open the possibility of nuclear escalation, but presents the difficult and perhaps insoluble problem of distinguishing between theater and central strategic balances. In Europe in particular it is important to exhaust every possibility for modernized conventional weapons and forces as an alternative to reliance on nuclear weapons in the theater.

Although it may seem to have but an indirect bearing on strategic arms limitation, we must nevertheless have a fuller and more accurate appreciation of the third actor in Soviet-American relations: the international political context in which their interests intersect. The turbulence of this period of international politics would make Soviet-American relations difficult even under the best of circumstances, for it inevitably involves both countries in local conflict situations that neither side may have created nor can control but in which their interests may collide.

It is evident from our review of Soviet-American relations during the past decade that a major factor in the deterioration of those relations was the Soviet exploitation of opportunities for the increase of its influence in third world conflicts. It clearly was not possible, as the Soviet Union wrongly calculated, to compartmentalize these actions from degrading the whole tone of the relationship, particularly in a period when the United States was recovering from its experience in Vietnam. While abstract commitments to restraint (as in the Basic Statement of the Principles of Coexistence) may have little value in practice, and while across-the-board codes of conduct for political competition in the third world may not be feasible, it does seem possible and indeed necessary that specific limitations in particular regional areas can be worked out, tacitly if not explicitly, governing the level and types of weapons to be transported to the area and the level of political intervention to be observed by both sides. Even more urgent is the evident necessity of strengthening international mechanisms for the management of conflicts as they may arise, in order to prevent their enlargement and to assist in their adjudication. Not only are such mechanisms necessary to keep within manageable limits the tensions that will inevitably accompany the continuing great power competition in the third world, but even more importantly they address the real possibility of general war arising out of the escalation of a local conflict.

At a more fundamental level, it is necessary to go beyond the management of third world conflicts as they arise to efforts to understand and address the causes of these conflicts at an earlier stage, before they become focal points of East-West competition. One of the bitter lessons of the recent past, illustrated in Vietnam, Iran, and many other instances, is that the general ignorance about local sources of conflict and local political cultures, needs, and concerns tends to result in belated great power intervention, after local conflicts have developed and become polarized to the point where only military resolutions remain.

Finally, the lessons of the recent past indicate that both the Soviet Union and the United States have choices to make. Unless both countries make determined efforts to deal rationally with the nuclear military competition, the continued qualitative and quantitative growth of that competition seems inescapable, despite the modest constraints that have been the meager results of a decade of half-hearted effort—with an inevitable increase in the possibility of nuclear war. If, however, reason should prevail on both sides and there should be a resumption of strategic arms limitation negotiations, the experience of SALT II suggests that the process should be shortened and simplified. The effort to negotiate a detailed and comprehensive agreement in SALT II involved seven years of negotiations, during which new problems continuously presented themselves. The result was a treaty of such complexity that public understanding and support became difficult.

If both sides are impelled by a growing consciousness of the consequences to take the problem in hand, it will be necessary to return to first principles and to seek early agreement on those few essential elements of the nuclear military competition that will result in a stable and secure balance at moderate levels. What Mr. Justice Holmes called "the parade of imaginary horribles" will always be there, but the essential elements of the problem are stark and simple.

5 POLITICAL IMPLICATIONS OF THE THEATER NUCLEAR BALANCE

Christoph Bertram

Since nuclear deterrence began, some of the forces providing that deterrence for the West have been stationed in Europe. In the early period when delivery systems did not yet enjoy intercontinental range, European real estate was essential for America's strategic deterrent. With the new intercontinental land- and sea-based nuclear missiles introduced in the 1950s, however, the United States could conceive of an effective nuclear deterrent without bases in Europe: The age of geographical identity between the deterrent requirements of the United States and its European allies had come to an end.

The military and political problems of the European theater nuclear balance have arisen since then. They essentially are caused by the distinctiveness of European theater issues from nuclear-strategic aspects. The many discussions and disputes to which problems of the European nuclear balance have given rise, in the final analysis, have been over the degree of this distinctiveness and the consequences that follow from it. This pattern runs from the trans-Atlantic debate over the Multilateral Force in the early 1960s to that over the function of tactical nuclear weapons in European defense, from political concerns over the withdrawal of U.S. Jupiter and Thor missiles in the early 1960s to the circumstances surrounding the first real alliance decision on theater nuclear forces, taken in December 1979, to station new U.S. Pershing II and cruise missiles on European territory. However painful that decision was for a number of European governments and however controversial it will become in the political debate of some, if not all, these countries, it is not the first nor will it be the last time that theater nuclear issues have strained the alliance.

The main reason for this does not lie in the degree of distinctiveness between the central and the theater nuclear balance in terms of weaponry; it lies in the distinction between the requirements of central and of extended deterrence. The former relies on the capability of the United States to launch a destructive second nuclear strike against a nuclear attacker. The latter, particularly as long as it has to compensate for perceived deficiencies in conventional defenses, relies on the credible potential for the United States and its NATO allies to make first use of nuclear weapons. Political strains are thus inherent from the start and aggravated by the advent of strategic vulnerability: for the United States, whether to risk her own survival for the sake of that of her allies; for the allies, whether the United States might seek to separate her own security from theirs, either by seeking to contain nuclear wars to their soil or by refusing to protect them with an effective nuclear umbrella.

This chapter discusses the political implications of theater nuclear weapons by taking the December 1979 alliance decision as its major example. This seems justified for three reasons. First, it is currently the most important issue to which both political and military consequences attach. Second, it represents the first occasion when the alliance—as opposed to individual nuclear weapon states—took a decision on the production and not merely the introduction of nuclear weapons. Third, it occurred against the background of Soviet-American strategic parity and bilateral attempts to limit arms. Finally, as the widespread opposition to the NATO decision in Europe testifies, it emphasizes the probably inseparable connection between nuclear and political matters in the alliance of the West.

The issue will be examined in four parts: (1) a look at the military and political background of the 1979 decision; (2) an analysis of the procedure implied by the decision concerning the procurement of the new systems and the arms control proposal that accompanied it; (3) a look at the problems raised by implementation of the program for political cohesion in the alliance; and (4) against this background, a suggestion of some prospects for arms control before a concluding section summarizing the major consequences of the chapter for the future.

THE BACKGROUND: MILITARY NEED OR POLITICAL SYMBOL?

Major military decisions rarely can be traced to one cause or to one justification; this is as true for the LRTNF (long-range theater nuclear forces) decision of December 1979 as for any other. There were both ostensible and underlying causes and military motivations combined with political ones.

Military Concerns

The reasons for the new program fell into two related categories: the advent of strategic nuclear parity between the superpowers and the growing Soviet threat to theater nuclear forces in Europe. In the 1950s and 1960s and even during much of the 1970s, the United States' superiority in strategic nuclear forces was so manifest that little attention had to be paid to the military requirements of theater nuclear forces; their deployment was—as the fate of the Multilateral Force proposal of the early 1960s or the introduction of thousands of nuclear warheads for theater purposes at the same time underlined— more an instrument for alliance policies than a military addition to the alliance's deterrent. The Soviet strategic disadvantage and the commensurate U.S. advantage created a general conviction, not seriously affected by General de Gaulle's doubts, that the United States could afford a nuclear exchange while the Soviet Union could not. The U.S. surplus of strategic deterrence provided regional deterrence for America's allies as well.

Three developments changed this picture of confidence. First, and most important, the Soviet Union caught up with the United States and attained numerical parity during the 1970s. Second, the strategic arms limitation agreements between the superpowers had the effect of distinguishing strategic from theater nuclear forces, thus highlighting the deficits of the latter, which in the past had seemed of little conseqence. Third, this distinction was reinforced by the advent of ICBM vulnerability in the 1980s: It would clearly be even more difficult for an American president to authorize a nuclear strike in Europe if a Soviet response could destroy much of America's land-based strategic missile forces.

Developments on the strategic level thus tended to call attention to the theater level, and here the picture looked far from reassuring, again due to the extent and reach of the Soviet military effort of the past decade. There was justified concern that NATO's longer-range nuclear systems (all of them aircraft) were aging and increasingly vulnerable to Soviet preemption. Moreover, with the buildup of the Soviet SS-20 medium-range missile, there was concern that escalation dominance—the ability to control the level of exchange by effectively deterring the other side from escalating—was being obtained by the Soviet Union and would have to be offset by new, more survivable, missiles capable of reaching targets in the Soviet Union.

Yet, significantly, none of this argumentation is entirely compelling. Despite the rough parity between the United States and the Soviet Union in the number of strategic launchers, the American lead in deliverable nuclear warheads remained impressive. Even as it declines toward the mid-1980s, new theater-based missiles would make only a marginal difference. The buildup of Soviet theater-range nuclear weapons only adds to but does not create military options that the Soviet force of medium- and intermediate-range missiles has not enjoyed from the late 1960s. There is no compelling military reason for arguing either that U.S. strategic forces would no longer be sufficient to provide adequate deterrence against the use of these weapons or that the new Pershings and cruise missiles would be.

The limitations imposed by SALT on strategic forces would make regional imbalances more dangerous only if either the remaining strategic forces were clearly insufficient to counter unfavorable regional asymmetries (and they are not) or if they implied that Soviet advantages could not be offset by commensurate U.S. force programs (they also do not). If protection of nuclear launchers against preemptive destruction were the prime consideration for the new program, then the Pershing II, only marginally more mobile than the Pershing I missile, seems less significantly suited than the ground-launched cruise missiles, and both of these two land-based systems are more vulnerable than in a —rejected— sea-based mode. Escalation dominance, finally, suggests a tidiness of categories of nuclear weapons and a tidiness in nuclear escalation processes that belongs more to the theoretical scenarios of Western strategic analysts than to the realities of a world in crisis or at war.

Still, it is probably unfair to require clear and compelling military justifications for any nuclear program that goes beyond minimum deterrence, whether in the strategic or the theater nuclear realm. Since there has never been a nuclear war, calculations about it inevitably lack empirical support. Since deterrence is in the eye of the beholder, one's military decisions can be taken on the basis of no more than a crude plausibility assessment of the other's perceptions and likely responses. Moreover—and partly for these reasons—NATO has continuously failed in its attempts to provide a clear doctrine for its theater nuclear forces. There is no accepted framework within which the December 1979 LRTNF decision can be placed and sustained. The margins, therefore, between correct and inadequate, necessary and desirable, tolerable and unacceptable nuclear decision are highly blurred, the yardsticks relative.

Military decisions cannot always wait for a clarity of concepts that all too often is elusive. While there are aspects of the 1979 LRTNF program that are open to criticism, its major military features strengthen deterrence and crisis stability, and emphasize the deterrence identity between West Europe and the United States. As long as Western Europe's security cannot be assured by conventional forces alone and the nuclear deterrence link to the United States' strategic forces remains necessary, then:

- U.S. nuclear forces in Europe will be both a more credible and a more proportionate demonstration of that link than if the alliance were to rely exclusively on strategic nuclear systems to deter a regional Soviet attack;
- These forces should be able to survive a Soviet attack so that the danger of slipping inadvertently into a nuclear exchange would be minimized; the 464 ground-launched cruise missiles and 108 Pershing II ballistic missiles of the NATO decision are less vulnerable to attack than the present U.S. intermediate-range arsenal in Europe;
- These forces should make the limitation of nuclear conflict to the European continent less likely; the capability of the new systems of reaching, from European soil, targets in the Soviet Union gives them the effect of widening the conflict beyond the immediate European conflict theater; and, finally,
- These forces should provide additional deterrence but not an offensive option against the Soviet Union; neither the cruise missiles that require a flight time of two to three hours to reach their targets nor the Pershing II missiles, which are well below the quantitative level required for an effective disarming strike against Soviet military installations, provide serious, independent offensive options.

Political Concerns

Nuclear decisions are almost by definition not only military but political matters, even more so for an alliance that links fourteen small to medium-size countries to a nuclear superpower. The 1979 NATO program is no exception. Indeed, political concerns have shaped the decision. This has introduced a new ambiguity into the issue: If it were measurable against a defined and constant Soviet threat alone, then the rationale would remain defined and constant for the duration of this threat.

Politics, however, have a dynamic quality. What may be desirable today, for political reasons, may become for other political reasons less desirable tomorrow. The history of NATO's LRTNF decision is full of examples of the way in which political concerns and motivations can change.

At first, the call for the new weapons came from Western Europe, while the United States was significantly less impressed with the need for their introduction. As Soviet opposition and domestic controversy over the program picked up, enthusiasm waned in Europe. For many in the United States, however, the implementation of the program had become a test by which the alliance would prove it could stand by its decisions. At first, European concern over the Soviet SS-20 was coupled with suspicion over the SALT process and, in particular, the way in which "grey area weapons"—weapons outside the SALT definition but of direct relevance to the European theater—were treated in the Soviet-American negotiations. Today, European governments come close to claiming that the ratification of the SALT II Treaty is a condition for implementing the 1979 program.

At the beginning, Europeans tended to see American readiness to go ahead with the program as a much needed manifestation of U.S. leadership and continued commitment to European security. Today, the United States (probably irrespective of the political philosophy of the administration) would see the collapse of political support for the TNF modernization as a sure sign of Finlandization—of Europe bowing to the preponderance of Soviet power. The contrast between then and now highlights not only the importance of political rather than military considerations in the shaping of the decision. It also suggests that these considerations lay, in the decisive instance, not so much in Soviet behavior as in an uneasiness over political relations in the alliance itself. This was particularly so in U.S.-German relations.

It is no coincidence that it was the German Chancellor, Helmut Schmidt, who was the first alliance leader to raise the issue publicly,[1] confirming a law of the alliance and especially of U.S.-German relations that has been in effect since the early 1960s: Strained political relations find an expression in nuclear issues. The ability of the United States to offer credible security to its European allies depends on nuclear weapons and the will to use them, in the final event, for the sake of Europe. Since there can be no guarantee to that effect, the credibility of the U.S. commitment depends, in the first and last instance, on the recognition of a mutuality of vital interests and on mutual trust. Once the trust is questioned—and European sensitivities are always highly developed—nuclear weapons become the most visible expression of the commitment.

It is, however, an awkward psychological mechanism. Nuclear weapons, as earlier experience has shown, cannot cure a political malaise of the kind that developed between Europe and America in the early Carter years or in the early Reagan months; only the reestablishment of political trust can. Moreover, as the alliance once again was to experience over the TNF issue, nuclear weapons are both the most reassuring and the potentially most controversial symbol of alliance cohesion: reassuring if they underline America's willingness to risk her own security for that of Europe but controversial if they suggest that the primary theater of nuclear war would be Europe. Only political trust makes these tensions tolerable. To seek remedies to political strains in the alliance through the nuclear route is, therefore, not only inadequate, it is also shortsighted: It is simply the wrong instrument.

It is tempting to speculate whether there would be a LRTNF program today if trans-Atlantic trust had been firmer in the late 1970s. European governments might then have been more confident about the U.S. commitment and more relaxed over the Soviet effort in theater nuclear forces. Perhaps a more self-assured U.S. administration than that of Jimmy Carter would have stuck to what was, after all, its immediate reaction: that the U.S. strategic nuclear arsenal was quite sufficient to cope with the Soviet medium-range threat, just as it had since Soviet SS-4 and SS-5 missiles were first deployed in the late 1950s. It seems likely that NATO would have responded in one way or the other to the growing Soviet program, and, as has been pointed out above, the LRTNF decision is not an unreasonable response. It would have been able to do so, however, without the mortgage of political symbolism that now weighs upon the program and weakens both its military purpose and its erstwhile political objectives.

THE PROCEDURE

The 1979 decision was a novelty in two respects: For the first time, it made a U.S. nuclear weapon program dependent on prior allied consent, and it linked the decision to procure the new arms with an undertaking to negotiate their limitation through bilateral U.S.-Soviet arms control. It is the novelty of this procedure that has tended to accentuate the political impact of the issue, in particular, and of theater nuclear matters in general.

Collective Responsibility for Procurement

The 1979 program was a collective decision of alliance governments. Before the new weapons were even produced, U.S. allies were asked to commit themselves to deploy them on their territory. The United States' refusal to proceed without this commitment amounted in practice to a collective decision by non-nuclear member states of the alliance to produce and deploy two major new weapon systems.

The significance of this novel procedure has been little noticed, yet it cannot be overstressed. Nuclear procurement decisions for the preceding thirty years of the alliance had been made by the United States alone (and Britain and France for their respective forces), and only afterwards, through a bilateral arrangement, were the countries on whose territory the weapons were to be stationed asked to agree to the specific deployment. This practice was abandoned for the first time in the neutron bomb affair in 1978, which was probably one major reason for its ill-fated demise.[2] Yet while the alliance generally, and the American and German governments in particular, took great pains in the TNF decision to avoid the mistakes of the neutron bomb experience, they again employed the specific deployment requirement.

That practice is an unfortunate one that serves to both complicate and politicize nuclear decisions in the alliance. To ask European non-nuclear countries to endorse a nuclear weapon program invariably forces them to protect that decision within their domestic political contexts by devices that are not conducive to the program itself. It was this that led the government of Helmut Schmidt to insist that West Germany should not be the only continental European country to agree to the deployment of the new weapons, thus both prolonging the decisionmaking process and provoking strong antinuclear emotions in Holland, emotions which later were to spill over into the debate on the German left. Similarly, the request to European non-nuclear alliance states to stand up and be counted in a nuclear procurement decision practically invited those governments to attach conditions and caveats to the decision and, in order to gain domestic political support, to link it to an arms control initiative in a way that rendered the whole program ambiguous.

There will be those who believe European (and particularly German) insistence on the need for linking the program to arms control was the result less of the chosen procedure than of a growing European respect for the weight of Soviet military power and growing doubts over American consistency. As so often is the case in the social sciences, one cannot prove the contrary. To this observer, however, it is not a convincing argument. After all, concerns over nuclear weapons have long been voiced in the European political debate, most energetically in the late 1950s (in Germany and in Britain in particular) when American strength and commitment were undoubted and detente with the Soviet Union enjoyed considerably less political support than it would twenty years later.

A more probable suggestion is that there exists in Europe—particularly but not only in those countries that have foresworn a nuclear military capability for themselves—a profound and continuous allergy to all nuclear military matters. It inevitably surfaces if their governments are asked to take responsibility for nuclear weapon programs, and it must be taken into account by responsible politicians in these countries. One cannot ask European governments both to be involved in the decision and to avoid the controversy. The one follows from the other.

Why, then, was this not taken into account as the LRTNF decision was shaped and the lesson from the neutron bomb debacle not learned? Two explanations seem probable: First, that part of the lesson was not sufficiently recognized, and second, political perceptions on both sides of the Atlantic assured that, even if the lesson had been recognized, other considerations then seemed weightier.

For the Carter administration, the lesson did not seem to be recognized at all. The American critique of the neutron bomb fiasco centered on the lack of clear leadership by the United States and on the belief that a more subtle diplomacy within the alliance could have provided a smoother result; there also was justified anger over the foot-dragging of West European governments in the matter. This, therefore, suggested to Washington that what had gone wrong was a lack of firmness by the United States and that, on the LRTNF issue, it was more essential to prove U.S. leadership than it was to be perceptive about European political requirements.

There also was logic to the U.S. approach. Since the new weapons were designed specifically for, and could only be relevant in the military context of Europe, it made little sense for the United States to go ahead with production unless those on whose soil the weapons were to be stationed gave their prior agreement. The absence of such agreement might well have jeopardized the budget request in the U.S. Congress. Moreover, was it not natural for a mature alliance that there should be no "nuclearization without participation"? Unfortunately, logic is not usually the best guide to successful politics since it suggests a tidiness that rarely reigns in the political arena. More important, the same logic might have applied to the Thor and Jupiter missiles in the late 1950s or to Lance, Honest John, and Pershing I missiles or nuclear artillery shells in the 1960s. Yet in none of these procurement decisions had the United States insisted on a prior deployment commitment from her allies.

It is useless to speculate whether European governments, if they had so wished, could have won an American agreement to follow this same procedure again in the LRTNF case. The fact is that they—at least the major ones—did not try for reasons of their own. First, concern over the supposed gap in Eurostrategic systems had been voiced with authority initially not by a leading U.S. politician but by the West German chancellor; it was scarcely possible for the Germans to limit themselves to voicing concern but not to accept a degree of visible responsibility for the program designed to allay it. Second, European governments had become increasingly unhappy with what they saw as American unilateralism in alliance nuclear issues—in the SALT negotiations or over the March 1977 Carter proposal for limiting cruise missiles. As a result, the trend in European Chancelleries was toward committing the United States to closer, more intimate, and comprehensive consultation and even coordination in nuclear matters. If the American ally now offered such coordination, both on the LRTNF procurement decision and on arms control in this field, it was not for Europe to reject it.

The question for the future is to what extent the full participation of European governments in specifically Europe-related nuclear weapon decisions is desirable or unavoidable. In spite of the cost in domestic political controversy, participation may be desirable if this is what is necessary for European governments to become involved from the start in all nuclear questions that affect them and if that, in turn, is desirable for the future of the alliance. But is it? The answer depends essentially on whether or not one believes that to leave these matters to the United States would change substantially the reliability of the U.S. security commitment to Europe. That commitment is defined essentially by America's strategic interests, and since these are unlikely to change, a greater European say on alliance nuclear matters might therefore superficially be more satisfying, even though in substance it would be marginal.

Has such involvement, in a political sense, become inevitable, now that the LRTNF precedent has been established? Will it be possible for future U.S. administrations to obtain the funding support in Congress for nuclear programs specifically designed for the European theater unless the endorsement of European governments has been obtained beforehand? Similarly, would European governments regard U.S. unilateral decisionmaking as politically decoupling, thus awakening the never dormant European fear that the United States would disregard European interests where they clash with its own? The answer was provided by President Reagan's August 1981 decision on the production of the neutron warhead. By deciding unilaterally on the weapon program and promising to seek later the agreement of host countries for the deployment, the United States returned to the pre-1978 practice. Nor was there much doubt that Congress would support the decision even in the absence of prior European agreement to have these weapons stationed in Europe. From the American perspective, therefore, the LRTNF procedure does not constitute a precedent for future decisions. Indeed, President Reagan's administration has probably been confirmed in its unilateral instincts by the LRTNF experience.

Is the precedent unavoidable for Europe? The first reaction in West European capitals, and particularly in West Germany, to Reagan's neutron bomb decision might suggest so; the administration was bitterly criticized for its unilateral decision and for not having consulted its allies. Two factors put this in perspective. First, President Reagan's decision was deliberately and unavoidably exploited in the European campaign against the LRTNF program. It served those who have argued against the decision as a means of allowing the United States to conduct its nuclear wars on European soil as additional evidence for their thesis. The central issue of critique, therefore, was not the specific procedure but the substance. Second, the experience with the LRTNF program has already been a thorny one for most European governments, and they are unlikely to want to repeat it once the present controversy has been overcome. While it is possible that Western Europe's governments would ask for a more defined responsibility in America's nuclear decisions, it is not very likely; more probably, they would want to return to the convenient position of criticizing U.S. nuclear decisions without being accountable for them. It happens to be a position that reflects the different nuclear status in the Western alliance and also minimizes the political controversy surrounding nuclear issues in Europe. This may not be sufficient as a durable formula for alliance nuclear diplomacy in the future, but it will remain one of its essential elements. The nuclear burden-sharing represented by the 1979 LRTNF decision is too costly a formula, accelerating as it does the latent divisive nature of extended deterrence. It must be hoped, therefore, that instead of providing a precedent it will prove an aberration.

Collective Responsibility for Arms Control?

The 1979 decision is two-tracked: The military program should be pursued as far as necessary, and arms control negotiations as far as possible. While the first constituted the alliance's first multilateral nuclear production decision, the second was put firmly in the context of bilateral Soviet-American talks and agreements. The reasons for this distinction are many: Originally, LRTNF negotiations were to be set firmly in the context of SALT in order to avoid the impression of decoupling theater forces from strategic deterrence, and, more frequently, that a U.S. administration reluctant to embark on SALT might be induced to do so through the backdoor of LRTNF negotiations. These are valid reasons, but they represent an incomplete assessment of the dynamics produced by the "double track." In order to protect their involvement in the former procurement programs and to ensure domestic political support for its implementation, European governments have had to take recourse to raising hopes for arms control—a matter that they do not control.

We owe the revelation of this built-in contradiction to the avowed skepticism of the Reagan Administration toward arms control. It is an awkward one for European domestic politics, for the East-West relationship, and for West-West relations. Domestically, it means that European governments that have obtained support for the first part of the December 1979 decision under condition of the second find that with the doubts over arms control political support for the program is waning. They can do little more than make appeals to the United States, appeals that lack credibility since they clearly are not dictated by arms control but by domestic political difficulties.

In East-West relations, it means that European governments are the Achilles heel of the decision and one that the Soviet Union quite legitimately seeks to exploit. Since Europeans control the deployment but not the negotiations, the Soviet Union uses their anxieties to put pressure both on the European domestic debate and, indirectly, on the United States. It also means that the Soviets are less pressed to make substantial concessions in the negotiations, as long as they can hope to delay the program's implementation without such concessions.

In West-West relations, it is a situation that is bound to create misgivings. European impatience over the slowness of arms control all too readily will be interpreted in the United States as a desire to renege on the deployment decision and to kowtow to the Soviets—a picturebook example of self-Finlandization. Even the most arms control-minded U.S. administration—and this scarely applies to the Reagan team—would resent what it must regard as unhelpful pressures to enter potentially premature agreements. Conversely, European governments are pushed by their domestic politics to show that they are doing something and, if nothing much happens, might be tempted to blame not the Soviets but the Americans for the lack of results.

It is true that the latter reactions also would have arisen if the procurement decision on LRTNF had been taken by the United States alone. European public opininon tends to respond to deteriorations in Soviet-American relations by calling for more arms control, and this would have been the case even if the LRTNF program had not been accompanied by a specific commitment to arms control. The question is not, therefore, how these frustrations could be avoided but how they could be made less disruptive politically.

One answer frequently heard in the Washington of the Reagan Administration is that the fault lies in the double-track nature of the decision itself: Procurement should not be made conditional on arms control. I do not share that view, for reasons developed later in this paper. But it clearly is a combination that requires more thoughtful presentation and management than was provided by the governments that endorsed it in 1979. One reason why the link as agreed is politically counterproductive lies in the combination of a collective procurement decision with bilateral arms control; it exacerbates, rather than alleviates, the political tensions inherent in alliance nuclear policies. Instead of containing the political controversy surrounding nuclear weapons—as had originally been hoped—this specific procedure has tended to fuel it.

Would that be any different with more direct participation of European governments in the negotiating process? The arguments that point against the wisdom of such participation are, on the surface, profound: As long as only Soviet and American systems are involved, only Soviets and Americans control the substance of the negotiations, and only they can decide on the result. To include America's allies formally would not only bring the differences between them to bear on day-to-day negotiations but also risk that European nuclear systems would be dragged into the process, against original intentions. The negotiations, already fraught with a good many complexities, would become even more complicated.

Yet these arguments leave major doubts. For one, there is the experience of the Vienna negotiations for mutual and balanced force reductions (MBFR). Here, Europeans are involved, with their own forces, in a collective negotiation, and in spite of differences over timing, domestic pressures, and attitudes to East-West detente, the alliance has shown a remarkable degree of cohesion over an unprecedented period of time—the negotiations are now entering into their eighth year. The MBFR talks also have shown that the primarily bilateral issue of Soviet and American conventional force reductions could be addressed in a multilateral forum and that through the device of a two stage procedure, inadvertent slippage from one negotiating arena into the other could be controlled. Moreover, that same experience indicates that political differences within the Western alliance may be reduced more effectively when West European governments have a seat at the table than when they have not: It is not difficult to imagine a major domestic politicization resulting from the troop reduction talks had the protracted negotiations been of a purely bilateral, Soviet-American character.

Why should the MBFR experience not also apply to the LRTNF negotiations? After all, nuclear questions were discussed in that context, too; witness the famous Option 3 in NATO's negotiating stance, that intended to offer reductions in American theater nuclear warheads in exchange for the withdrawal of Soviet tanks from East Germany. Both in MBFR and in the earlier Helsinki process of the Conference on Security and Cooperation, fears that these multilateral gatherings might aggravate Atlantic dissonance were disproved; indeed, it seems to have been precisely the direct participation of West European delegates in these negotiations that led not only to effective alliance coordination but also to the determination of all Western governments concerned to sort out their differences *in camera* and not in the public political arena.

There is a more profound political reason for this, and one not merely of procedural dynamics. It lies in the basic European attitude to the military balance in Europe. By and large, the European instinct is that a balance exists as long as the United States remains committed to and present in Europe. For this reason, asymmetries in the strategic nuclear forces of both major powers have generally been viewed with much less concern in Europe than in the United States. Arms control, much of the rhetoric notwithstanding, has for European elites generally been important not for its (so often disappointing) results but for its political symbolism of tying the United States and Europe to the pursuit of a cooperative modus vivendi with the Soviet Union, and the Soviet Union to greater respect for the interests of the Western Alliance as a whole, including Europe. For Europeans, this is the "bargain" in arms control, not precise force limitations or reductions.[3] Full participation in negotiations, whether on conventional or on nuclear forces in Europe, responds to this approach.[4] If those concerned are tied both into the discipline of the negotiations and the responsibility for the outcome, the basic political objective would be met more effectively and more harmoniously. By contrast, the halfway house of LRTNF—European participation in the procurement but not in the negotiations—is a recipe for major difficulties in the pursuit of both.

This is not to suggest that everything would be clear sailing if European governments had a direct role in the LRTNF negotiations. Some allied governments, such as West Germany, have consistently shied away from direct responsibilities in the nuclear realm. The more the controversy over the LRTNF program fueled North Europe's latent nuclear allergies, the more difficult it would be to bring those governments into co-responsibility for the negotiations. However, the 1979 decision already has imposed on them direct responsibility for the nuclear program. If the United States were to persist in the approach started in the Carter years—namely, to ask European governments to be committed to nuclear procurement decisions relevant to the European theater—their involvement in the arms control issues would follow. It is a major interest for the alliance that the process of this involvement is one that reduces, not increases, political controversy, frustrations, and mutual suspicions on both sides of the Atlantic. Merely the establishment of more High Level or Special Groups in NATO are unlikely, to judge by recent experience, to meet this requirement.

Yet there remains one major political counterargument: the fear that multilateral negotiations on LRTNF separate form SALT would be decoupling in their political effect. To open LRTNF negotiations to America's allies might underline that separateness, a development that the alliance has sought to combat by its repeated emphasis that these negotiations should be conducted in the framework of SALT. There can be no doubt that a rapid resumption of the SALT talks would reduce much of the political pressure on the LRTNF program in Europe, at least temporarily, or that the most relevant arms control framework would be that of SALT. The separation of LRTNF from the SALT issue, however, is underway in any case, not least due to the conviction of the present U.S. administration that serious talks on the limitation of strategic forces would make sense only if America were clearly embarked on correcting what are perceived as serious deficiencies in its strategic posture. This, together with European impatience, is likely to lead to a deliberate effort to keep the two issues separate, for fear of drifting into a SALT negotiation before conditions in the strategic nuclear field were judged ripe.

Would it then not make sense to accept the separateness of the LRTNF negotiations and to involve European governments more directly in them? Decoupling is less the result of weapons and procedures than of trans-Atlantic frustrations and misgivings. If multilateralizing the negotiations could, as has been argued above, reduce the latter, would they not serve, rather than undermine, the cohesion of the alliance?

PROSPECTS FOR IMPLEMENTATION

Rarely has a NATO decision been as carefully prepared to assure political support during its implementation than that taken by the Council of Ministers in December 1979.[5] Yet within a short time, the consensus achieved has become shaky, to the extent that it cannot be foreseen with certainty whether the program will be implemented. What makes this even more surprising is the fact that the NATO position, in theory at least, should be strengthened by the continuing Soviet military buildup. Why has it come to this?

Two reasons have been suggested above: the agony that direct European involvement in nuclear production decisions arouses and the lack of direct European involvement in preparation of the arms control aspects. Yet these would apply to all nuclear decisions in the alliance (as the neutron bomb affair underlined). There are three additional reasons why this particular program has run into trouble.

The first is that it was announced at a time of deteriorating Soviet-American relations. Only two weeks after the NATO ministers signed their communique, Soviet forces marched into Afghanistan, and the United States decided to bring home to the Soviet Union their profound concern by putting bilateral detente on ice.

The European political reaction was predictable. European public opinion in 1979 feared for the consequences in their immediate region of the deterioration between the superpowers and tended to play down the significance of Afghanistan. Instead, governments generally sought to emphasize that detente was not dead, but alive in Europe. It fitted badly with this instinctive reaction that, at the same time, they were involved in the first major nuclear modernization program since the early 1960s.

A traditional European attitude to superpower detente thus was manifested anew. Europeans are worried if Soviet-American relations are progressing smoothly since it might imply a "deal over our heads"; only twelve months before the 1979 decision many European governments had been concerned, for instance, that some of the provisions of the emerging SALT II agreement could harm their military options. Yet they are even more worried if Soviet-American relations are in difficulty, and understandably so: The effects are felt most directly in Europe. The result, then, is often not to rally to the Western against the Eastern superpower, but to resent both as spoilers of European detente. This sentiment was strengthened both by the frustration over Mr. Carter's inconsistencies and the uneasiness over Mr. Reagan's pronouncements, reviving, in the political and in the public mood, the old "Europe for the Europeans" dream. The unfortunate presentation of Presidential Directive 59,[6] together with the apparently irrepressible enthusiasm of some American nuclear theoreticians for elaborate options for limited nuclear exchanges, combined with and rationalized this resentment. In the simplification of European concerns, doubts over the United States acquired a new and disturbing respectability: Was the alliance with a United States bent on acquiring military superiority, on fighting limited nuclear wars, and on delaying arms control in Europe's interest? Or, on the contrary, was the United States becoming a liability for Europe? These doubts could not but render that most visible symbol of the alliance, nuclear weapons in Europe, even more controversial.

The second, related reason why the LRTNF program has floundered lies in the intensity of the Soviet reaction and the clear Soviet willingness to go to considerable lengths to stop the LRTNF program, preferably through political interference in the Western, and particularly West German, debate. In retrospect, there can be little doubt that NATO treated the question of Soviet reactions less than adequately when it prepared the program. Perhaps a more careful assessment of Soviet nuclear thinking and likely responses would have led to a different emphasis in the LRTNF program (e.g., an emphasis on cruise missiles alone rather than including the—in Soviet eyes—eyes—ambiguous Pershing II as well) and to its presentation (less on the SS-20 threat than to protect NATO nuclear forces against Soviet preemptive capabilities). As it was, the long-range capabilities of the new systems were seen by the Soviets as a strategic, not a theater, threat, which either had to be prevented by a cancellation of the Western program or, if that were not successful, by a strategic response. NATO's opportunistic stance of justifying its own program by the growth of the Soviet SS-20 arsenal meant that this program was vulnerable politically to Soviet offers of a moratorium: If tomorrow the Soviet Union declared that it had stopped all SS-20 procurement and would take it up again only as NATO systems are being deployed, political support for the LRTNF program could be in considerable trouble.

The third reason lies, paradoxically, in the novelty of the LRTNF decision, namely to link the go-ahead for the production of the new weapons to an offer to negotiate their limitation. This link had been designed in order to assure political support in Europe for the program, to make it more palatable for the latent nuclear allergies. The combination of production and arms control, in itself, is a promising model for arms control since it avoids a familiar obstacle—the weapon programs that one wants to constrain are usually completed before the negotiations. Imagine how much better the situation would be today if the Soviet Union, before embarking on its earlier massive nuclear modernization program, had adopted a similar stance.

Nevertheless, the net effect of the particular combination chosen by NATO has not been to secure European public support for the program but to make implementation of the program more doubtful. The mistake lies not in the combination itself but in its ambiguity, an ambiguity for which European governments have to take most of the blame. It was they who insisted that, theoretically at least, arms control could lead to agreements that would render the deployment of a single new American missile in Europe unnecessary (the so-called zero solution). The result has been predictable: Arms control in much of the European debate is no longer seen as parallel to the deployment but as its alternative; moreover, deployment has become, for much of the critical European public, counterproductive to arms control. The eagerness of European governments to make the deployment decision politically more palatable has thus made it more, not less, controversial. Raising unrealistic hopes for a zero solution through arms control has deprived the military arguments for the LRTNF program of much of their credibility. What would have made sense, both in the interest of credibility and of getting the Soviets to make serious concessions, was to announce the minimum number of forces required and to extend the program beyond that conditional on Soviet restraint. Instead, the entire Western program has now become conditional on Western restraint by proving that the West—and not the Soviets—is serious about arms control.

All this does not mean that LRTNF modernization will not take place. Contrary to the agitation of the debate, there remains instinctive majority support in all the major West European countries for responding to the threat caused by Soviet nuclear forces. It does mean that more is now needed to assure implementation than was thought necessary in 1979.

First of all, it is no longer sufficient to base the modernization of Western LRTNF on the Soviet SS-20 program alone. Instead, it will have to be based squarely on precise Western military needs, and this implies both a fuller and a more balanced presentation of the threat by pointing to the whole range of Soviet delivery systems that threaten the survival of nuclear missiles in Western Europe—not just the SS-20 missiles and the Backfire bomber but the modernized shorter-range missiles (the SS-21, SS-22, and SS-23) that the Soviet Union is now beginning to deploy.

Second, and most important, it will be necessary to make clear that the new weapons are a means of deterring, not of fighting a war, and that notions of limiting a nuclear conflict to Europe are without foundation. For any democratic society to consent that their security be based on nuclear weapons requires credibility that these weapons would not be used except in extremis. To pretend—as much of the American debate on limited nuclear options and nuclear war-fighting suggests—that nuclear weapons are in fact usable and that nuclear exchanges can be kept limited and controlled is technically highly doubtful given the uncertainties of command and control on which such limitability would have to rely.[7] It is also dangerously apolitical since it forgets that no strategic doctrine can endure in a democratic society that frightens its own citizens at least as much as it does the leaders of the opposing camp. To make the nuclear weapons of the LRTNF program acceptable politically, deterrence itself has to be made again credible as a valid concept and not one that is indistinguishable from fighting with nuclear weapons.

Third, there would have to be visible progress toward arms control. The start of Soviet-American negotiations on limiting theater nuclear forces has taken some of the pressure off beleaguered European politicians for some time, but more is needed than gaining some time. Even assuming that the first of the U.S. LRTNF systems would be deployed on schedule, that is, by late 1983, the full program would not be completed before the late 1980s. Political support for the program needs to be maintained not for a mere few months but for years. Willingness to negotiate would suffice for the former, not for the latter. What will be needed, rather, is either indisputable evidence that the United States, as the West's negotiator, has done everything to reach agreement—and that can never be proven to everyone's satisfaction—or an agreement that, by defining mutual limitations also defines the extent to which the 1979 decision should be implemented.

PROSPECTS FOR ARMS CONTROL

It is this latter consideration of political expediency that determines what can be sought through arms control. It is now too late to change course; many of the suggestions made earlier in this chapter might have applied if NATO were still to take its decision. Now that the decision has been made and the political dynamics have evolved around it, these suggestions might be useful for the next round, but not for today. The political pressures are now such that any major change in procedure or substance would lead to an unravelling of the program as a whole and to political consequences for the alliance of much greater potential damage than the imperfect implementation of an imperfect decision.

Together with the familiar problems of reaching arms control agreements, this argues against overambitious limitation concepts. It would be desirable that agreements should lead to a nuclear force relationship in Europe that effectively excludes the option of a preemptive strike, such as replacing ballistic delivery systems by cruise missiles on both sides, but this is unlikely to be attained in the near future. Similarly, it could be hoped that agreements would regulate the whole range of nuclear systems threatening the survival of nuclear delivery systems on each side—including the SS-21, SS-22, and SS-23, not only the long-range varieties—but such comprehensive control cannot be expected realistically. The same applies to suggestions for linking LRTNF to agreements on strategic arms limitations[8]—a logical answer since it would include all systems that constitute a strategic threat to either of the major powers or their allies but scarcely a practical one within the constraints of time and political rationale that determine the LRTNF and SALT issues. This inevitably implies that a realistic agreement will not be ideal—but there is the mitigating circumstance that more ideal types of arms limitation also would not be without their shortcomings.

What is a realistic approach to LRTNF arms control?[9] First, the West is right to insist that negotiations, at least initially, should deal with longer-range missile systems alone. To include shorter-range systems or to accept the Soviet request for an "organic" link with forward-based systems would amount to delaying agreement. While clearly these weapon systems have to be taken into account in formulating the negotiating position (for instance, their existence rules out that the West could accept very low ceilings for LRTNF) and might be considered specifically at a later stage, they should not be the subject of negotiations in the first phase.

Second, the aim should be an equal numerical ceiling, and the "unit of account" should be warheads on missiles deployed, not those in launchers. To concentrate on launchers would, in the short run, favor the Soviet Union but in the longer run would encourage the West to seek ways to proliferate the number of warheads on NATO systems.

Third, the Soviet SS-4 and Ss-5 missiles would either have to be disbanded or put under a composite ceiling on the Eastern side, which would also imply a higher ceiling for Western LRTNF. The first of these alternatives is clearly preferable, and it would be difficult for the Soviet Union to argue both that the SS-20 is merely a modern replacement of the older systems *and* that they must be retained.

Fourth, the West should seek a prohibition of new medium-range systems on both sides, beyond the current modernization. If agreed, this might also provide some kind of a barrier against the upgrading of range capabilities in other, formerly short-range systems—such as the Soviet Frog, Scud, and Scaleboard missiles—that are currently being upgraded.

Fifth, there should be an attempt to formulate major principles of nuclear balance in Europe that might apply beyond the LRTNF systems to other theater nuclear forces. The West clearly must be concerned that if it agrees to limitations on LRTNF, it will—due to the political controversy aroused by nuclear modernization in Europe—have few other bargaining chips to encourage restraint in the modernization of shorter-range Soviet systems. The Soviet Union has already emphasized that U.S. forward-based systems (nuclear delivery systems capable of reaching Soviet territory from supporting points in and around Europe) should be "organically linked" to the negotiations. Perhaps there is a chance to profit from the obvious Soviet concern over the new missiles to push the negotiations beyond the mere regulation of the existing balance to an understanding of the rules that should govern it in the future.

Two important obstacles remain. The first is that of verification. The dilemma that modern arms control has been forced to address increasingly—that less and less of what is militarily relevant can be adequately verified—is even more acute in the case of theater nuclear forces, with their multiple range and multiple purpose systems, their small size, and considerable mobility. The West—and particularly the United States, where verifiability has become a dogma of arms control—will have to face the choice between agreements that restrict the weapons of concern, but with less than assured verifiability, and agreements that, although verifiable, can cover only a section of those weapon systems determining the theater nuclear balance. This choice might be made less sharp with the help of associated measures to assist the monitoring of agreements, but it will not disappear.

The second obstacle is that of political will—the readiness to make concessions for the sake of an honorable agreement. For the United States—particularly for an administration that, through its early verbal opposition to SALT II, has tied itself into a position from which it would be hard to emerge with undiminished credibility—a separate LRTNF negotiation would seem preferable to one integrated into SALT. It also would serve as a symbol that the United States is not fundamentally opposed to exploring ways of promoting security other than increasing the national defense effort. European governments are primarily concerned to get the talks going; they would certainly not object to an early agreement.

How will the Soviets respond? Soviet behavior over the past two years suggests that there is indeed profound concern over the Western program. Once it becomes clear that the program cannot be successfully torpedoed politically, the Soviets are likely to be willing to accept some restrictions on their own efforts in exchange for restrictions on the Western one. The difficulty will lie in making this clear to Soviet leaders when the continuing controversy surrounding the LRTNF program in Europe might give rise to hopes in Moscow that a *de facto* Western restriction—the collapse of the 1979 decision— might be had without restrictions on the Soviet effort. The temptation will be there for the Soviet Union to use the negotiations in order to delay the deployment of Western systems, not in order to reach agreement. The antinuclear forces in Europe, in this respect, are also anti-arms-control forces: The more effective their opposition to the LRTNF program, the bleaker the prospects for agreement.

It is doubtful that the Soviet temptation to delay agreement could be overcome unless a number of factors combine. It would need, first, on the part of European governments, a more confident and informative campaign to rally support around the LRTNF program than they have generally displayed to date; it would no longer be enough to merely react to Soviet proposals or to point to the number of SS-20 missiles deployed against Europe. It would require, second, that the commitment of the United States to arms control in general and to LRTNF limitations in particular become credible to European public opinion and to Soviet leaders alike. Third, it may have to involve a readiness by the United States to make the LRTNF negotiations a test case for nuclear arms control or such. Soviet delaying techniques would then not only make agreement on theater nuclear forces difficult but also darken the prospect for negotiations on strategic nuclear weapons likely to be the more important objective for Soviet diplomacy in the 1980s.

On November 18, 1981, President Reagan made public the U.S. proposal for the Geneva talks that were to begin a few days later. He formally endorsed the "zero option" that some European governments had advocated: The NATO program would not be implemented if the Soviet Union in return were to dismantle its intermediate-range nuclear capabilities.

This proposal has the fault of its merits. It is simple but scarcely negotiable, and the Soviet Union did not hide its profound opposition from the start. It formally links the rationale of the Western program to the Soviet SS-20 build-up and thus exposes European political support to the temptations of Soviet offers to stop the almost completed SS-20 deployments.

It is, for some time at least, an effective political counter to the pressure against the program that had been building up in Western Europe, but it is at the expense of an arms control approach that considers the long-term rationale for theater nuclear forces for Europe. If the Soviet Union were to accept the U.S. proposal, the effect would be to rule out a modernization program that, for the reasons stated earlier in this chapter, makes military sense while locking NATO into an existing theater nuclear posture which does so much less.

The Reagan proposal, therefore, will not avoid the problems that have been discussed in these pages. Rather it confirms the political-tactical approach that has for so long guided decisionmaking on NATO's nuclear issues. European governments at least will not be able to blame the United States for following an example that they themselves have set. But it is imperative that the alliance now take a serious and longer term look at its theater nuclear requirements, quite apart from the prospect for arms control.

CONCLUSIONS: THE 1979 DECISION
AND BEYOND

NATO's 1979 decision on LRTNF procurement and arms control is neither the first nor will it be the last time that nuclear issues have to be addressed by the Western alliance. It provides both the latest and probably the most penetrating lessons of how to deal with these issues. What are these lessons?

First and most important, do not try to solve political problems within the alliance by nuclear remedies. Nuclear weapons are simply too terrifying a symbol for alliance cohesion; for maximum acceptability, they should be assumed but not seen. Moreover, the malaise within the alliance is rarely one that nuclear weapons programs can cure; if the past thirty years are any guide, then malaise springs from European uncertainty not over America's military strength but over its willingness to exercise it for the sake of Europe. Finally, nuclear programs require a lead and implementation time that exceeds that of political cycles: They cannot be realized fast enough to allay a low in alliance trust, and they are still around when alliance political relations require other than nuclear medication.

Second, do not overload the European political process by asking from it more than it can sustain. The nuclear allergy will remain a factor in European politics for the foreseeable future. Non-nuclear states are, by definition, more sensitive to this allergy than those who have a tradition of nuclear weapons. European governments should not, therefore, be asked to share in any procurement decision for U.S. nuclear weapons in the future, although their agreement to deployment on their soil remains essential. If, however, that rule is neglected—as in the 1979 LRTNF decision—then European participation needs to go beyond the responsibility for procurement and include direct involvement in negotiations for the control of nuclear arms.

Third, take care how you present the case for nuclear weapons. The only basis on which those who must fear that they will be obliterated by nuclear war can tolerate nuclear weapons is as an essential means of deterrence. Talk about nuclear war-fighting and limited nuclear war is not only highly doubtful in its strategic assessment, it is also profoundly and disturbingly ignorant of the need in democracies to find and maintain support for the policies of security. This applies to the alliance countries as a whole: while the phenomenon, at present, is most articulate in the protestant north of Europe, it is by no means absent from other alliance societies, including the protestant north of America. There is a high political price for talking about nuclear weapons as if they were merely a more powerful type of conventional explosive.

Fourth, take care how you plan the use of nuclear weapons. This is not just a matter of presentation, but it is very much of substantive policy. The uncritical way in which Western, and particularly American, strategists have welcomed limited options for nuclear use may, in a strategic sense, be an affordable luxury; in a political sense, it is an unaffordable liability. It is clear that some options beyond that of the secure second-strike capability continue to be required, but it is a failure of the strategic community that to date it has failed to define how many are enough. The option for limited first use with nuclear weapons remains essential for effective deterrence in Europe; this very fact makes it even more necessary to make clear that this is not an option for nuclear war-fighting, as distinct from deterrence. Two consequences follow from this. One, that nuclear weapons do not provide an effective remedy for conventional military weakness—a banality by now, but one that is still insufficiently recognized in NATO's conventional military posture. The other, that the alliance should pay maximum attention to crisis stability in its nuclear posture; battlefield nuclear weapons that, if at all, have to be released in the fog of war, are much less suitable for this task than are mobile LRTNF stationed in the rear of the theater.

Fifth, resist the temptation to engage in precise nuclear doctrines. The more precise the doctrine, the more controversial nuclear weapons for extended deterrence become. For the United States they imply an unacceptable automaticity of nuclear response; for Europe they imply the contradictory combination of two concerns—that of decoupling and that of nuclear war-fighting. An American nuclear doctrine that emphasizes endurance and suggests limited nuclear conflicts will undermine European political support for nuclear weapons in Europe and, with it, for the alliance.

Sixth, and last, respect that the search for arms control is the necessary companion of nuclear deterrence. The fear of an uncontrollable arms race is a deep-rooted one in all our societies. It will not be dismissed merely by pointing out that the other side is moving ahead, at least not in the nuclear domain. Once deterrence and balance are seen as a danger to, rather than a condition for peace, as is

the case in much of the European peace movement, even the most
persuasive military arguments become mute. The credible search for
an alternative to the dangers of uncrontrollable arms competition is
thus an essential corollary of prudent deterrence.

The Uncertain Future

How far into the future will these lessons be relevant? It was argued
at the beginning of this chapter that the political problem of extended
deterrence began when the age of geographical deterrence identity
between the United States and Europe ended. Since then, many of
the political implications of theater nuclear forces have been due to
their technical distinctiveness, which in turn led to the definition,
however inadequately, of nuclear balances distinct from the overall
strategic balance. That period is now coming to an end. The cruise
missiles on B-52 bombers may be classified as strategic, but they are
not substantially different from those to be launched from European
soil and classified as theater weapons. As William Kincade has put it:
"Cumulative technological innovation is ushering out the era dominated by large limited-mission strategic systems. . . . Alongside improved models of these behemoths will be smaller, more flexible,
more interchangeable and faster weapons with greater firepower and
more supple control mechanisms."[10] In other words: Technological
distinctiveness will soon be a thing of the past, technological flexibility
the theme of the future.

It is too early to be certain about the implications of the LRTNF
decision for political cohesion and nuclear issues in the alliance. One
desirable possibility is that the disappearance of weapons distinctions
would again reunite the European and the North American con-
tinents into one strategic zone, where deterrence can function irrespective of geographical distances.

There is also another, more daunting possibility. A Europe that
continues to depend on the readiness of the United States to fire
nuclear weapons first would make demands on the United States that
in the strategic conditions of the 1990s may not be satisfied. To quote
again Kincade: "Americans will have to accustom themselves to the
kind of insecurity their West European allies have long lived with,
their survival dependent on decisions made in distant capitals, and
possessing no immunity from nuclear weapons effects."[11] If Euro-

peans cannot show that their reliance on nuclear weapons is not merely the consequence of insufficient conventional military efforts of their own, will they then still be regarded as a tolerable risk by their American ally?

NOTES

1. Helmut Schmidt, "1977 Alastair Buchan Memorial Lecture," *Survival* (January-February 1978):2-10.
2. See the analysis of the International Institute for Strategic Studies, *Strategic Survey, 1978* (London: IISS, 1979), p. 10.
3. See Philip Windsor, "West Germany and the Alliance," *Adelphi Paper 770* (London: International Institute for Strategic Studies, 1981).
4. David Owen's suggestion to include West Germany in the talks is incomplete but goes in the right direction. See David Owen, *Survival* (May-June 1980):122.
5. For a full account of these preparations see David D. Elliot "Decision in Brussels." April 1981, unpublished.
6. President Carter's directive on U.S. strategic doctrine of August 1980 was leaked to the press as a major new stance of toughness vis-a-vis the Soviet Union implying the actual use of nuclear weapons, as a doctrine of deterrence. *Strategic Survey 1980/81,* p. 44.
7. See Desmond Ball, "Can Nuclear War be Controlled?," Adelphi Paper No. 169 (London: International Institute for Strategic Studies, 1981).
8. For much of the following discussion in this section I am indebted to Lynn Davis "A Proposal for TNF Arms Control," *Survival* (November/December 1981):242-246.
9. Suggested originally by West German sources and discussed further in Lawrence Freedman, "The Dilemma of Theatre Nuclear Arms Control," *Survival* (January/February 1981).
10. William Kincade, "Over the Technological Horizon," *Daedalus* (Winter 1981):122.
11. Kincade, 1981:125.

6 TECHNOLOGICAL PROSPECTS

William J. Perry

Four distinct characteristics of strategic forces have a direct effect on their capabilities:

1. Lethality—the ability of forces to destroy an assigned target even if the target is hardened; lethality is determined by the accuracy with which the nuclear warheads can be delivered and the number and yield of those warheads;
2. Survivability—the ability of delivery systems to survive a surprise attack while they are still at or near their bases;
3. Penetrativity—the ability of missiles and aircraft to defeat or evade an active defense while carrying out their strike mission;
4. Connectivity—the ability of national command authorities to determine the status of, and transmit commands to, the various elements of strategic forces in the presence of a variety of disrupting factors, including nuclear detonations and countermeasures.

Current U.S. strategic forces were conceived in the 1950s and for the most part developed in the 1960s. The technologies of that era allowed the development of strategic forces that could survive any attack then considered plausible and could penetrate known active defenses with a residual force whose lethality was more than adequate to execute their deterrence mission. During the 1970s, there were dramatic changes in the technologies that affect these four fundamental characteristics of strategic forces and that continue unabated in this decade. These changes necessitate a review of the assumptions that originally defined U.S. strategic forces in order to determine how to maintain viability throughout the rest of this century.

LETHALITY

Well-advanced technical developments in the U.S., which lag about five years in the Soviet Union, are converging toward infinite lethality for nuclear weapons. Because of improvements in guidance technology, reentry technology, and propulsion technology, we are developing weapons that approach perfect accuracy and that have ever increasing numbers of warheads.

1. Accuracy

The inertial guidance systems already on our operational weapons have accuracies that give them some probability of destroying even very hard targets, such as missile silos. In the course of the next decade, improvements will be made in inertial systems that will reduce delivery error to about one-half of what it is now. Given the lethal radius of nuclear warheads, this approaches what could be called zero circular error probable (CEP), since it assures destruction of each target that is engaged.

In a sense, this is the nuclear equivalent of the precision-guided munitions now being deployed with conventional forces. Nearly equivalent accuracies will be achievable for submarine missiles in the near future, using the same inertial components combined with a stellar (star-seeking) system to compensate for the inaccuracies that come from the uncertainty of the submarine position at launch.

Even greater accuracies could be achieved by employing a terminal guidance system. The cruise missile employs a form of terminal guidance called TERCOM, which has accuracies several times better than those derived from the inertial systems on land-based intercontinental ballistic missiles (ICBMs). A similar scene-matching guidance system is used with the Pershing II missile and could be adapted to

ICBMs or submarine-launched ballistic missiles (SLBMs). Another form of very accurate guidance system positions itself by reference to new navigation satellites (NAVSTAR). Six of those satellites are already in orbit, and the program calls for eighteen to be in orbit by the late 1980s. With the appropriate radio receiver and computer, any vehicle can locate itself at any time and any point to very fine accuracies. NAVSTAR is intended for navigational purposes for ships, airplanes, ground vehicles, and Trident submarines. Also, during the test program of the Trident missile, it is being used as an instrumentation system to check on the accuracy of the missile's stellar-internal guidance system. Had it been decided to "close the loop," NAVSTAR could have been converted into a very accurate guidance system for either submarine-launched missiles or for ICBMs. Richard Garwin has proposed a variation of this scheme called inverted NAVSTAR. This system envisions beacons like those in the satellites but deployed on the ground in quantities of hundreds to allow a guidance input to SLBMs or ICBMs from any position within line-of-sight of those ground beacons. ICBM accuracies better than those based on advanced all-inertial systems could be achieved with such a system. In sum, a variety of different technical paths to extremely high accuracies for either ICBMs or SLBMs are available by the end of the decade.

2. Reentry Technology and Propulsion Technology

Coupled to improvements in accuracy will be further developments in the technology of multiple, independently targetable reentry vehicles (MIRVs). The MX missile will be able to carry from ten to fourteen warheads the size of the current Minuteman warhead (Mk 12A). It could be designed to carry up to twenty warheads of the size of the Trident warhead. The latter option would be technically attractive with guidance system accuracies on the order of 100 meters. The Soviets have considerable potential for increasing the number of RVs on their SS-18 and SS-19 missiles if they made improvements in the efficiency of their warhead designs or if they accepted a lower yield warhead as they improved guidance accuracies. Both the SS-18 and SS-19 could accommodate at least twice as many Minuteman-size warheads as they now carry and three times as many Trident-size warheads.

The net effect of improvements in reentry technology will be to allow the United States (and the Soviets) to put more warheads in a given payload. At the same time, propulsion efficiency is improving significantly, which allows more payload to be put on a missile of a given size. These two factors taken together indicate that, for a missile of a given size, the number of warheads and destructive power is going to increase many fold in the next decade. The United States, for example, could develop the capability to carry twenty to thirty warheads on a single ICBM. Already, twenty cruise missiles are being placed on one B-52 bomber, and that number could increase to thirty with propulsion improvements in current cruise missiles. An alternative way of using these technologies would be to go to a missile with one warhead and build it very small; for example, one could build a 20,000-pound missile capable of delivering a single warhead to ICBM ranges. Thus, technology might lead in either of two directions: It could result in large quantities of small, low-cost missiles with single warheads, or it could lead to a multiplication of warheads using the same number and same size of missiles as are deployed today.

3. Summary of Lethality Improvements

The net effect of advances in guidance, warhead, and reentry technology will be to make ballistic missiles into even more fearsome weapons than they are today. Each ballistic missile will be able to carry twenty to forty warheads, and each warhead will be directed to its target with "zero-CEP"—that is, it will bring the target within its lethal radius virtually 100 percent of the time, even if the target were very hard. At an even earlier date than these ballistic missile improvements are available, cruise missiles would be entering U.S. strategic forces with equivalent lethality. These improvements will not require technical breakthroughs but only a continuation of the guidance technology, MIRV technology, and propulsion technology that already is well advanced.

An ironic consequence of these improvements in ICBM capability is a dramatic increase in ICBM vulnerability. That is, ICBMs could be used in a counterforce mode to attack other ICBMs, and no amount of silo hardening would offer adequate protection. This emerging vulnerability of ICBMs to surprise attack could be extremely destabilizing. At the same time that the ICBM is becoming more powerful and more threatening, especially when used in a surprise attack, it is also becoming more vulnerable to a surprise attack. ICBMs will therefore evolve from a highly stabilizing component of strategic forces, which they were in the 1960s and 1970s, to a dangerously unstable component in the 1980s and 1990s unless substantial reductions in their vulnerability to surprise attack can be negotiated. We are led then to seeking ways of enhancing the survivability of ICBMs—that is, increasing the ICBM's ability to ride out a surprise attack or actively defending them against such an attack.

SURVIVABILITY OF U.S. STRATEGIC FORCES

It is a matter of overriding importance to devise ways of reducing the vulnerability of U.S. strategic forces—that is, improving their survivability, which we define as the ability of a system to avoid being destroyed at or near its base.

1. Launch Under (or Before) an Attack (LUA)

For years, U.S. strategic planning has accepted that those bombers and submarines still at their bases during a nuclear attack would be destroyed. When we talk about the survivability of submarines and bombers, we mean only those submarines and bombers that are no longer at their bases. This means further that high operating costs to maintain a high percentage of submarines and bombers on operational alert are accepted. More than 60 percent of U.S. strategic submarines are at sea at any one time and are thus invulnerable to surprise attack. Of U.S. bomber forces (depending on the level of strategic alert), 30 to 60 percent are on strip alert and could be airborne in a matter of minutes if an attack were detected.

Likewise, if the ICBMs were not at their bases when attacked, they would not be vulnerable either. However, a very significant difference with ICBMs is that once they leave their bases they cannot be recalled; the bombers and submarines can be recalled, of course. In a presumed counterforce attack—ICBM against ICBM—the president would have only minutes to decide whether to move either bombers or ICBMs from their bases. While, in the past, ambiguous warnings have been sufficient to require the removal of bombers from their bases, no president has ever decided on the basis of any alert to move ICBMs from their bases, for that is an irrevocable action.

Launching ICBMs under attack has been proposed as a viable way of dealing with the vulnerability problem. It would be an extremely destabilizing and dangerous situation, however, to have the president believe that the country's security depended on his decision to launch ICBMs on the basis of a computerized assessment of a possible attack. This would make the United States vulnerable to the unlikely, but not impossible, risk of a computer malfunction. Consequently, U.S. planners are seeking to restore the previous situation in which ICBMs could "ride out" an attack.

2. Survivability of ICBMs

For two decades, ICBMs have achieved their survivability through hardened basing (silos). The guidance accuracy already achieved by U.S. and Soviet ICBMs allows them to destroy missiles in these hardened silos with a single shot-kill probability greater than 50 percent. Improvements in accuracies that could be achieved during this decade would increase that to nearly 100 percent. Further hardening (up to fivefold increases) can be achieved but would be overwhelmed by expected improvements in accuracy that would place the silo within the warhead's fireball. Hardening is thus no longer a viable means of insuring the survivability of the ICBM force. The obvious alternative to hardening is stealth; that is, basing the missile so that its location is unknown and thus it could not be targeted effectively, even with a zero-CEP weapon. Submarine-launched ballistic missiles already use a combination of mobility and stealth to achieve survivability. Indeed, if their locations were known, they would be substantially more vulnerable than land-based missiles because of their concentration of relatively large numbers of missiles on one relatively soft launching platform.

A number of alternatives have been considered for giving land-based missiles this same combination of mobility and stealth. Air mobility presents no significant technological problems. The issues are security and cost. Security could be compromised if over-the-horizon tracking systems to track airplanes were developed, and life-cycle costs for air mobile systems could be higher than for ground mobile systems—substantially higher if some fraction of the force were required to maintain a continuous airborne alert. Mobility on roads is a relatively inexpensive option but would require continuous movement of nuclear missiles on public highways to give a target area broad enough to withstand a barrage attack (since the transport vehicles would be relatively soft). This poses a risk, probably intolerable, of nuclear accidents occurring in populated areas. If the road mobile system were concentrated in a small, sparsely populated area, it would have to be in hardened shelters to avoid a barrage attack and moved deceptively to present many more targets than missiles. This is the so-called multiple protective shelter (MPS) system approved by the Carter Administration. This system would be effective but expensive, both in dollars and political costs, and could require a supplemental ballistic missile defense system if the Soviets escalated the threat posed to it. The option of defending ICBM sites with an ABM system is discussed below.

The other viable alternative is to give up trying to preserve the ICBM as an independently survivable component of the strategic forces and instead put major emphasis on the modernization of other components, primarily submarines, cruise missiles, and bombers. ICBMs would be retained; we would not spend tens of billions of dollars to build new ICBM forces but recognize that the vulnerability of the ICBM force does not equate to the vulnerability of strategic forces in general.

3. Survivability of Bombers

To abandon ICBM survivability clearly would place a heavy burden on bomber and submarine survivability, so let us consider maintaining survivability of those forces. In the case of bombers, only a certain percentage would safely escape their bases in a surprise attack— 30 to 60 percent, depending on the stage of strategic alert that may exist. Of those that made it into the air, what chance would an opposing force have of destroying them while airborne?

The airplanes being built today have a fairly wide radius of vulnerability to a nuclear airburst. A nuclear bomb fired at them doesn't have to hit them. It has only to come within a few miles of the aircraft to destroy it in flight. The aircraft could therefore be subjected to a barrage attack. If an attacker devoted a dozen or two warheads to attacking a single airplane, then he would have to know the location of the airplane only to within a radius of several tens of miles to be effective. That means, then, that the bombers would have to be widely dispersed, that they would have to get away from their individual dispersal points quickly, and that they should not be detectable in flight.

We therefore are interested in the long-range techniques for detecting airpanes in flight. Two systems in development today are relevant to this problem. One is called an over-the-horizon (OTH) radar; the United States could have by the late 1980s an operational over-the-horizon radar that could detect at several thousands of miles airplanes flying at any altitude. This radar could locate an aircraft within a circle of perhaps a ten mile radius; while that is a crude location, it is good enough for a barrage attack. The second kind of a system—a spaceborne infrared detector—could be operational by the early part of the next decade. These detectors are sophisticated heat measurement devices in satellites that look down at the earth and measure small changes in temperature, thereby detecting the presence of airplanes, particularly those flying at high altitudes.

These two technologies could be used to detect and locate airplanes while they are on their way to targets. Neither country has that capability today, but either could have operational OTH radars by the late 1980s and infrared satellites by the early 1990s. In the face of such detection systems, maintaining the survivability of aircraft while in flight would require the development of countermeasures that could degrade the range and accuracy of those detection systems.

4. Survivability of Submarines

Attacking missiles while they are still in a submarine requires locating the submarine and mounting an attack on it. It is a mistake to think of this problem in terms of tactical antisubmarine warfare (ASW), where a submarine detects another submarine and fires a torpedo at it. The greatest threat to strategic submarines would arise from a global ocean detection system that could locate submarines in open ocean areas and then direct a missile attack at them. In a barrage attack on submarines, much as in the case of the bombers, twenty or thirty warheads could barrage a large area of the ocean. If a submarine could be localized to twenty or thirty miles, barrage attacks would become feasible. The goal in submarine survivability is to prevent the Soviets from locating to accuracies of twenty or thirty miles our submarines on patrol in broad ocean areas.

The Soviets cannot do this at present nor will they be able to, I believe, for a good many years in the future. A crucial question, however, is the extent to which technological improvements over the next two decades could change this assessment.

A prominent form of technology used in tactical submarine detection is sonar—transmitting a sound wave that bounces off a submarine and comes back. No existing sonar system is useful for the detection of strategic submarines, nor is one likely to be useful in the foreseeable future. A closely related technology, which might be called passive sonar, uses acoustic receivers to monitor the acoustic energy unintentionally emitted by a submarine, including noise from the screw, the main engine, and auxiliary engines. These sounds are propagated at very long ranges in open ocean areas and can be received by sensitive acoustic sensors. Acoustic technology has advanced sufficiently so that a global network of acoustic sensors could be deployed to monitor the location of submarines in broad ocean areas. Such a system would take advantage of submarines that generate high levels of noise. U.S. submarine designers pay a great deal of attention to suppressing noise, so that U.S. submarines presently have a low vulnerability to this kind of noise detection.

Even if a submarine is noisy, performing successful detection requires very sophisticated sensor devices—very long acoustic arrays and super computer-processing systems—technologies in which the United States has a preeminent position. In short, the situation in acoustic detection is asymmetrical. The United States has a very significant capability today, which could be extended and improved in the future. The Soviets do not. As in the case of other technologies, the Soviets might eventually catch up with U.S. detection technology. One element of the equation, however, the noise characteristics of submarines, is under U.S. control. As long as the United States continues to emphasize quiet submarines, it can probably avoid open ocean detection by acoustic means.

Another technology of potential significance in submarine detection involves the internal waves made by a submarine. As a submarine moves through the water, it pushes the water aside causing waves below the surface. Eventually, these waves reach the surface, causing a visible disturbance. A very sophisticated system might be able to discriminate that disturbance from the disturbances already present on the surface of the water—the natural waves. Although that sort of detection system can be described, its realization is exceedingly difficult and would require a sophisticated high-powered computing system. While the United States is performing research and development on these techniques, I do not anticipate broad ocean-search systems to become operational in the foreseeable future.

A third technique, known as blue-green lasers, uses a laser in a radar mode to detect a submarine. Radar waves at radio frequencies bounce off the water without penetrating to submarine depths, but a laser of the wave length corresponding to blue-green light can penetrate the water down to submarine depths and reflect energy back to the surface. (Clear water appears blue-green because it is transparent to the blue-green component of sunlight but opaque to other components.) To realize this capability would require deployment of a satellite sensor system not yet developed. Moreover, even the light of a wave length best able to penetrate could not make a round-trip to submarines cruising below a certain depth, and this limitation could not be improved by increases in laser intensities beyond those now contemplated. In short, development of blue-green ASW lasers would require the solution of many technical problems, including development of high-power laser sources. Of course, such laser detection systems would be sensitive to the turbidity of the ocean; under conditions of high turbidity, no laser could penetrate very far. Even in clear water, the submarine might avoid laser detection by cruising at great depths.

Finally, the probability of submarine detection is always threatened with a breakthrough or discovery that might come next year or next decade but that is not now predictable. Even if a system were developed that were capable of detecting submarines in the ocean, it would still face the threat of countermeasures that might be deployed against it. If it were acoustic, for example, it would be susceptible to acoustic decoys; if it were a blue-green laser, greater depth and other countermeasures could be used to degrade or defeat it. Both the United States and the USSR are pursuing intensive efforts in submarine detection research and development. During this decade, we likely will have a high degree of technical progress in various techniques now under development, but the operational systems resulting from such technological progress do not necessarily pose a threat to our strategic forces. Even if they did pose a threat, we probably could devise effective countermeasures for such a threat. In this field, the offense will continue to have the advantage over the defense; that is, strategic submarines should be able to maintain their high degree of invulnerability.

It is likely that by the 1990s however, strategic submarines will no longer have a free ride. Even so, scientists are likely to have developed operational countermeasures to maintain the relative invulnerability of submarines to detection in open ocean areas.

PENETRATIVITY OF U.S. STRATEGIC FORCES

"Penetrativity" is the ability of strategic forces to survive an attack by active defense systems at or near the target area; that is, it is the ability to penetrate active defenses. A discussion of penetrativity must consider only two categories of strategic forces: Bombers and cruise missiles may be lumped together since they both must penetrate the Soviet air defense systems; submarine missiles and ICBMs both have to penetrate any Soviet ABM defenses.

1. Penetrativity of Bombers and Cruise Missiles

The ability of U.S. bombers to penetrate Soviet strategic air defenses today is very good. It is achieved by flying low, which masks bombers in the ground clutter returns of Soviet radars and prevents the Soviets from extracting the bomber targets with sufficient signal strength to track them. More than ten years ago, the United States developed radars capable of extracting airplane targets out of that kind of ground clutter. The simplest way is to employ the so-called Doppler radar, which is able to detect signals from moving targets and reject signals from stationary targets. Since ground clutter is stationary, a Doppler radar can be used as a means of separating airplanes from ground clutter. Such radars are now operational on airborne warning and control (AWACs) systems, as well as F-14, F-15, and F-18 fighter aircraft, and are used to detect and track low-flying airplanes in the presence of ground clutter.

The Soviets have not had such a radar for years, allowing the United States the same kind of "free ride" in bombers that it gets in submarines. But the free ride for U.S. bombers is almost over. In the last five years, the Soviets have developed and are beginning to deploy such a "look-down, shoot-down" radar and associated missile.

When that system becomes operational in quantity in about the mid-1980s, the tactic of flying low will no longer be sufficient as a way of evading Soviet strategic air defenses. At that time, the effectiveness of the U.S. B-52 force as penetrators will be greatly reduced.

Any solution to that problem must involve defeating those radars or avoiding the use of penetrating aircraft. Two techniques are in hand for doing that: stealth and electronic countermeasures. The cruise missile system is already becoming operational with a sufficient degree of stealth to defeat existing Soviet air defenses. Additionally, cruise missiles can degrade the effectiveness of the new generation of Soviet look-down radars, since none of the look-down radars can extract perfectly a moving target from the backround; some background clutter remains, which can obscure small targets. The first generation of American look-down radars and the present Soviet version can extract medium to large aircraft from background noise but not aircraft with small radar cross-sections. In particular, current U.S. cruise missiles are small enough to defeat first generation look-down radars, but U.S. second generation look-down radars, already operational, are capable of detecting cruise missiles. It is only a matter of time, therefore, before the Soviets develop that same capability and then would be able to track first generation U.S. cruise missiles.

When that happens, the continued effectiveness of these forces would depend on revolutionary, but feasible improvements in electronic countermeasures and stealth technology. Stealth technology will be applied to all future tactical airplanes and missiles. Technology also is rapidly changing in microelectronics, which will allow dramatically different things to be done with electronic warfare systems. Little more than a decade ago, ten transistors were put on a single chip; today a few thousand transistors can be put on a chip, and these large-scale integrated circuits will be used in ever-increasing quantities in military equipment in the years to come. Even more important is the revolution in very large-scale integrated circuits (VLSI) that is about to begin. VLSI technology will reduce element spacings on chips from four to five microns, which is the state of the art today, to 0.5 microns—a 10-to-1 compression in linear dimensions—that will result in a 100-to-1 improvement in the number of transistors on a chip, a 100-to-1 improvement in processing speed, and a 100-to-1 reduction in cost per transistor. That will provide the basis for truly revolutionary changes in electronic warfare systems. It is obvious that we will be able to make ECM systems smaller, lighter, and more cheaply. We also will see substantial increases in computer power, which probably is the real heart of the ECM revolution.

I have discussed stealth systems and ECM systems as two separate technologies, each of which will have a revolutionary impact on our ability to penetrate Soviet defenses. Perhaps most interesting of all is the synergism between the two. For example, reducing the cross section of an airplane by only ten or fifteen decibels is not enough to make it immune to an air defense system, but it does reduce the requirement for power on the ECM system defending the vehicle. ECM systems with tens of watts of output power would provide the same protection that a kilowatt ECM system could do with a larger cross-section vehicle. The introduction of stealth technology would therefore allow the use of low-power ECM systems, which will result in the entire ECM system being put on a few microchips.

In sum, the advantage will continue to be with the offense; that is, we will continue to build missiles and bombers capable of defeating any conceivable Soviet air defense system. It will be difficult and expensive, but technology will permit the United States to stay ahead of improvements in Soviet defenses at a significantly lower cost than the Soviets spend on their air defense system.

2. Penetrativity of Ballistic Missiles

There was a great debate in this country in the 1960s over whether antiballistic missiles should be used to defend the country against an ICBM attack. For a variety of reasons, they were vetoed. This decision reflected a doubt that ABMs would be effective. It is therefore important to examine the new technological developments that have occurred since the 1960s that might make this decision worth reconsidering.

In the last fifteen years or so, both ABM radars and interceptors have improved in evolutionary ways. There are no dramatic differences, but technological advances have permitted improvements that make the current generation of ABM experimental systems more efficient at shooting down ballistic missiles. The radar, however, is still vulnerable to a saturation attack by large numbers of reentry vehicles. Therefore, the parallel development in the Soviet Union of MIRVed offensive missiles, with large numbers of MIRVed delivery vehicles, more than offsets the improvements made to U.S. radars and interceptors. It is still a reasonable projection that ballistic missiles would achieve a high percentage of penetration against even these improved ABM systems.

On the other hand, newly developed exoatmospheric technologies are a revolutionary departure from the technologies developed during the 1960s. Optical detection systems, the same technology used in tactical precision-guided munitions, provide extremely accurate guidance that allows an interceptor warhead to make a direct hit on a reentry vehicle, thereby destroying it by the kinetic energy of the collision and without using a warhead. The intercept vehicle could thus be quite small, allowing the ABM interceptor to be MIRVed. Twenty or thirty interceptor warheads could be placed on a single ABM, in effect deMIRVing the offensive force—that is, cancelling the penetration advantage of MIRV systems deployed on ICBMs by matching them with a MIRV capability on ABMs.

However, as it is conceived today this system would still be vulnerable to penetration tactics. In particular, it would be vulnerable to decoys, such as balloons. A balloon could be built that when blown up is the size and shape of a reentry vehicle. It could be very light and have a thin coat of metal to look like a reentry vehicle to either an optical system or a radar. Instead of releasing ten reentry vehicles, for example, the ICBM could release nine reentry vehicles and hundreds of balloons. Currently available experimental data suggest that it would be very difficult for even advanced detection systems to discriminate between balloons and warheads outside of the atmosphere, so there is no reason to be optimistic about our ability to deal with the decoy problem. Even though we may be able to deMIRV the ICBM attacking force and remove the threat of RV saturation, we still would face a saturation threat from effective decoys.

The advantage, therefore, still lies with the offense. The offense will continue to be able to penetrate more readily than the defense will be able to figure out ways of dealing with each kind of penetration, resulting in unacceptable leakage through the defenses.. It is worth pointing out that an ABM system 90 percent effective for defending the United States against an ICBM attack would still allow 10 percent of a few thousand reentry vehicles—that is, a few hundred one-megaton warheads—to strike the United States. Technological developments presently identified do not provide a high-confidence defense of the United States against a determined ICBM attack that includes several thousand reentry vehicles and huge quantities of sophisticated decoys.

Space-Based ABM

One other revolutionary change in the ABM field is still in the early stages of development. Directed-energy weapons, high-energy lasers in particular, theoretically could be placed on space vehicles and attack an ICBM during its launch phase by burning a hole through the booster while the missile was still under powered flight. The ICBM might thus be destroyed, not only before it reached its target but before it even had a chance to release its warheads. To put adequate levels of energy on an ICBM target would require deploying the laser on a low-altitude satellite that must be located over the launch area when it fires its laser beam. This means that not one but a whole constellation of satellites—about twenty—would be necessary to be able to shoot down any particular ICBM at any given time that it were launched. A few seconds would be required to detect, track, lock on, and dwell on the target long enough to burn a hole through it. Therefore, any given laser is tied up for a few seconds in this operation, which has to occur during the few minutes the ICBM is in powered flight. The twenty satellites required for continuous coverage of the launch area could attack in sequence perhaps a few tens of ICBMs that were launched simultaneously, but they could not handle a mass attack of a few hundred or one thousand ICBMs. Therefore, the base number of twenty satellites would have to be multiplied by five or ten to deal with a mass attack. In other words, one to two hundred satellites continually orbiting around the world would be needed to maintain enough laser beams to deal with a mass attack against the United States.

Assuming it were feasible to orbit one hundred or more of these space stations, there is still the question of the feasibility of developing the necessary laser weapons. Space-based ABM lasers would require a pointing and tracking accuracy of a few inches at a range of a few hundred miles; that is, better than one part in a million accuracy. While not impossible to achieve, this is many factors better than anything that has been demonstrated in ground-based systems so far. A feasible but difficult and expensive development program would be required to achieve a pointing and tracking system of sufficient accuracy and stability. With the beam properly pointed, it must have sufficient energy to burn a hole in the missile skin; this would require a more than tenfold increase in power over what has already been demonstrated for high-energy lasers. Finally, the reflecting mirror for this whole system would need to be about a factor of ten in linear dimension larger than any that have been built so far, and that would mean a factor of 100 larger in area. These very substantial engineering developments would have to be demonstrated before we could begin to build an operational weapon system.

Once a laser system were developed with these capabilities it would be too large to be launched from the space shuttle. Four or five shuttle launches would be required to place the components of one of these space stations in orbit, which would then be assembled in space. Thus, four or five launches of a shuttle would be necessary for each of 100 or 200 battle stations. The most optimistic view is that such a program would cost well in excess of $100 billion in today's dollars and could perhaps reach a beginning operational status by the end of the century. Estimates of lower costs or more rapid availability are, in my view, unrealistically optimistic.

If the United States embarked on such a program and, in fact, achieved the developmental objectives that have been cited, it would still have to worry about the countermeasures that might be adopted, some of which are straightforward. The most obvious would be to use infrared decoys to simulate the heat sources of missile launchers. Another obvious one would be to coat the ICBM skin with the same kind of heat-absorbent material used on reentry vehicles so that higher levels of energy would be required to burn through the skin, requiring increases in laser power or in the mirror size of the laser weapon. Direct countermeasures against the space stations also might be possible. For example, space mines would have to be reckoned with. The space-based laser would be most vulnerable, ironically, to ground-based lasers.

4. Silo Defense by ABMs

Even if ABM systems do not have the potential of providing a high-confidence defense of the United States against an ICBM attack, ABMs might be employed to defend ICBMs from an attack by opposing ICBMs. A 50 percent leakage rate could be tolerated in an

ABM system defending hardened ICBM silos, whereas a 10 percent leakage rate is unacceptable for population defense. The United States has under development a system called LOADS (low-altitude defense system), which is designed to provide a "bloody-nosed" defense of fixed, hardened sites. This type of ABM system is deployed at the site and fired at the incoming RV at the end of its trajectory to allow the atmosphere to separate out the decoys from the real missiles. Once this separation has occurred and the ABM system has decided which target is a real missile, it has only tens of seconds left to operate, so it requires a missile with very high acceleration, which is feasible with current solid fuel technology. It also requires a nuclear warhead to be sure that the incoming warhead is destroyed.

A LOADS or similar defense system should provide a high probability of defending a silo against a single RV attack. However, it would be very difficult to defend against a multiple RV attack because the nuclear warheads may interfere with each other. A LOADS or similar system could stop the first RV and probably the second, but its effectiveness against additional RVs would become doubtful because of the self-interference effects of nuclear weapons. A silo defense system could therefore raise the cost of an attack by a factor of three or four, but it could not provide a total defense.

Past arguments used against ABMs are not applicable to a silo defense ABM system. A decade ago it was argued that the ABM did not have any hopes of performing its mission. The defense of the United States seemed then and today still seems totally beyond our ability to achieve, but it is not totally out of the question to provide a level of defense for a silo. In fact, the only application for which ABMs would be seriously considered in the next decade or two will be defense against a counterforce attack. Although there are substantial engineering, economic, and arms control problems with such a system, the one glaring technical weakness of all ABM systems—their vulnerability to leakage—is not a disqualifying factor for silo defense.

CONNECTIVITY

The system controlling U.S. strategic forces comprises three components:

1. Sensors that monitor activity in the Soviet Union and at sea and assess whether an attack is underway;

2. The national command authority (NCA), which receives this and other information and decides what action to take; and
3. The operational commands who execute decisions made by the NCA, by deploying weapons as appropriate.

Each of these components consists of a variety of units in widely different locations. For each component to perform its function in a timely manner, its scattered units are interconnected by a communications network. Additionally, each of the three components is interconnected by redundant communications links.

We say that strategic forces have connectivity whenever each of the three components is functioning and when they are able to communicate with each other. The loss of connectivity of strategic forces can be as detrimental to their mission as losing the weapons. The loss of connectivity for even twenty minutes at a critical time could cause the loss of a major part of the force to a counterforce strike.

The present system could carry out its mission if the operating environment were sufficiently benign, but the system is fragile; that is, it would be susceptible to interruptions or malfunctions. The most serious generic problems for the system prior to a nuclear attack are:

*   Susceptibility to interruption because of equipment failure;
*   Susceptibility to false alarms because of equipment malfunction;
*   Susceptibility to sabotage of ground stations;
*   Susceptibility to a nonnuclear attack on warning satellites; and
*   Susceptibility to interference (jamming or natural) with radio links.

During or after a nuclear attack, the system would face all of these problems plus the very real possibility that command and control centers and communications satellites would themselves be targeted. Even if they were not, the communication systems' connectivity would suffer some degradation by the disturbances to radio propagation that would follow a nuclear detonation.

In recognition of these problems, a degree of redundancy and failsafe circuits have been built into the system that give it a reasonably good immunity to radio failure or computer malfunctions, but it would be difficult and expensive to render the system invulnerable to a precursor attack. If the Soviet Union were to launch a deliberate preemptive attack on U.S. strategic forces, however, surely they would consider a covert precursor attack against the brain and nervous system that might otherwise command the targeted weapons to leave their bases before the strike arrived. In the event of a surprise attack, our system should be capable of alerting the NCA in time to deploy recallable and alert forces, but there would not be sufficient time to deploy forces not on alert. Additionally, it is quite possible that U.S. leaders might not have sufficient confidence in their assessment to launch the ICBM force, which could not be recalled.

It is even more difficult to render the system resistant to nuclear bombardment, which could occur simultaneously with or shortly after a nuclear attack on U.S. strategic forces. By its very nature, command, control, communication, and intelligence (C^3I) equipment is scattered over the globe and in space, usually in inherently exposed positions. Many sensor systems must have a line of sight to the Soviet Union—which means that weapons in the Soviet Union also would have line of sight to them. The ground stations are at fixed locations, the satellites are in known orbits, and all antennae necessarily must have a degree of exposure to function efficiently. After a nuclear attack in which the command structure were not targeted, we could quickly recover virtually complete capability to communicate since the propagation disturbance effects would be relatively short-lived at microwave frequencies. However, if the command structure were targeted extensively, very little would survive beyond those forces airborne or moving on the ground at the time of the attack. Reconstituting the command structure and restoring its connectivity would involve a long, difficult undertaking with uncertain results.

A major effort is planned to improve this situation for the 1980s. This will involve changes in operational procedures and changes in equipment, both of which are necessary.

Sensors in the warning system could be improved in both sensitivity and jam resistance. Missile launch detection systems currently use a scanning infrared sensor. Their performance could be substantially improved by shifting to an array of infrared detectors that has hundreds of simultaneous beams staring at the target area (this is called a mosaic sensor). These new sensors would have substantially more sensitivity than present sensors, so that smaller targets (including high-altitude aircraft and cruise missiles) could be detected; they would provide more refined tracking data to improve attack assessment characteristics and would be much more resistant to laser jamming. To further improve jam resistance, they could be multi-color; that is, operate at several different frequencies in the infrared band.

Ground detection systems could be similarly improved by upgrading the Ballistic Missile Early Warning System (BMEWs) to include phased array radars, such as those used in the Pave Paws SLBM detection system. Additionally, a redundant ground radar system based on over-the-horizon techniques could be installed. An OTH radar operates in the 3 to 30 MHz band, at which frequencies the ionosphere bends the radio waves back to earth instead of allowing them to pass into space. It therefore could be used to detect targets inside the ionosphere that are considerably beyond the line of sight limitation of ordinary radars. In particular, OTH radars could be installed in the northern United States to look at ICBMs during their boost phase over the Soviet Union. These systems would not have the same reliability as microwave radars because of their inherent susceptibility to interference—both manmade (jamming) and natural. In particular, since such a radar would be looking approximately over the North Pole, it would have substantial interference from the aurora borealis, which could render it inoperable at unpredictable times. However, as a redundant system with independent failure modes, compared to microwave radars or infrared satellites, OTH radars are well worth considering.

It is also possible to put radars and infrared detection systems on aircraft. To maintain such a system on continuous airborne alert would involve very substantial procurement and operating costs. Illustratively, a fleet of fifty or so aircraft would be needed and ten or so would need to be airborne at any one time in order to provide geographic coverage of the most obvious attack corridors. The system would be of only doubtful effectiveness against an ICBM attack but could provide warning of a bomber attack. On balance, it does not seem likely that the life-cycle costs would be justified by the value of the information however, since it is unlikely that the Soviets would launch a bomber attack on the United States prior to an ICBM attack.

Finally, it is important to consider combinations of these sensor systems. Because of the susceptibilities described—to physical attack, to jamming, to natural interference, to equipment malfunction—it is desirable to have redundant sensors that fail in different ways and under different conditions. We should have both ground and satellite sensors; the satellite sensors should be multi-color and the ground sensors should include both microwave and over-the-horizon systems.

Survivability of communication links also could be improved by multi-color (called frequency diversity in communication systems) and by having redundant paths—ground, airborne, and satellite—for connecting stations. A fair amount of redundancy is already built into the system, but more is desirable and would be relatively inexpensive. Additionally, there are three other features that should be built into some of the communications links coming into operation in the 1980s—hardness, stealth, and fail-soft. Communication antennae do not lend themselves to high levels of hardness when functioning. In some ground systems the antennae can be stored in a hardened shelter when not in use, much like a missile, but some antennae in the warning system must be exposed to allow the system to be alerted to a surprise attack. Moderate hardness could be achieved on such antennae—low-frequency antennae may be buried to depths of a few feet; microwave antennae may be embedded in plastic radomes; electronics may be shielded to protect them from EMP effects. None of these provisions, however, would protect the system from a direct attack, but would only increase its probability of surviving an attack on a nearby target. Since ground and satellite links are fixed or predictable targets, only airborne links have high confidence of surviving a direct attack and then only if the location of the aircraft is unknown to the attacker. Today, this is true of any aircraft flying outside the coverage of Soviet air defense radars. As the Soviets develop more sophisticated aircraft detection systems (OTH or satellite-borne), it may be desirable to incorporate stealth features in our communication relay aircraft. This may not be feasible because the aircraft would have to be hardened as well as stealthy, since the Soviets could barrage a large operating area with relatively few warheads if the airplanes were as vulnerable to nuclear effects as commercial transport aircraft are. Future military communication satellites also could be designed to make attacks against them very difficult. This would require a combination of redundancy, stealth, and hardening. If such a system were designed and deployed, it could have greater endurance than the airborne links.

Since redundancy of links is a key to survivability, it is important that a viable communications network be able to be reconstituted after a number of its links had been destroyed. This fail-soft feature can be accomplished most effectively with a new technology known as packet switching. A message on a packet radio is digitized and segmented into a number of packets that are transmitted sequentially over the packet network. At each junction of the net, a microprocessor assesses the best route to the destination. Depending on traffic density or link outages, each group may go to its destination by a different route, but they are then reconstituted into the original message at the destination point. A packet system can therefore give good performance in the face of overloaded circuits, jamming, or a physical attack on part of the network. A reasonable strategy for a survivable system is to connect hundreds of stations by packet switching. Even if each station were soft, the network may still be able to carry a message to its destination.

Today the attack assessment system is effective when the data it handles is not "noisy," but in an operational environment where we can expect jamming, loss of stations, and propagation disturbance, the data would be noisy and difficult to interpret. One solution to this problem is lowering the threshold; that is, assessing that an attack is under way even if the confidence level is not high because of noisy data. This, of course, raises its vulnerability to false alarms, which if acted on by the NCA could lead to tragic results. It is imperative that we insist on a high threshold in our assessment system, even in the face of noisy data. Current computer software technology permits major improvements in this respect. Error-correcting codes can be employed in computer software that virtually eliminate any probability of computer false alarms on noise. Similarly, much more sophisticated algorithms could be introduced for attack assessment calculations—which compare the data being received with a variety of stored models—so that data which violate certain physical or operational constraints would be rejected. These algorithms also would protect against false alarms on noise. Both the error-correcting codes and the comparison algorithms are costly in terms of computer memory and computer speed and are not compatible with the relatively old computers presently in the attack assessment system. Modern computer designs could easily accommodate these software improvements with even less computer time than is presently used and could provide higher hardware reliability as well.

In sum, the present C³I system works, but it is susceptible to countermeasures, physical attack, and accidents. It is useful for alerting the NCA to a surprise attack in time to deploy alert and recallable forces. It is of questionable reliability for deploying nonrecallable forces like ICBMs, however, and it would have little endurance after a nuclear attack.

Technology permits us to make substantial improvements in the survivability and endurance of this system. These include new infrared mosaic sensors, new OTH ground radars, new hardened command aircraft, and a new computer system with state-of-the-art hardware and error-correcting software. It is very important to pursue these improvements; if we do not, we allow an instability to develop that could even be an incentive for a surprise attack.

Technology, however, no matter how diligently applied, cannot provide complete security. There will always be a finite possibility of a computer false alarm, especially in a high stress environment. That is why we continue to prefer that nonrecallable forces like ICBMs be capable of riding out an attack. Technology cannot give us high confidence that we will be able to control our forces days or weeks after a nuclear war has started: These links have a basic vulnerability to a nuclear attack, and a host of unpredictable effects would attend any mass nuclear attack. Above all, there is a very real question of how those humans in the command structure who survived a massive attack would perform under those unpredictable and unimaginable conditions.

CONCLUSIONS

Both the United States and the Soviet Union are pursuing these technologies at the highest level of national priority. As a result, they will continue to advance at a rapid pace during the next decade. This inexorable application of technology to strategic weapons will create a dynamic new environment that poses new problems for arms control but that also presents new opportunities.

The technologies that are leading to infinite lethality for strategic weapons probably cannot be limited meaningfully by arms control agreements. They already have advanced too far in systems that are either deployed or are in an advanced stage of development. They also make obsolete the previous controls on launchers, since one launcher in the coming decade could have the destructive capability of twenty or thirty launchers as envisioned at the signing of SALT I. These new technologies also present an opportunity: Because of the increased efficiency they give to strategic weapons, it is possible for both the United States and the Soviet Union to make major reductions in the numbers of weapons they deploy and still have an equivalent deterrence level.

New weapons also will have greatly increased levels of mobility because new guidance and MIRV technologies (on the other side) make it necessary and because new guidance and propulsion technologies (on our side) make it possible. This presents an opportunity for new arms control agreements on theater nuclear forces because it reduces the military advantage (to both sides) of forward basing and allows for an agreement for stand-off basing of SLBMs so that bombers are not threatened by a surprise attack that destroys them at their base. This increased mobility also presents a new problem for arms control because it makes verification by national technical means much more difficult. While it is true that these national technical means are also becoming more sophisticated and more effective, the problems posed by mobile systems, especially deceptively based mobile systems, still require some form of cooperation to supplement the national technical means.

New technology will allow ballistic missile defenses (BMD) to be designed during the 1980s that would be much more effective than those envisaged when BMD deployments were prohibited in 1972. On the other hand, the technology to penetrate BMD defenses has also advanced, so that neither side could have confidence in defending his country from ballistic missiles. Therefore, it remains to the advantage of both sides to not begin such a competition. However, if neither arms restraint nor mobility is seen to solve the ICBM vulnerability problem, it is possible that a BMD silo defense system would be invoked as one of several means of dealing with that problem.

The exotic BMD system—a space-based directed-energy weapon—is in such early development stages in both countries that it could effectively be limited by arms control agreements if both countries decided that this would be in their best interest. While it would be very difficult to control research and development in this field, it would be easy to control deployments, since any effective deployment program would take many years to implement and would be highly visible.

New microelectronic and computer technology will lead to major improvements in warning and command systems, thereby improving our confidence in these links and reducing their vulnerability to false alarms. Bilateral agreements could also help, whether or not these agreements were part of a formal arms control treaty. Agreements to improve communications operations are particularly important—continuation of and expansion of the hot line is an important example. Confidence-building measures such as prior announcements of maneuvers and missile test firings also could reduce the probability of false alarm, and an agreement that limited antisatellite weapons to their present low altitude capability would reduce the vulnerability of communication satellites.

In sum, technology has created substantial improvements and efficiencies in strategic weapons this past decade. These technologies will continue to evolve at a rapid pace during the next decade. In aggregate, they are creating strategic weapons that are incredibly lethal. In spite of advances in defensive technologies, the advantage will remain with the offense for the foreseeable future. The main threat to offensive weapons will be from other offensive weapons. We therefore will be faced with the extremely destabilizing situation that these highly lethal weapons are also highly vulnerable to a surprise attack. In a partial attempt to deal with this problem, we will make our weapons more mobile and improve our warning system, but we will also try to reduce this danger by arms control. In this pursuit of arms control, we will face both the problems and the opportunities presented by technology. Our challenge will be to seize the opportunities and overcome the problems.

7 THE POLITICS OF ARMS CONTROL AND THE STRATEGIC BALANCE

Alan Platt

Since the 1980 presidential campaign, many observers both in the United States and abroad have been closely watching the Reagan Administration's policy toward nuclear weapons. In essence, the administration's approach is two-tiered: (1) to build up significantly America's own nuclear capabilities, and (2) to pursue cautiously arms control as an instrument of national security policy. Concerning the latter, the administration has adhered to the terms of the SALT II treaty, signed in 1979 but never ratified by the U.S. Senate. It has begun negotiations with the Soviets on limiting intermediate-range nuclear forces (INF), and it favors talks on reducing intercontinental strategic arms (START).

Whatever the ultimate outcome of these talks, negotiations are likely to be protracted, and it is not too soon for the Reagan White House to begin thinking about managing the politics of these arms control negotiations. Yet all the evidence indicates that, thus far, no high-level or systematic attention has been paid to this matter. To devise an appropriate strategy for managing the domestic politics of its arms control efforts, the Reagan Administration would be well-advised to look at and learn from the Carter Administration's unsuccessful experience in managing SALT II.

There are now two major schools of thought about why the SALT II Treaty was not ratified. One school, reflected in a recent work by

155

Charles Kupperman of the Committee on the Present Danger,[1] holds that the SALT II Treaty—because it is fatally flawed substantively—does not promote U.S. security interests and accordingly was not approved by the Senate. A second school of thought holds that the treaty, while not a perfect document, does in fact enhance American security and would have been approved by the Senate had it not been for coincident Soviet behavior challenging American interests in various parts of the world. This is the reasoning, for example, behind Zbigniew Brzezinski's shorthand references to SALT being "buried in the sands of Ogaden."[2]

Both of these arguments implicitly downplay a very important reason why the SALT II Treaty was not ratified by the Senate—the overall ineptness of the Carter Administration with respect to the political management of difficult legislative issues. The central thesis of this chapter is that the Carter Administration made a series of political misjudgments and mistakes, largely prior to the June 1979 signing of SALT II, which undermined congressional and public confidence in the executive branch's stewardship of strategic issues and which, cumulatively, significantly hurt the treaty's chances for ratification. At a minimum, these misjudgments and mistakes helped shape a political environment in which Soviet behavior in places like the Horn of Africa and Cuba, to say nothing of the December 1979 invasion of Afghanistan, created a bipartisan political consensus such that consideration of the SALT II Treaty had to be deferred.

If strategic arms control is to play an important role in American defense security policy in the future, it is crucial for policymakers and the attentive public to understand the precise reasons why the SALT II Treaty acquired such a poor reputation during the years of the Carter Administration and thus was not ratified by the Senate. This chapter is intended to contribute to such understanding, first by examining recent popular American attitudes toward strategic arms control and then by analyzing selected aspects of the Carter Administration's management of the politics of SALT during 1977-79. The discussion of the Carter Administration, while largely critical, is intended to provide useful lessons for future efforts at strategic arms control. The chapter concludes with a discussion of some of the policy implications of these lessons.

AMERICAN PUBLIC OPINION
AND STRATEGIC ARMS

Recent trend in American public opinion set the backdrop for the negotiation of SALT II as well as Senate consideration of the treaty.

They probably will be important in terms of any future efforts at strategic arms control. When the Carter Administration took office in January 1977, SALT was not an important or familiar issue to the American people. A 1977 Roper Organization poll showed that approximately 33 percent of those interviewed had never heard of SALT. In January 1979 a CBS/New York Times poll indicated that a substantial majority of the American people did not know which countries were involved in the strategic arms talks.[3] A poll commissioned by the Committee on the Present Danger, taken in March 1979, reinforced earlier polling results, showing that a large majority of Americans did not have any substantive knowledge of the provisions of the SALT II Treaty.[4]

While ignorant about SALT per se, American public opinion was and continues to be supportive of strategic arms control in the abstract. In March 1977 a Harris poll found that 77 percent of Americans would "favor the United States and Russia coming to a new SALT arms control agreement that would limit the number of nuclear warheads and missiles they can deploy." Subsequent Harris polls in 1977, 1978, and 1979 all found support for a SALT agreement, in the abstract, among 67 to 80 percent of the respondents, and in a late 1980 poll, 83 percent of the respondents agreed that it was "vital for the United States and the Soviet Union to reach an agreement to limit nuclear arms." It should be added that the concept of strategic arms control has been supported consistently by all the various strata in American society. Not surprisingly though, the young, the best educated, and the best informed segments of the populace have tended to be the most supportive. Furthermore, urban, female, and East Coast respondents have consistently registered higher levels of support than other respondents.[5]

These same polls over the last several years have shown that discussions between the United States and the Soviet Union to try to control nuclear weapons are widely viewed as likely to lead to a reduction in tensions between the two countries. In addition, many Americans believe that the talks and resulting arms control agreements are likely to reduce the risk of nuclear war. As such, the idea of strategic arms limitation talks has been strongly and consistently supported by the American people.

At the same time, popular support for the SALT II Treaty itself has declined over the past few years. According to the Gallup organization, the ratio favoring ratification of SALT II in March 1979 was three to one (of those in the sample who were considered "informed,"

27 percent favored approval, 9 percent were opposed, and 9 percent had no opinion). By June 1979—the date the treaty was concluded, signed, and sent to the Senate for ratification—this ratio had declined somewhat to five to three. In September 1979 and March 1980, Gallup surveys showed those supporting and those opposing the treaty were in about equal proportions. The March 1980 poll, for example, indicated that 26 percent of the "informed" public favored Senate approval, 26 percent opposed, and 9 percent had no opinion.[6]

NBC News/Associated Press polls showed an even steeper decline in public support for SALT II in the course of 1979. In April 1979, when asked whether they favored or opposed "this new SALT agreement," responses indicated 72 percent in favor, 19 percent opposed, and 8 percent not sure. By July only 50 percent favored the treaty, 40 percent opposed, and 10 percent were not sure. By September 1979, 43 percent were in favor, 50 percent were opposed, and 7 percent were not sure.[7] In a Harris poll taken soon after the 1980 presidential election, 64 percent of the respondents said that they agreed with President-elect Reagan that "the SALT II treaty should be scrapped and negotiations should be started again for a new nuclear arms agreement with the Russians." In this poll, 28 percent of the respondents disagreed with the new president's position, while 8 percent were not sure.[8] Of course, there is some question whether this November 1980 poll indicated dissatisfaction with the SALT II Treaty per se or if it represented popular sentiment rallying around a newly elected president, particularly as that president may have been perceived to have a better chance to get a SALT treaty ratified by the Senate if negotiations were begun anew. Nevertheless, the precipitous decline in popular support for the SALT II Treaty between 1977 and 1980 is indisputable.

Why has public opinion consistently supported strategic arms control in the abstract while forsaking the SALT II Treaty itself? A partial explanation of this seeming paradox lies in the public's perceptions about the negative effects of a SALT II agreement on the U.S.-Soviet strategic balance. To many, SALT II, setting equal limits and sublimits on different categories of strategic nuclear delivery vehicles, was seen as ratifying a state of nuclear equality between the two superpowers. To others, however, the treaty was seen as dangerously weakening U.S. forces by setting certain limits on such important new weapon systems as cruise missiles, while accelerating an ongoing trend toward Soviet superiority over America by failing to restrict sufficiently the Soviet's Backfire bombers and heavy missiles. To still others, the SALT II Treaty was perceived as a deterrent to the resurrection of a dynamic American strategic weapons program. Among these observers, there was a fear that ratification of SALT II would lull America into a false sense of nuclear security and prevent the development of a consensus in the Congress that would allow the United States to compete effectively with the Soviets in the military sphere. These observers often pointed out that the Soviets have made impressive military advances since the 1972 SALT I accords went into effect.

Coincident with these negative perceptions of the SALT II Treaty itself has been a discernible trend in recent years in the United States in favor of the adoption of a stronger military stance vis-à-vis the Soviet Union. Today, a majority of Americans believe that it is necessary for the United States to be militarily superior to the Soviet Union, rather than equal in strength. This has not always been true in recent years. In July 1978, for example, a plurality of respondents queried by the ABC News/Harris survey felt that it was a necessity for the United States to be as strong as the Soviets but not stronger. This viewpoint changed in the course of 1978–79, and by October 1979 a follow-up survey found that 49 percent of the respondents felt that it was necessary for the United States to be militarily stronger than the Soviets, while 43 percent felt that being equally strong was the preferable foreign policy objective.[9] By January 1981, 52 percent of the respondents in a CBS News/New York Times poll felt that the United States should be superior militarily to the Soviets, with only 39 percent of the respondents believing that we should be equal in strength.[10] Not surprisingly, the SALT II treaty, representing at best strategic equality and to some strategic inferiority, was perceived by a growing percentage of Americans as being at odds with this necessary military posture.

Similarly, attitudes toward increased American defense spending changed rapidly. In a 1981 poll, the Gallup organization found the highest level of public support for increased defense spending in more than a decade. Asked about the adequacy of spending for national defense, 51 percent of the respondents felt that the amount of the budget for defense was "too little," 23 percent felt it was "about right," and 15 percent thought that "too much" was being spent on defense. This marked the first time that the Gallup organization had ever found that a majority of Americans believe that the defense budget was "inadequate." By way of comparison, when this question was asked in 1978, 32 percent thought that the United States was spending "too little," 45 percent thought the amount "about right," and 16 percent "too much." When the question was asked in 1969, when opposition to the Vietnam war and American entanglements abroad was growing, only 8 percent of the public supported increases in defense spending for military purposes and 31 percent thought we were spending about the right amount for defense.[11]

These changing general attitudes on SALT and defense spending are in part attributable to the decline of the impact of American involvement in Indochina and, in the words of Louis Kriesberg and Ross Klein, the fading of "the Vietnam trauma" that produced "antimilitarism" in America and a "hands-off" approach to international relations.[12] In part, they are traceable to the growth of popular anti-Soviet feeling in the 1970s, a sentiment that has been strongly reinforced by continuing increases in Soviet defense spending, a growing perception that the USSR has moved ahead of the United States in armed strength, and frequent examples of assertive Soviet behavior in the international arena. Finally, these popular attitudes have been fueled by the broad-ranging efforts of influential individuals and interest groups alarmed by what they perceive as a declining American strategic position in the world. United in their perceptions and concern about ascendant Soviet power and American retreat, these individuals (e.g., Senator Henry Jackson, Daniel Graham) and special-interest groups (e.g., Committee on the Present Danger, Coalition for Peace Through Strength) seem to have been effective in the past few years in influencing both elite and popular attitudes with respect to the trends in the American-Soviet strategic balance and how the ratification of the SALT II Treaty would accelerate those trends. In an article on why and how the SALT II Treaty should be defeated, syndicated columnist Patrick Buchanan summarized this line of argument against SALT in the following way:

> The country must be instructed in the new math of the 1980s. The United States has surrendered strategic superiority; we are in the process of losing parity; we are entering an era in which the West will be militarily inferior to the East—ripe for Soviet blackmail, Soviet bullying and, conceivably, Soviet attack.[13]

If the United States in the late 1970s had continued to enjoy the position of superiority it unquestionably enjoyed during much of the postwar period, these arguments may have fallen largely on deaf ears. However, given general American disenchantment with detente, the loss of American influence in the third world, and declining public confidence in America's institutions and leaders, these arguments carried a good deal of weight and appeared to play an important role in shaping the backdrop for, and also the terms of the debate on SALT II.

THE CARTER ADMINISTRATION AND SALT II

Notwithstanding these trends in American public opinion, popular support for strategic arms control in the abstract might have been translated into Congressional support for SALT II had the Carter Administration been more adroit at legislative political management. However, in the main, this was not the case—certainly not in comparison with the Kennedy Administration's handling of the 1963 Limited Test Ban Treaty or the Johnson Administration's management of the 1968 Non-Proliferation Treaty or the Nixon Administration's handling of the ratification of SALT I in 1972. Indeed, with effective political management, the Carter Administration might have succeeded in getting SALT II ratified in essentially its present form, since the major problems associated with its ratification were due less to substantive weaknesses in the treaty, as was apparent during the summer 1979 Senate Foreign Relations Committee hearings, than to a series of political and tactical mistakes that helped doom the administration's SALT ratification efforts.

The Carter Administration's political mistakes regarding SALT strategy and tactics were most serious with respect to: (1) communicating the treaty's importance; (2) establishing public confidence in the negotiating effort; (3) internal organization; (4) lobbying individual Senators; (5) timing. In each of these areas, there are important lessons to be learned from the Carter Administration's experiences that undoubtedly will have relevance for any future strategic arms control efforts.

SALT II, as concluded in 1979 and sent to the Senate for ratification, is clearly not an ideal document. As the congressional hearings on the treaty demonstrated, several provisions in SALT II theoretically could have been significantly improved, particularly those concerning the relatively high ceilings and subceilings on different types of strategic weapons. Nevertheless, the treaty does place equal aggregates on both sides' strategic nuclear delivery vehicles and in so doing enhances the effectiveness of the American deterrent against nuclear attack and its retaliatory power if war did break out. It excludes from the aggregate limits American forward-based missiles and nuclear-capable aircraft that could reach the Soviet Union from their bases in Europe. It constrains significantly the quantity and quality of planned Soviet ICBMs, the most threatening part of the Soviet arsenal. And it significantly improves both sides' ability to assess the other's strategic forces and thus to verify compliance with the treaty.

The Carter Administration was faced with a choice of at least two alternative ways to communicate, in terms of tone and content, these values of the emerging SALT II Treaty to the Congress and the American people. On the one hand, it could have adopted the approach that the Nixon Administration purposefully followed regarding SALT I, constantly underscoring the absolutely vital, global importance of the new SALT agreement. This approach would have highlighted SALT II as an extremely important document in its own right in capping and stabilizing the nuclear arms competition between the superpowers and in winding down, although clearly not ending, the arms race. This approach also would have stressed the critical importance of the ratification of SALT II for the preservation of NATO, to say nothing of its role in preventing a nuclear holocaust. On the other hand, the Carter Administration could have adopted an approach that posited that SALT II was certainly no worse than SALT I and that, marginally, the United States would be better off with the treaty than without it. This approach would have emphasized that SALT II was only one stage in the process of American-Soviet discussions on the control of nuclear weapons and the maintenance of rough strategic equivalence and that after SALT II was ratified, negotiations would commence immediately on SALT III, which would be much more meaningful in terms of reducing the strategic arsenals of the two superpowers. The dilemma of which approach to use in publicly communicating SALT II's importance clearly confounded the Carter Administration, as it did the Ford Administration, and will undoubtedly be a tactical issue to be resolved regarding any future strategic arms control agreement.

In reality, the Carter Administration followed both approaches at different times, although the second—the marginalist approach— seemed to be dominant, particularly in the period before the actual signing of SALT II in June 1979.[14] To some extent, the use of the marginalist approach was unavoidable: It is hard to assert with any credibility the critical importance of a treaty that is not yet concluded. The marginalist approach was consciously adopted, though, by the Carter Administration, a result of a series of interagency meetings in late 1977 and early 1978. This approach was chosen on the pragmatic grounds that it was likely to be the more successsful tack in gaining congressional and public acceptance of SALT II.

In fact, this was an important political miscalculation. By stressing the marginality of SALT II and its importance as a stepping-stone to truly meaningful arms control efforts, statements by administration representatives frequently had the effect of focusing attention on specific shortcomings in the treaty rather than on the accord's overall worth. This, of course, enhanced the influence of anti-SALT senators, columnists, and interest groups, whose own views about the treaty's shortcomings were thus accorded valuable credibility and reinforcement. The marginalist approach, ironically, also had the effect of undermining support for the agreement among a number of senators, who otherwise might have been expected to back it (e.g., Hatfield, McGovern, Moynihan, Proxmire, and Stevenson), as well as similarly minded interest groups who came to question the utility of the treaty on arms control grounds. Most importantly, the marginalist approach failed to take into account and capitalize on the public's general support for strategic arms control as a way to stabilize American-Soviet arms competition and to lessen significantly the risk of nuclear war. If one accepts former chief SALT negotiator Paul Warnke's view that arms control is an unnatural act, it is clear that it is politically useful to emphasize, and at times purposefully overstate, the significance of any given strategic arms control agreement to the avoidance of nuclear war. This point was largely lost on the Carter Administration until perhaps late 1979, by which time the SALT II Treaty had acquired a marginal or negative image in the minds of many members of Congress as well as among much of the public-at-large. On the other hand, had the administration followed the Nixon Administration's example and adopted a more positive and expansive public approach on SALT from the outset, the executive would have been in a far better position later on to move decisively to crystallize this public disposition, mobilize it, and transform it into a potent political force.

The effectiveness of the administration's communications about SALT II's importance also was badly hurt, perhaps more significantly, by the executive's inability to generate public confidence in its treaty negotiating effort. Throughout 1977–78, both administration and independently sponsored polls showed that the single most important factor influencing popular attitudes on SALT was the relatively low confidence the American people had that the treaty's negotiators would protect American security interests. This was the case even when this factor was compared to such other factors as the relative military strength of the United States and the Soviet Union.[15]

Public confidence in the Carter Administration's SALT II negotiating effort got off to a bad start in early 1977 as a result of the confirmation hearings of Paul Warnke to be chief SALT negotiator and the director of the Arms Control and Disarmament Agency. To many, Warnke was an ideal choice for these two positions given his extensive background in arms control and defense matters and his high-level experience at the Pentagon during the 1960s. Warnke was opposed for these posts, however, by a number of detractors in the Senate and elsewhere who felt, among other things, that he was not likely to be "tough enough" with the Soviets in negotiating a new SALT agreement.

The Warnke confirmation process provided the new administration with an early opportunity to take its case about SALT's vital importance and its competent stewardship of this major foreign policy issue to the Congress and the American people. This opportunity was not effectively seized. Indeed, instead of building public confidence in the new administration's approach to SALT, the confirmation hearings and vote seriously—perhaps fatally—undermined the public's sense that the Carter Administration could negotiate a new SALT agreement that would protect American security interests.

Facing well-organized and well-financed opposition to the Warnke nomination among interest groups and the media, the administration should have launched a major political campaign prior to the nomination's public announcement, with the idea of winning a resounding vote of confidence in both Paul Warnke and the administration's planned SALT efforts. Instead, it reacted defensively and somewhat naively, privately hoping that the opposition would in time wither away. On the other hand, the opposition forces well understood that a negative or even a close vote on the nomination was of great potential importance, for such a vote would have the effect of seriously undermining public confidence in the new administration's leadership on SALT-related issues.

In any event—first in the Senate Foreign Relations Committee and then in the Committee on Armed Service, whose membership included several outspoken SALT opponents (e.g., Jackson, Tower, Thurmond, Scott, Goldwater, Garn)—the Warnke confirmation hearings were widely followed. The Armed Services Committee hearings were particularly closely covered by the national news media and proved to be a highly visible sounding board for arguments against SALT and

Warnke's leadership of the negotiating effort. In the end, the Senate confirmed Warnke for both posts, but the vote on the SALT negotiator nomination was fifty-eight to forty. The forty votes against Warnke for the SALT position represented six votes more than were needed to defeat a new SALT treaty. Anti-SALT forces, in effect, had successfully sent a message to the President and the Congress that there was a substantial segment of opinion in the Senate that lacked confidence in the new administration's proposed approach to SALT II.

The negative impact of the Warnke confirmation fight might have been significantly mitigated had the Carter White House understood the central importance of having the administration's top national security team play an active, publicly visible role in explaining the general terms of SALT II prior to its final conclusion. On an issue as important and complex as SALT, most members of Congress as well as the majority of the American people look to the president, their commander-in-chief, and the military for leadership. Early in the Carter Administration, however, the president and his principal military advisors—Secretary of Defense Harold Brown and Chairman of the Joint Chiefs of Staff David Jones—dissipated significant congressional and public confidence in their toughness and reliability on national security issues as a result of the decisions not to go ahead with the B-1 bomber, to close down the Minuteman III production line, to withdraw American troops from Korea, and not to proceed with the deployment of the neutron bomb. Whether or not these decisions were well-founded on their merits is debatable—their political effect, however, was clear. Public leadership by the president and the military on SALT II prior to the treaty's submission to the Senate for ratification was even more critical than it might otherwise have been because of these other defense decisions as well as the fight over the Warnke nomination, periodically lukewarm public confidence in President Carter, and a continuing stream of anti-SALT press leaks. Morton Kondracke summed up this situation very well when in 1978 he noted:

> If there is any area in which trust in the President is crucial, it is SALT. The issues are so complex, so higher-mathematical, so apocalyptic that most citizens and even many Senators ultimately will decide what they favor on the basis of whose arguments seem to have credibility. . . . Carter is entering the battle with a severe confidence problem. . . . [16]

Nevertheless, it was Carter Administration policy that while the SALT II Treaty was still being negotiated, the executive branch would severely restrict the quantity and quality of information publicly disseminated on SALT II. There was great fear that if there was too much public discussion of the treaty's contents, particularly concerning verification and Soviet concessions, the successful conclusion of the treaty would be jeopardized. To the extent that any case was to be made publicly in behalf of SALT II prior to the treaty's signing, it was to be made by the State Department, the Arms Control and Disarmament Agency, and middle-level civilians at the Pentagon. Defense Department personnel at the assistant secretary level or above, for example, were not authorized to speak publicly on behalf of the treaty prior to its submission to the Senate for ratification. In the words of one senior administration official, "The President, Harold Brown and the Chiefs were to be the big guns after the treaty was signed and the ratification fight really began."

The absence of sustained presidential and military leadership on SALT II during the first two-and-one-half years of the Carter Administration would not have been so consequential had the Secretary of State been of a different temperament. Cyrus Vance, an inherently low-key lawyer, was not given to frequent public educational efforts on SALT or most other issues, and he consistently rejected public-speaking opportunities and media interviews that would have afforded the administration the opportunity to make the best case for the emerging SALT II Treaty. As Zbigniew Brzezinski subsequently acknowledged in an interview, "Secretary of State Vance had various strong qualities, but an inclination to engage in what might be called a sustained effort to educate the American public was not among them."[17] This aspect of Vance's personal makeup significantly hurt the administration's SALT public education effort.

Furthermore, largely preoccupied with other issues during the first several months of the new administration, Secretary Vance did not initially master the detailed intricacies of SALT. This was unfortunate because when asked to testify about the details of the U.S. SALT II negotiating posture in the fall of 1977, he was not able to answer many of the detailed questions put to him by the members of the Senate Armed Services Subcommittee on Arms Control, chaired by Henry Jackson. At one closed-door hearing in mid-October 1977, Senator Sam Nunn, a key swing vote on SALT, was so taken aback by Vance's seeming lack of familiarity with the details of the U.S. negotiating position that he asked rhetorically—"Who in fact is in charge of overseeing the negotiations?" In short order, Vance learned the SALT brief and soon became an eloquent defender of every nuance in the Joint Draft Text of the SALT II accord, but his initial performances before the Jackson subcommittee, combined with his personal reticence to give public speeches, did little to bolster confidence in the U.S. negotiating effort.

Of course, the lion's share of responsibility for the administration's misjudgments with respect to the political management of the SALT II Treaty must rest ultimately with the president. However, part of the explanation for a number of tactical mistakes can be traced to the way that the Carter Administration was organized and staffed for SALT matters. Until June 1979 when the SALT II Treaty actually was signed and White House Counsel Lloyd Cutler was put in charge of ratification efforts, most matters related to SALT were handled by technical experts, not politically experienced professionals.

To deal with daily matters regarding SALT, including communications with the delegation in Geneva, an interagency group called the Special Coordinating Committee (SCC) met regularly at the White House.[18] The members of this group, all substantive experts on the technical complexities of weapon systems, typically had limited political experience. Yet, the mini-SCC and its subgroups, not the White House or any interagency political group, was responsible for the management of political—as well as technical—SALT issues on an ongoing basis. In the period prior to the actual signing of the treaty, this group did not welcome nor were they inundated with political advice from the president's key political advisors—Hamilton Jordan, Jody Powell, Patrick Caddell, and Charles Kirbo. Moreover, several of the members of the mini-SCC had previously worked on SALT I during the early 1970s and had largely been excluded from dealing with any of the political issues associated with strategic arms limitation, that being the preeminent domain of Henry Kissinger. Not surprisingly, these people now relished and closely guarded their new responsibilities.

Probably the mini-SCC's greatest mistake in the management of SALT politics was its failure to understand the critical importance of generating and maintaining public confidence in the SALT negotiating effort prior to the treaty's submission to the Senate. Had this been widely understood, the group would have taken steps to modify the previously noted marginalist approach. It might also have discretely disclosed the more significant Soviet concessions at various points in the course of negotiations. As it was, the members of the mini-SCC worried principally about two matters—the possible overselling of the terms of the treaty and the premature disclosure of any sensitive information about the actual details of the negotiations, most particularly concerning Soviet concessions. These were views one might expect from technical experts familiar with the relatively modest accomplishments of the treaty. But they were hardly shrewd political judgments, particularly in the face of the multi-million-dollar campaign being waged against the treaty during 1977-79.

The absence of a White House-directed SALT political coordinating group perceptibly hurt the administration's lobbying in the period prior to June 1979. This was particularly true concerning the arrangement of briefings about the emerging treaty. A few examples illustrate some of the political wounds the administration inflicted on itself. In one instance, when a group of several influential senators visited Geneva in the spring of 1978 to be briefed on SALT II, both chief negotiator Warnke and his deputy Ralph Earle were not in Switzerland. A State Department representative was chosen to lead the Geneva briefings. Unfortunately, the briefer, while technically knowledgeable, was unable to respond effectively to inquiries about the policy implications of several of the treaty's provisions. After their return to Washington, a few of these senators met privately with Secretary Vance to complain about the Geneva SALT briefing, confiding that they were now considerably more concerned about U.S. efforts at SALT than they were prior to the trip. Soon thereafter, the State Department official was recalled and reassigned but not before perceptible damage had been done to the confidence of several important senators in the U.S. negotiating effort. In another instance, when an important, undecided southern senator requested a briefing on SALT, two technical experts made the presentation. Their remarks focused largely on a number of the more arcane provisions of the treaty. After the briefers left the office, the senator, unimpressed and unconvinced, commented graphically to his staff aide, "No wonder SALT is in trouble; those guys couldn't sell a prostitute on an Army train." In a third instance, more than a few people in the executive branch and the Senate were appalled to learn that a very junior Foreign Service officer, who had been working on SALT for a matter of months, had been sent to New York City in the spring of 1978 to brief former vice-president Nelson Rockefeller, among other notables, on the emerging SALT treaty. These and other arrangements regarding SALT briefings could have been handled more skillfully, and to a significant extent they were after the treaty was concluded and a White House group, under Lloyd Cutler, was established.

Moreover, the lobbying of individual senators on SALT might also have been managed more adroitly in the pre-June 1979 period. The treatment of three key senators, all of whom ultimately opposed SALT II—Howard Baker, Henry Jackson, and John Glenn—illustrates the kinds of tactical errors the administration made in its lobbying efforts.

Howard Baker, Senate Minority Leader and a member of the Foreign Relations Committee, clearly should have been viewed from the outset of the Carter Administration as a crucial vote on SALT, both for his own vote and his potential influence on eight to ten moderate Republicans. Baker's backing was essential if bipartisan support for the treaty was to be built. Somewhat surprisingly, Baker was not treated as carefully as one might have supposed, and the administration ultimately paid dearly for its inattention. The Carter Administration consulted Baker sporadically[19] but failed to meet or allay his privately expressed substantive reservations about the treaty. It also declined to accept his spring 1979 offer to play the role of "honest broker" between the White House and moderate senators who were skeptical of SALT II as it was emerging but might have supported an "improved" treaty. Worse still, President Carter personally intervened in Baker's 1978 reelection campaign on behalf of his Democratic opponent, a candidate who tried to build her campaign on the charge that Baker had voted with the administration to give away the Panama Canal. It is conceivable, given Howard Baker's substantive reservations about SALT II and his 1980 presidential ambitions, that after a 1978 vote to support the Panama Canal Treaties he would not have voted for the SALT II Treaty under any circumstances. Nonetheless, the administration's treatment of the Tennessee senator never put this hypothesis to a fair test and lost whatever support he might have been willing to give to the treaty privately.

While the Carter Administration treated Howard Baker relatively shabbily regarding SALT, it paid too much attention to Henry Jackson. Jackson, chairman of the Senate Armed Service Subcommittee on Arms Control, was the leading Senate critic of SALT II during the Nixon and Ford Administrations. Yet, for the Carter Administration, in the words of Thomas Franck and Edward Weisband, "(Jackson) was early targeted for very special care and feeding by the disarmament negotiators."[20] The special attention that was paid to the Washington senator was manifested in numerous ways, including: (1) a willingness on the part of the administration to study seriously and ultimately incorporate a number of Jackson's SALT recommendations into the comprehensive U.S. proposal presented to the Soviets in March 1977; (2) an unprecedented commitment by Secretary Vance in October 1977 to meet with Jackson's Armed Services Subcommittee on Arms Control every two weeks; and (3) President Carter's agreement to reappoint General Edward Rowny, Jackson's choice, to be the representative of the Joint Chiefs of Staff on the SALT delegation. All three of these measures, and several other initiatives, were undertaken in significant part in the hope of gaining Jackson's support for SALT II. However, none of these steps proved particularly helpful to the SALT ratification effort. Some were perceptibly damaging, such as the presentation of the March 1977 comprehensive proposals wherein the administration set benchmarks to which all subsequent proposals were unfavorably compared. An alternative lobbying approach would have been to leave the door open to Henry Jackson but to focus special attention on several other more open-minded Senators.

One such Senator was John Glenn, the former astronaut and a senior member of the Foreign Relations Committee. From early 1977 onward, Glenn was outspoken in his belief that verification was the key issue regarding the SALT II Treaty. In line with his concerns about the government's ability to verify Soviet compliance with the emerging treaty, Glenn requested in November 1977 that the executive branch prepare for him "a simple matrix" that would reflect the verifiability of the different weapon systems that would be covered by SALT II. This information was not provided to the senator until June 1978, roughly eight months after the request was made initially and only then as a result of Glenn's persistent personal prodding. Even when the information was forwarded to the Ohio senator, there were continuing differences within the executive branch about some of the numbers and attendant conclusions contained in the matrix. Accordingly, it was submitted to Glenn by a middle-level State Department official and was represented as the product of a low-level group of technical experts rather than as a document that had the concurrence of the President, the Chairman of the Joint Chiefs of Staff, and the Director of Central Intelligence. This procedure afforded those technical experts in the executive branch who disagreed with some of the material contained in the matrix the opportunity to disown the document at a later date.

However, the time delay and unofficial submission procedure also had the effect of contributing to already existing doubts in the minds of John Glenn and several of his colleagues about the verifiability of the emerging SALT II Treaty. Particularly in view of the fact that verification is to some extent a matter of confidence in the executive branch's judgment, the administration's dealings with Glenn concerning the matrix and other matters regarding SALT verification should have been handled more authoritatively and expeditiously through the president. Many senators ultimately found persuasive the generally affirmative findings of the Senate Intelligence Committee, which had primary responsibility for judging SALT II's verifiability. Other senators, including Glenn, eventually opposed the treaty, in part because of their concern about the executive branch's ability to monitor the treaty's provisions adequately. [21]

The dilatory handling of John Glenn's request for a "simple matrix" regarding SALT verification vividly underscores another important tactical political mistake the Carter Administration made: It never truly sensed the urgency of moving quickly to conclude SALT II and have it ratified. To be sure, some administration officials sensed that given the mistrust between the two superpowers SALT might be vulnerable to the vicissitudes of overall U.S.-Soviet relations and that the longer the SALT negotiations went on, the greater the chance that Soviet behavior might jeopardize the successful conclusion and ratification of a new SALT treaty. At times, various officials expressed hope for a speedy conclusion of the negotiations, as in October 1977 when President Carter declared publicly that SALT II might be signed "in a few weeks." As an operational matter, however, there was no pervasive sense of urgency among most of the senior officials working directly on SALT, and, in truth, several initiatives were adopted in 1977–78 that significantly prolonged and complicated the SALT negotiations. Most important among these initiatives was the presentation of a comprehensive SALT proposal to the Soviets in March 1977. In addition, the Carter Administration's human rights policy, particularly as it concerned Soviet dissidents, the conclusion and ratification of the Panama Canal treaties, and the normalization of relations with the People's Republic of China all made the conclusion of SALT II significantly more complicated. These measures and others, in combination with a Soviet tendency to negotiate with glacial speed, perceptibly contributed to delaying the actual conclusion of a SALT II treaty until two-and-one-half years into the Carter Administration. This was despite the fact that the treaty that was eventually signed in Vienna was based largely on the 1974 Vladivostok Accord.

This delay in timing was not without consequence. It permitted subsequent Soviet assertiveness in the Horn of Africa and Afghanistan, *inter alia,* to make positive Senate action on SALT II significantly more difficult. In a January 1981 interview, Zbigniew Brzezinski speculated that "the Senate would 'probably' have approved the strategic arms limitation treaty if it had been negotiated 8 to 12 months earlier."[22] Another student of U.S.-Soviet relations, Strobe Talbott, has written about the impact of timing on SALT ratification in the following unequivocal way:

> . . . the single biggest problem with SALT was delay. The negotiations had dragged on for too long. The saga of SALT II had become a shaggy dog story of anticlimaxes and missed deadlines. . . . American domestic support for a new treaty lost much of its momentum, while opposition gained steadily, in a political climate of growing anger, fear and frustration directed at the Soviet Union.[23]

In short, while one cannot be certain, it does seem likely that Senate consideration of SALT II would have been less complicated had the negotiations been concluded, as they almost were, during the Fall of 1977.

LESSONS FOR THE FUTURE

To be sure, a number of mistakes in the managment of the politics of SALT II are more apparent in hindsight. Nevertheless, these failings do suggest some guidelines for future efforts to gain support from both the right and the left for new strategic arms control initiatives.

First, persuading the Senate to ratify a new SALT agreement is likely to require the direct, continuous, and active participation of the president. The Congress and the American people clearly look to the president as commander-in-chief for leadership on a critical national security issue like strategic arms control, particularly given the complexity of the subject and the public's general lack of knowledge about it. Nothing can fully substitute for the president's direct involvement and the use of the presidency as a bully pulpit to educate the public. Extreme presidential secrecy and noninvolvement—however attractive for reasons of negotiation, personal operating style, or foreign relations—are likely to prove self-defeating. Among other things, the president can and should seize early opportunities to shape the terms of the public debate. In so doing, he should attempt to cast the emerging accord—in the face of inevitable damaging press leaks and public criticism—in as reassuring a public light as honesty and prudence will permit.

In this regard, it is critical that the president be concerned with projecting an image of himself and his negotiating team as tough but responsible stewards of America's national security. This could mean persuading the military to support publicly the ongoing negotiating effort. Particularly given recent trends in public opinion regarding the Soviet Union, it may also mean that the tougher a president is perceived to be with the Russians, the easier it will be to get a future SALT treaty ratified. As Milton Viorst has noted, the credibility of future SALT treaties may depend on the president's ability to convey to the public that he is "an unyielding defender of the national interest and can confront the Russians when he must."[24]

Second, the task of persuading the Congress to approve a new strategic arms control agreement, if it is to be successful, must be viewed early on by the president and his administration as a major political campaign. The negotiations themselves, of course, should be pursued with all deliberate speed and professionalism, but it is not sufficient to begin the effort to sell the emerging treaty to the Congress and the American people only after the accord is formally submitted to the legislative branch for approval. The campaign must be planned and appropriately implemented long before a treaty is formally concluded. Contrary to the urgings of a number of pro-SALT senators, the Carter Administration acted as if such a campaign could usefully be carried out only after all the details of the treaty were firm. This, in fact, missed an essential point. The best reasons for supporting SALT II or any future arms control agreement are likely to lay not in the accord's detailed provisions but in its implications for stability and predictability, as well as in its beneficial effect in reducing the danger of nuclear war. By not moving with an appropriate sense of urgency, treaty proponents allowed the treaty's opponents, inside and outside the government, to set the terms of the debate. By the time the treaty was submitted to the Senate, the litmus test regarding SALT II's worth hinged for many on the detailed provisions of the treaty. From an administration point of view, a strategic arms agreement should be weighed in terms of the treaty's potential contribution to U.S. security, global stability, and the moderation of U.S.-Soviet arms competition.

Third, future strategic arms control agreements must be perceived as reducing the level of armaments on both sides if they are to be successful politically and must be portrayed as such, positively and expansively, within the United States. This means that future negotiations must in fact be directed, as START is supposed to be, at reducing the strategic arsenals on both sides, not at merely capping them at relatively high levels. Such an approach will make more likely active support from traditional congressional backers of arms control. It will also help spur interest in and private financial contributions to groups supporting arms control and help translate popular support for strategic arms control in the abstract into public support for a concrete agreement. In essence, future strategic arms control agreements, if they are to command broad political support, must be widely perceived as beneficial rather than marginal or harmless.

Fourth, persuading the Congress to approve a future strategic arms control agreement will require the administration to have its most trusted political professionals continuously and intimately involved in managing the politics of strategic arms control. The Carter Administration's mistakes in 1977 and 1978 with respect to SALT briefings and lobbying vividly demonstrate some of the problems that can result from having SALT technical experts responsible on a day-to-day basis for overseeing important political decisions. Persuasion and coalition-building with respect to ultimately gaining Congressional approval of strategic arms control agreements are tasks for politically experienced personnel who understand SALT, rather than for SALT technicians willing to learn about political matters.

Fifth, it is necessary to have one senior official coordinate the political effort. This individual would have a close personal relationship to the president and no other responsibilities and would be given the authority and legitimacy to speak for the chief executive both within the administration and on Capitol Hill. Only such a person—a czar for strategic arms control—would be able to iron out inevitable interagency differences, coordinate effectively with supportive interest groups, and manage congressional lobbying and public education campaigns smoothly. The operations of Lloyd Cutler regarding SALT ratification after the treaty was submitted to the Senate and the activities of Robert Strauss with respect to the negotiation and ratification of the 1979 Trade Agreements Act both provide models that should be closely studied.

Sixth, in order to gain congressional approval of a future strategic arms agreement, it will be necessary for an administration to be clear about the relationship between strategic arms control and the overall context of U.S.-Soviet relations. The Carter administration oscillated regarding the notion of linkage, sometimes saying that SALT was too important in its own right to be tied to other aspects of U.S.-Soviet relations and at other times blaming assertive Soviet behavior in different parts of the world for delays in the SALT negotiations. Ultimately, of course, the December 1979 Soviet invasion of Afghanistan dealt a mortal blow to SALT's chances in the Senate, but this was only after some senior officials had explicitly linked SALT to Soviet activities in the Horn of Africa.[25] In so doing, as J. Brian Atwood, former Assistant Secretary of State for Congressional Relations, ruefully observed, "the administration had inadvertently legitimized the opponents' most telling argument and had itself undermined the chances for [SALT] ratification."[26]

Future administrations would be well-advised to be unambiguous about linkage. Either they should make it very clear from the outset that strategic arms control negotiations will be affected by certain aspects of overall U.S.-Soviet relations and be specific about what those aspects, expectations, and linkages will be, or they should argue and proceed as if equitable, verifiable strategic arms control agreements are useful in their own right and should not be tied to other elements in the U.S.-Soviet relationship. It is impossible to say with any certainty which of these two approaches should be chosen in the future. The choice should turn on a number of considerations, including contemporary U.S.-Soviet relations, the political climate in the United States, and the military and political importance of the arms control accord being negotiated. In any case, executive branch invocation of contrary notions of linkage is likely to be confusing, counterproductive, and suggestive of the absence of a coherent, overall policy for linkage to serve.

Seventh, and finally, an administration interested in having a new strategic arms control agreement ratified by the Senate will have to plan and implement an effective strategy to deal with the legislative branch. The recent experiences of the Carter Administration should be looked at with particular care because despite the aforementioned missteps a number of inspired initiatives were undertaken that may be worthy of emulation in the future. For instance, the Carter Administration began the practice of having a selected number of senators and representatives visit Geneva periodically to make a firsthand assessment of the ongoing negotiations and to offer advice to the negotiating team. By most measures, this practice was quite useful.

Among other things, it led the administration to respond constructively to important substantive concerns of several key senators.[27]

The Carter Administration also encouraged the establishment and active operation of the Cranston Group, a bipartisan group of twenty-three senators who were not generally members of the Foreign Relations or Armed Services Committees but who were interested in learning about the detailed intricacies of SALT II. This group received frequent, in-depth briefings from, among others, the chief SALT negotiator, the National Security Advisor, and the Director of Central Intelligence. In time, several of its members became the administration's pointmen in the Senate, arguing the details of the treaty with anti-SALT senators and hostile representatives of the media and special interest groups. Finally, in concert with its lobbying activities on Capitol Hill, the Carter Administration convened conferences in various parts of the United States on SALT and U.S.-Soviet relations. These public affairs conferences, in which key opinion leaders in a selected number of states were exposed to the pros and cons of SALT II, were one of the administration's few effective efforts at public education.

To be sure, the Reagan Administration—with its high credibility on national security issues and the Senate controlled by the Republican Party—will be in an excellent position politically to pursue ratification if either the intermediate-range force negotiations or the strategic arms reduction talks come to fruition. Nevertheless, particularly in light of the recent SALT II experience and aggressive Soviet behavior, President Reagan is likely to face criticism from the right and the left regarding virtually any new strategic arms control agreement. Even if all of the recommendations and criticisms of the past administration herein noted were taken seriously, it is unclear whether the Reagan Administration could persuade the Senate to ratify a new agreement. It is certain, though, that without effective political management, any administration will have a very difficult task in the future in persuading the Congress to approve a new strategic arms control treaty.

NOTES

1. Charles Kupperman, The SALT II Debate (Ph.D. dissertation, University of Southern California, 1981).
2. See, for example, "Brzezinski Calls Democrats Soft Toward Moscow," *The New York Times* (November 30, 1980).

3. See CBS/New York Times poll on SALT (Mimeo released November 7, 1979). For detailed discussion, see also William Kincade, *U.S. Civil Defense Decision-Making: The Ford and Carter Administrations* (Ph.D. dissertation, American University, 1980).

4. Committee on the Present Danger, "Public Attitudes on SALT II: The Results of a Nationwide Scientific Poll of American Opinion" (March 15, 1979).

5. ABC News/Harris Survey, November 25, 1980, vol. II, no. 148. ABC News/Harris Survey, June 16, 1977, vol. I, no. 74; May 22, 1978, vol. I, no. 64; and May 14, 1979, vol. I, no. 58.

6. William Lanouette, "The Public and Arms Control," *Arms Control Today* (June 1980):1.

7. These findings are similar to those found in Roper Organization polls taken during 1979 regarding SALT. "SALT Support Shaky," *Public Opinion* (October/November 1979):40.

8. ABC News/Harris Survey, November 25, 1980, vol. II, no. 148.

9. ABC News/Harris Survey, February 28, 1980, vol. I, no. 59.

10. CBS News/New York Times Poll, January 1981 (Mimeo released February 2, 1981).

11. Gallup Poll (Mimeo released May 7, 1981).

12. For an empirical analysis of the effect of American involvement in Indochina on U.S. defense spending and policy during the 1970s, see Louis Kriesberg and Ross Klein, "Changes in Public Support for U.S. Military Spending," *Journal of Conflict Resolution* (March 1980). See also Daniel Yankelovich and Larry Kaagan, "Assertive America," *America and the World, 1980* (New York: Council on Foreign Relations, 1981), pp. 696–713.

13. "The Coming Battle Over SALT: How to Defeat the Treaty," *Public Opinion* (November/December 1978):7–F.

14. For example, see "Address by Secretary of State Cyrus Vance to the American Society of Newspaper Editors," *The New York Times* (April 11, 1978).

15. David Moore, "SALT and Beyond: The Public is Uncertain," *Foreign Policy* (Summer 1979).

16. "Carter's Nuclear Confidence Gap," *The New Republic* (April 15, 1978):16.

17. George Urban, "A Long Conversation with Dr. Zbigniew Brzezinski," *Encounter* (May 1981):14.

18. David Aaron, Deputy Assistant to the President for national security affairs, chaired the mini-SCC. The other regular participants were Walter Slocombe, Director of the Defense Department's SALT Working Group; Leslie Gelb, Director of the State Department's Bureau of Politico-Military Affairs; Spurgeon Keeny, Deputy Director of ACDA;

178   RETHINKING THE U.S. STRATEGIC POSTURE

General William Smith of the Joint Chiefs of Staff; and Robert Bowie, Deputy Director of the CIA. These men were deputies to the most important interagency group on national security matters, the Special Coordinating Committee (SCC). For a detailed discussion of the operations and personalities of the members of the mini-SCC, see Strobe Talbott, *Endgame* (New York: Harper and Row, 1979), pp. 94-98.

19. Baker was not consulted at all during the period from just prior to Secretary of State Vance's March 1977 trip to Moscow until October 1977. Yet, in the interim, the administration significantly changed its approach to the negotiations, adopting the so-called three-tiered approach (Treaty, Protocol, Joint Statement of Principles). When Baker first learned of the changes in the U.S. negotiating posture at a closed-door October hearing on SALT, he was furious and threatened to oppose any future SALT agreement unless he was consulted on a regular basis, something the administration thereafter earnestly sought to do.

20. Thomas Franck and Edward Weisband, *Foreign Policy by Congress* (New York: Oxford University Press, 1979), p. 259.

21. For a detailed discussion of this point, see Senate Foreign Relations Committee, "Additional Views of Mr. Glenn," *The SALT II Treaty, A Report of the Senate Foreign Relations Committee* (Washington, D.C.: Government Printing Office, November 1979), pp. 484-486.

22. "Brzezinski Says his Critics Are Irked by his Candor," *The New York Times* (January 18, 1981).

23. "U.S.-Soviet Relations: From Bad to Worse," *America and the World, 1979* (New York: Pergamon Press, 1980), p. 529.

24. Milton Viorst, "The Coming Battle Over SALT," *Public Opinion* (November/December 1978):5-F.

25. For example, see "Brzezinksi Sees Ethiopia Issue Slowing Arms Talks," *The New York Times* (March 2, 1978).

26. J. Brian Atwood, "The SALT II Treaty: A Victim of Self-Inflicted Linkage" (Address to the Harvard Club of Boston, December 17, 1980), p. 11.

27. For example, the administration responded constructively to Sam Nunn on permitting sharing of cruise missile technology with our European allies; Charles Mathias on establishing a "data base" for the strategic weapons of both sides; Dennis DeConcini on precisely defining the terms under which cruise missile technology would be limited; Dale Bumpers, John Culver, and Thomas McIntyre on establishing a suitable timetable for Soviet dismantlement of certain systems. For further details, see Franck and Weisband, pp. 290-291; and Talbott, pp. 96-7, 197-8.

8 SHOULD THE ABM TREATY SURVIVE?

Michael Nacht

When the antiballistic missile (ABM) treaty took effect in October 1972, a broad segment of the American electorate greeted the event enthusiastically. The U.S. Senate had overwhelmingly approved the treaty by a vote of eighty-eight to two. Most Americans seemed to feel that the agreement contributed significantly to stabilizing the Soviet-American nuclear balance and thus reducing the risk of nuclear war. Moreover, they considered the accord an important step in mitigating the potential risks of superpower competition, an advantage emphasized by President Richard M. Nixon and National Security Advisor Henry A. Kissinger.

Ten years later, in the aftermath of the Soviet invasion of Afghanistan, the U.S. failure to ratify the SALT II Treaty, the crackdown in Poland, and the general deterioration of Soviet-American relations, the future status of the ABM Treaty is being increasingly questioned. The United States faces the decision of whether to leave the treaty intact, seek its modification through negotiation with the Soviet Union, or withdraw from it unilaterally as is provided for, in certain circumstances, by its Article XV.[1]

At one extreme, some argue that any missile defense system, even one that only marginally reduces the vulnerability of U.S. offensive strategic forces, is better than none and should be deployed regardless of the terms of the ABM Treaty. Those who advocate scrapping the

179

treaty contend that it is the product of the now-discredited policy of detente pursued by Presidents Nixon, Ford, and Carter and that the most effective way to signal a tough policy toward the Soviet Union would be to dismantle the entire structure of negotiated arms control agreements that were a central feature of this policy.

At the opposite extreme, some hold that the ABM Treaty contributes significantly to the prevention of nuclear war. If the treaty was discarded, these observers assert, both the United States and the Soviet Union would deploy additional sophisticated offensive and defensive weapon systems that would increase significantly the likelihood of a nuclear exchange. To prevent such a catastrophe, not only must the ABM Treaty not be altered, but even discussion or analysis of such possibilities should be shunned to avoid undermining the treaty's effectiveness.

These extreme positions fail to take into account the fact that treaties between two sovereign states are political documents reflecting compromises. Each side usually obtains certain advantages and simultaneously incurs discrete disadvantages. Treaties are serious expressions of intent that should not be treated lightly. Treaties are rarely abrogated, for abrogation often induces severe and adverse consequences for the parties involved. Circumstances change, however, and given the dynamic quality of advanced weapon technologies, U.S. officials should address periodically whether the balance of advantages and disadvantages that prompted U.S acceptance of the ABM Treaty has alterd sufficiently to warrant reconsideration of the treaty's terms.

Currently, both sides have denied themselves the deployment of significant ballistic missile defenses (BMD) of any type. If the ABM Treaty were modified or terminated, that step alone would not simply permit the United States to solve some particular military problem (e.g., reducing the vulnerability of its land-based missile force). Instead, the treaty's modification or termination would facilitate the transition from a world without effective ballistic missile defenses to one in which both sides deployed such forces. In large measure, then, the U.S. position on the future status of the ABM Treaty should be based on whether the preservation of a world without extensive ballistic missile defenses is preferable to a world in which BMDs play a significant role in the strategic nuclear arsenals of *both* superpowers.

THE BALANCE SHEET

For the United States, the ABM Treaty offered numerous advantages. The treaty limited Soviet ballistic missile defenses to insignificant levels, thereby assuring that U.S. strategic missiles that survived a first strike could retaliate against the complete array of Soviet military, industrial, and civilian targets. Given the absence of significant Soviet defenses (the Soviets restricted their deployments to one obsolescent ABM system around Moscow), American strategic planners could concentrate in their weapon acquisition and deployment decisions on maximizing the number of targets covered. The introduction of multiple independently targetable reentry vehicles (MIRVs) greatly increased the U.S. ability to target Soviet cities and military installations.

Doctrinally, the establishment of this mutual vulnerability to retaliatory missile attack was thought to strengthen the mutual deterrence of nuclear war. In particular, Soviet acceptance of the treaty was believed to add validity to the concept of assured destruction as the dominant criterion of American nuclear strategy. With such relative and mutual vulnerability it was believed that the incentive for either side to acquire additional offensive forces would be reduced, thereby also lending stability to the offensive arms competition. More important, the absence of meaningful defenses meant that in terms of expected damage from a nuclear war there would be little to choose between initiating an exchange and retaliating following an opponent's first strike. Hence, the incentive to preempt in a crisis would be minimal, and the crucially important objective of stabilizing the behavior of the superpowers during crises would be realized.

Moreover, an agreement of such significance, it was thought, could lead toward major offensive arms control agreements involving substantial quantitative reductions in the number of nuclear weapons on each side and important limitations on the qualitative characteristics of weapons permitted to be still deployed. The ABM Treaty also won the support of those concerned about the proliferation of nuclear weapons, since the treaty was a concrete demonstration of the commitment of both superpowers to arms control and disarmament, a pledge both states had made in the Nuclear Nonproliferation Treaty.

In international political terms, this demonstration of Soviet-American cooperation and of the utility of negotiated arms control agreements was fully consistent with and supportive of the Nixon-Kissinger detente strategy. This policy envisioned building a complex array of economic, political, and security ties with the Soviet Union that would provide incentives for the Soviets to alter their foreign policy goals, moderate their international behavior, and reduce their investment in military programs.

In domestic political terms, the signing of the SALT I agreements—of which the ABM treaty is a part—was carefully orchestrated to strengthen President Nixon's political position. His impeccable anti-communist credentials secured him the support of conservatives in both political parties. His efforts to improve simultaneously Sino-American and Soviet-American relations—the former dramatically symbolized by his trip to China in February 1972 and the latter demonstrated at the Moscow summit in May 1972—were therefore calculated to broaden his political base, secure his reelection, and codify for the historical record his credentials as a statesman of the first rank.

In budgetary terms, the ABM Treaty meant that the United States did not have to proceed with the substantial investments necessary to deploy the Safeguard ABM system and could reduce funding for BMD research and development programs to modest levels. Indeed, some Americans applauded the ABM Treaty simply because they were skeptical of the military effectiveness of Safeguard—the ABM system developed by the United States—and thus opposed the system's deployment. A negotiated agreement in which both sides relinquished the deployment of ABM systems would prevent the Safeguard system from being completed.

Criticisms

At the same time, the treaty carried with it certain disadvantages for the United States, some of which have taken on greater significance as Soviet-American relations soured in the mid- to late-1970s. Most important, the treaty simplified Soviet nuclear attack problems generally and enabled Soviet defense planners to develop higher confidence in their ability to destroy the U.S. land-based missile force. Because successive U.S. administrations have failed to resolve this land-based missile vulnerability problem, the argument for modifying the treaty to permit the use of BMD systems to protect ICBMs has gained considerable strength and has been cited as a realistic option by Secretary of Defense Caspar Weinberger on several occasions.

In addition, the risk that the United States would become vulnerable to attack if the Soviets developed a BMD system clandestinely and then deployed it suddenly (thereby "breaking out" of the ABM Treaty) has always disturbed some members of the American defense community. The U.S. ability to verify Soviet compliance with the treaty, particularly those terms relating to the development of new types of ABMs, has therefore been a highly charged political issue since the treaty was signed. Critics also feared that the treaty made the United States vulnerable to nuclear attacks by countries other than the Soviet Union, although this objection has declined as Sino-American relations have continued to improve.

Those who contend that the U.S. emphasis on the doctrine of assured destruction represents an unrealistic nuclear policy have also consistently opposed the ABM treaty. They have long argued that an ability to deter nuclear war must include a spectrum of capabilities and contingencies. These analysts insist that having the ability to destroy Soviet cities in a retaliatory attack is not sufficient to deter a variety of Soviet actions less than an all-out nuclear strike. Such an action, for example, might be a first strike on U.S. land-based missiles. They argue that the United States must develop limited nuclear options, including a flexible ability to target Soviet nuclear forces. In this regard, some view the ABM treaty as a hindrance because they believe it has kept too many Americans wedded to an unrealistic nuclear weapons policy—assured destruction—that they contend the Soviets have never accepted.[2]

Some also have criticized the ABM Treaty on the grounds that as a product of the SALT process it helped lull the American public and Congress into a false sense of security. This mood resulted in insufficient U.S. nuclear force modernization in the 1970s. Critics maintain that inadequate funding for U.S. BMD programs has been one consequence. Members of the U.S. BMD technical community assert that they have been caught in a vicious cycle as a result. They need more funds to demonstrate that it is feasible to develop a significant capability to defend U.S. missiles against a Soviet attack, but they have not been able to obtain congressional support for higher funding levels without first demonstrating this capability.[3]

One final concern about the ABM treaty is that it set a poor precedent for arms control because it is so technical and detailed. After the painful experiences of negotiating and then failing to ratify the SALT II Treaty, many have come to believe that for arms control to succeed the products of negotiations must be simple and easily understood by the electorate.

A necessary condition for American support of the ABM Treaty in 1972 was the significant doubt registered by the technical community concerning the feasibility that the Safeguard system or any other contemporary technology could perform effectively against a sophisticated Soviet attack. During the years immediately preceding the signing of the treaty, experts raised several technical questions about Safeguard that were never adequately answered. Critics pointed to the substantial vulnerability of Safeguard's radars and the system's inability to cope with large attacks that would saturate it. Decoys, chaff, and other penetration aids also could be used to degrade the Safeguard system's capabilities to discriminate among targets. The fundamental challenge to the prudence of deploying Safeguard, however, was its potential leakage. A large percentage of the attacking reentry vehicles (RVs) had to be intercepted and destroyed, or the system's mission could not be fulfilled.

The impenetrability requirement depends upon the purpose of the particular BMD system under consideration. A system designed for population center defense must be completely impermeable because even one or two nuclear weapons detonated on a city would cause enormous damage. For defense of missile silos, however, a certain amount of leakage could be tolerated without destruction of all the missiles under attack.

SOVIET ASSESSMENT

The Soviet Union derived different benefits and drawbacks from the ABM Treaty than did the United States. The treaty surely eased the Soviet leaders' concerns about the ability of Soviet weapons to penetrate defenses and reach U.S. targets, thereby preserving a preemptive counterforce option that some believe is consistent with Soviet military doctrine.

Soviet defense planners were probably more relieved than their American counterparts by this development. Although the Soviet

Union has made giant strides over the past several years in matching and in some cases surpassing American weapons technology, most observers agree that the United States holds the edge in technologies relevant to missile defenses. Effective BMD capabilities require the most advanced technological systems that blend sophisticated sensing devices, information processors, and ballistic missiles and warheads. In combination, these systems must locate the attacking RVs, discriminate between real RVs and accompanying penetration aids, then track and destroy the RVs. Soviet defense officials may have felt in the early 1970s that the U.S. technological edge in defensive and offensive systems was so pronounced that Soviet weapons would have had much greater difficulty penetrating a U.S. ABM system than U.S. weapon systems would have had penetrating a Soviet ABM system.[4]

The vulnerability of the United States to retaliatory attack, as codified by the ABM Treaty, must have reduced Soviet fears concerning the possibility of a U.S. preemptive strike in the event of a crisis. Moreover, given the large throw-weights of the generation of ICBMs that the Soviets were developing in 1972 and began to deploy in 1975, Soviet officials could have seen the ABM Treaty as a way to channel the arms competition into areas that favored them while constraining the area of greatest American advantage—high technology defensive systems.

Political considerations, however, very likely dominated Soviet thinking about the ABM Treaty. The SALT I agreements and the SALT process in general had the potential of satisfying several key Soviet objectives. First, by linking the United States and the USSR as equals, the treaties would codify the superpower status of the Soviet Union, an accomplishment that would benefit the Soviets in their relations with other nations, especially China. This achievement also would strengthen Soviet President Leonid Brezhnev's domestic political position.

Second, as the centerpiece of detente, SALT would contribute to better overall relations with the West that could stimulate stronger economic ties and provide the Soviets with access to Western technology. The Soviets could use such technology to benefit both their military programs and heavy industries. Third, the Soviets hoped that over time the SALT process might produce political friction between the United States and its European allies that the Soviets could exploit, particularly once U.S.-Soviet negotiations began to address

European-based systems. Fourth, by solidifying cordial Soviet-American relations, SALT in turn could provide disincentives for the United States to improve its relations with China.

Given the momentum of Soviet offensive weapon programs during the early 1970s, it is not obvious that the Soviets foresaw major economic benefit to be derived from the ABM Treaty. Any anticipated advantages probably featured the expectation that rubles previously budgeted for defensive strategic systems could be reallocated to offensive systems or to other military priorities. In this sense, the ABM Treaty may have provided budgetary support for the Soviets' planned offensive military buildup.

The Soviets probably did not consider the disadvantages of the ABM Treaty important. It restricted Soviet ABM deployments to one limited site in the Moscow area. Yet Soviet leaders surely realized that this system provided only marginal capabilities to limit the damage inflicted by a sophisticated American attack, especially in light of the continuing deployment of MIRVs on U.S. ICBMs and submarine-launched ballistic missiles (SLBMs).

Undoubtedly far more troublesome for Soviet officials to accept was what the treaty implied for Soviet vulnerability to third-party attacks. Unlike the United States, the Soviet Union must take seriously the threat posed by the other nuclear powers—Britain, France, and China—especially in light of the tension in Sino-Soviet relations since the mid-1960s. Soviet military planners who thought they could mount a credible defense against a Chinese, British, or French nuclear attack must have had to swallow hard when their government signed the ABM Treaty.

The Soviets probably viewed as an additional disadvantage the asymmetry in the respective vulnerabilities of the two sides' offensive missile forces. The Soviet Union has 75 to 80 percent of its total megatonnage invested in its land-based ICBM force; the United States has a much more diversified force with only 25 to 30 percent of its megatonnage in its Minuteman II, Minuteman III, and Titan II land-based missiles. Therefore, the absence of ballistic missile defenses places a much greater percentage of Soviet strategic nuclear destructive power potentially at risk than is the case for the United States. In theoretical terms, this asymmetry is a disadvantage for the Soviet Union, although operationally it would be of questionable significance if the Soviets perfected a substantial capability to destroy U.S. missile silos and the United States failed to develop a similar capability.

The ABM Treaty may have presented the Soviets more doctrinal and political or psychological problems than military difficulties. The Soviet Union, and Russia before it, ravaged by war throughout its history, traditionally has relied on large standing armies and quantitative superiority to compensate for its persistent inferiority in weapons quality, mobility, and innovation. Emphasis on defending the motherland has deep doctrinal and psychological roots, and contemporary Soviet military and political leaders have undoubtedly inherited this feeling. To forego unilaterally a marginally effective defensive system, even temporarily, must have been a wrenching experience for many Soviet officials.

Premier Kosygin's reaction of almost total disbelief when then-Secretary of Defense Robert McNamara first raised the idea of an ABM ban at the June 1967 Glassboro summit meeting is probably representative of the typical initial view of many Soviet leaders. The fact that they came to accept the merits of the ABM Treaty can only reflect a combination of their assessments of the advantages of the treaty, doubts about the technical merits of their own ABM system, and the substantial budgetary commitments they had already made to other components of the Soviet military program.

The treaty's attractiveness was bolstered by the Interim Agreement on Strategic Offensive Forces, which accompanied it. This agreement granted significant, although temporary, numerical superiority to the Soviets in ICBM and SLBM launchers and in ballistic missile submarines. Together, the SALT I agreements provided the USSR with substantial military, political, and economic benefits.

RENEGOTIATION VS. WITHDRAWAL

In both legal and declaratory terms, the United States set the stage for its own withdrawal from the ABM Treaty two weeks before the treaty was even signed and five months before it entered into force. In commenting on a possible withdrawal from the ABM Treaty, Ambassador Gerard Smith, head of the U.S. SALT I delegation, made the following statement on May 9, 1972:

> If agreement providing for more complete strategic offensive arms limitations were not achieved within five years, U.S. supreme interests could be jeopardized. Should that occur, it would constitute a basis for withdrawal from the ABM treaty.[5]

Of course, no such "complete strategic offensive arms limitations" were completed within five years of the signing of the ABM Treaty, nor, for that matter, were such limitations attained within ten years of this signing. But governments do not take the step of abrogating a treaty lightly.[6] Despite the rhetoric of some Reagan Administration officials reflecting a willingness to consider terminating the ABM Treaty, the likelihood of U.S. termination is not high. The United States has long criticized the Soviet Union for not living up to its international agreements. The Reagan Administration would suffer severe domestic and international criticism if it terminated the treaty, except under the most compelling of circumstances. Short of an acute international crisis or the development of an impregnable BMD system, neither the United States nor the Soviet Union is likely to terminate the ABM Treaty. The incentives to renegotiate the treaty should therefore be considered before termination is addressed.

Analysts have suggested several ballistic missile defense systems the United States could deploy if the ABM Treaty were modified. These alternatives include the following measures:

- Deployment of point defenses to protect either the existing Minuteman ICBM force or a new land-based missile that would be deployed in Minuteman silos or in a mobile basing mode;
- Deployment of an area defense system to protect American cities;
- Deployment of a limited ballistic missile defense system to protect the command, control, communication, and intelligence assets (C^3I) associated with U.S. strategic nuclear forces; and
- Deployment of a BMD system in Europe to protect U.S. nuclear forces abroad from Soviet intermediate- and medium-range systems.

Of these options, it is the first that is receiving the most serious attention. While it was long recognized that immobile, land-based missiles eventually would become vulnerable to attack, it was only after a series of tests of Soviet ICBMs in 1978 that American officials acknowledged publicly—in light of the demonstrated accuracy of those tests coupled with the projected number and yield of Soviet RVs—that the U.S. ICBM force would be vulnerable to attack by 1982. Specifically, theoretical calculations indicated that the Soviets would be able to destroy 90 percent of the U.S. land-based missile force using 30 percent of their MIRVed ICBMs, provided that none of the American missiles were launched while the attack was still underway. Although major questions exist about the technical feasibility and political realism of such an attack, the U.S. Government has taken the problem seriously for several years and has explored a number of missile-basing modes to alleviate the problem. The Reagan strategic program announced in October 1981 included funds to intensify research and development efforts on a BMD system that would defend MX land-based ballistic missiles in fixed silos.

The second option is not a pressing issue. Virtually no defense analysts who have examined the current and projected status of U.S. BMD technology and trends in Soviet weapons development claim that an effective area system to protect American cities could be deployed in the 1980s. It is conceivable, however, that were the first option to be adopted, the United States over several years could make the transition from a point defense system to protect missiles to an area network to protect cities. Indeed, one problem associated with amending the ABM Treaty to permit point defenses is the difficulty of discriminating between area and point defenses.

The third option could be incorporated into the first program, or it could stand on its own. In fact, because of the high priority being given to the reduction of missile silo vulnerability, it is most unlikely that the U.S. would seek to protect only its C^3I facilities.

The fourth option also seems to be only a remote possibility. The response to the deployment of Soviet SS-20s and other systems that threaten U.S. nuclear escalatory capabilities in Europe was the December 1979 NATO decision endorsing the double track of deploying Pershing II and mobile, ground-launched cruise missiles while offering to negotiate limitations with the Soviets on the number of long-range theater nuclear forces. This decision has generated such a complex web of political and military problems within the Atlantic alliance that it is virtually certain that the Reagan administration would not wish to complicate matters further by introducing BMD deployment issues as well.

DISINCENTIVES TO RENEGOTIATE

Renegotiating the ABM Treaty could present the United States certain disadvantages. Renegotiation would probably result in the deployment of point defenses by both parties. This development in turn would greatly increase the offensive force levels required to overcome those defenses. Since the United States seems determined to acquire at least as much counterforce capability as has the Soviet Union, renegotiation, which would encourage further proliferation of offensive systems on both sides, would not appear to be in the U.S. interest. The dilemma for U.S. policymakers, however, is that America has pursued with equal fervor two objectives: acquiring counterforce capability, which a renegotiation of the ABM Treaty might harm, and reducing land-based missile vulnerability, which renegotiation in theory could help.

A secondary military disincentive is that Soviet missile defenses deployed to protect Soviet ICBMs might be perceived as jeopardizing the ability of British, French, and Chinese forces to strike at Soviet military targets. These other nuclear powers might well interpret the deployment of Soviet point defenses as a first step of a BMD program whose net effect would be to weaken the deterrent value of their own nuclear forces. Thus renegotiation of the treaty could stimulate a rancorous debate between the United States and each of these nuclear weapon states.

Moreover, opening up the ABM Treaty to renegotiation and not achieving a new agreement could lead to abrogation of the present treaty and to the collapse of any hope for the continuation of negotiated Soviet-American arms control agreements. Although some would welcome this development as the destruction of the last remnants of cooperation with the Soviet Union, others wish to preserve at least those agreements that have served, and continue to serve, American military and political interests.

It would be particularly challenging to define BMD limits in a revised treaty that would permit point, but not area, defenses. With certain aspects of BMD activity permitted under the terms of such a treaty, U.S. confidence would be shaky concerning Soviet observance of the treaty's terms. Fears of Soviet breakout would be aggravated and if their subsequent behavior prompted American allegations of Soviet cheating, the already fragile Soviet-American relationship could be damaged still further.

The aim of renegotiating the ABM Treaty would be to deploy new BMD systems, which in turn would have quite a significant impact on U.S. expenditures for strategic nuclear forces in the 1980s. Despite the large increases in the defense budget proposed by President Reagan, authorized funds are unlikely to be sufficient for the programs already underway. BMD deployment expenditures, which might exceed $5 billion per year, would aggravate these problems. There is, therefore, an economic disincentive to open up the ABM Treaty since it is bound to generate still further demands for defense budget increases, which would have adverse economic effects and could run into serious political opposition.

Do the Soviets have incentives to renegotiate? It is not clear that they do. If they reached a point where they were confident they had enough RVs to destroy the U.S. ICBM force even if it was augmented with BMD systems, without fear of U.S retaliation, the Soviets could opt for renegotiation to buy some added protection for their own land-based missile forces. The Soviet Union is far from such an enviable situation, however, so this incentive does not exist.

A second incentive for the Soviets to renegotiate would be to protect themselves against third parties, particularly the Chinese, but this rationale also seems a bit far-fetched. The Chinese have long used dispersion and camouflage to minimize the vulnerability of their relatively modest nuclear arsenal. The inaccuracy of their own weapons suggests that the primary targets for Chinese nuclear retaliation against the Soviet Union would be civilian or industrial sites. Soviet defenses of ICBMs would be of marginal value against such a Chinese attack, despite the proximity of some Soviet ICBM fields to urban-industrial areas.

Only if the Soviets had developed a new, leak-proof BMD system, probably based on new physical principles, which they might wish to deploy to protect their cities, would they have an incentive to renegotiate. Indeed, if the system were truly impregnable, the Soviets would presumably abrogate the treaty and deploy that system because this action would tip the nuclear balance significantly in their favor.

Short of such a revolutionary breakthrough, the Soviet Union has two powerful disincentives not to renegotiate. The first is its strong desire not to help alleviate the U.S. land-based missile vulnerability problem. Why should the Soviet Union, after spending so much effort to target the U.S. ICBM force, participate in a process that would in large measure negate this very effort? Secondly, renegotiation could lead to the deployment of point defenses by both countries in which once again American technological prowess could win out. The net effect of the renegotiation, then, would be to transform a situation in which U.S. forces were vulnerable and Soviet forces were not, to the reverse. There is no reason whatever why the Soviet Union should participate in a process that ran the risk of producing such an outcome.

TECHNOLOGY AND TIMING

Given that much of the real debate about the ABM Treaty revolves around the desirability of deploying point defenses to protect ICBMs, what technological options are available to the United States and in what time frame? Informed assessments of U.S. BMD technology point to two categories of technology that might be available during the 1980s: (1) novel concepts using unsophisticated components that would create great uncertainty for the attacker but would also be of uncertain reliability from the defender's perspective and (2) components that are technological derivatives of programs from the early 1970s, especially the Low-Altitude Defense System (LoADS).[7] The first category includes such concepts as "beds of nails"—ground-based metal spikes that would be fired at incoming RVs. Theoretically, the warheads would be destroyed before they could detonate against the missile silos. The effectiveness of this and several other concepts in this category, however, would be very sensitive to the offensive tactics and to the specific kill technique employed. Moreover, some of these concepts would require renegotiation of the treaty before they could even be tested because they are inconsistent with Article V, which prohibits the testing of other than immobile land-based systems or systems with multiple launchers or rapid reload capability.

In any event, because of the uncertain reliability of these novel systems, the BMD technical community much prefers LoADS. LoADS is an advanced form of terminal defense involving the use of small radars, modern data processing systems, and a single stage ABM interceptor that would be designed to intercept attacking RVs between 50,000 and 200,000 feet within ten seconds of their location. In a sense LoADS is a high probability-high risk system because it is designed to intercept the incoming RV at the last possible moment. If the interception is not made at these low altitudes as planned, the defense has no second chance.

LoADS would be particularly attractive in defending MX in a multiple protective shelter system (MPS) because of the leverage it would provide the defense. "Leverage" is the number of additional offensive warheads necessary to overcome each interceptor missile deployed. The logic of the system is predicated on the idea that each interceptor would preferentially defend one shelter—the one with the MX. The LoADS unit itself would be housed within the MX shelter, and it would not be known to the attacker which shelter was being defended until the radar antenna commenced radiating. The attacker would consequently have to target an additional warhead against each shelter in order to have high confidence of destroying the single MX missile. In an MX squadron of K shelters, there would thus be a $K - 1$ numerical advantage favoring the defense.

However, since the essential feature of LoADS in defense of MX in a multiple shelter system would be its deceptive basing, it would run counter to the provisions of Article XII of the ABM Treaty. Deployment of LoADS would therefore require renegotiation of the treaty. In addition, the system's radars remain vulnerable to jamming; the entire system has not been designed to counter maneuverable re-entry vehicles (MaRVs), which the Soviet Union might be able to deploy by the end of the 1980s or the early 1990s; and the deceptive basing concept is contingent on the inability of the Soviet Union to determine quickly in which shelter the missile is hidden.[8]

The effectiveness of LoADS to protect fixed ICBMs is far more problematical than for a mobile MX system. Without deceptive missile basing, the leverage enjoyed by the defense with MPS is absent. The attacker could therefore resort to saturation attacks, decoys, and other penetration aids to defeat the defense. Unless these offensive options could each be countered, it would be difficult to justify the deployment of LoADS for fixed-based MX missiles.[9]

The LoADS system is expected to undergo extensive proof testing over the next several years. Therefore, even if it proves to be a very attractive system, it would be premature for the United States to initiate renegotiation of the ABM Treaty at the 1982 treaty review meeting of the Standing Consultative Commission (SCC). Based upon projected development of LoADS, it would be sensible for the United States to delay raising the issue of treaty renegotiation until the 1987 SCC review session;[10] of course, there is nothing to prevent the United States from calling for renegotiation in the SCC before 1987 if circumstances warranted.[11]

It is anticipated that within twenty years layered BMD systems would be available combining an exoatmospheric kill capability with a low-altitude BMD system like LoADS. This concept, calling for multiple nonnuclear warheads in individual kill vehicles, holds the promise of minimizing attacking RV leakage. Testing of many of the components of this system would require renegotiation of the treaty since both exoatmospheric systems and MIRVed interceptors are prohibited.

Based upon projections made in the early 1980s, it would not be until the twenty-first century that exotic missile defense systems involving satellites and directed energy weapons would be feasible. These systems—predicated on "other physical principles" capable of substituting for ABM interceptor missiles, launchers, and radars—would necessarily be the subject of negotiation between the parties as specified in Agreed Statement D of the treaty, if the treaty was to remain in force.[12] Therefore, there is nothing in the offing with respect to overlay or exotic systems necessitating renegotiation of the treaty for many years.

A MORE STABLE NUCLEAR BALANCE

The Soviet-American nuclear balance is being influenced most significantly by the introduction of very accurate weapon systems that render all immobile targets potentially vulnerable to attack. In a world dominated by such weapons, increased emphasis quite naturally should be placed on mobility, deception, and defense. In order to maintain a credible deterrent posture for a wide range of contingencies, and in order to sustain the hope of being able to engage, if necessary, in a limited nuclear exchange without it inevitably escalating to Armageddon, both sides will undoubtedly seek to acquire flexible targeting capabilities. This does not mean that assured destruction would vanish as a key element of American nuclear strategy. It does mean, however, that other criteria would also necessarily play a significant role in determining the composition and mission of U.S. strategic nuclear forces.

In this context BMD can, but does not have to, play an important role. Through mobility and concealment, but without defenses, the United States, at least conceptually, could reduce the vulnerability of its land-based missiles and acquire as much capability as it wished to target flexibly and to destroy hard targets. If, however, BMD is found to be technically attractive and mobile-basing modes are determined to be infeasible for technical or political reasons, "instability" need not occur. Carefully negotiated modifications of the ABM Treaty could in principle be worked out leading to the deployment of unambiguous point defenses by both parties. The net result would be a more stable nuclear balance, particularly during crises, since the vulnerability of the retaliatory forces of both sides would be reduced. The arms competition might indeed be accelerated, however, as both sides would seek to acquire new offensive forces to overcome the defenses of the other.

In political terms, the United States would have to expect severe criticism from its allies for moving down the BMD path, since it would leave the nuclear retaliatory forces of those states undefended while initiating a process that could eventually jeopardize their ability to penetrate to Soviet targets. Moreover, if BMD deployments were accompanied by termination of the ABM Treaty, negotiated arms control would be judged as having no future whatever and Soviet-American relations would be seen as being in their most difficult state since the 1962 Cuban missile crisis. Alternatively, the ability of the Soviet Union and the United States to cooperate in modifying the ABM Treaty to satisfy each party's objectives could provide needed assurances that the arms control process was still valuable and that the superpowers were seeking to avoid confrontation rather than to promote it.

It is especially noteworthy that the tough, anti-Soviet posture taken by the Reagan Administration has been greeted in Europe by vehement, widespread expressions of concern about the perceived growing prospect of nuclear war. At issue, in part, is the perennial European suspicion that the United States seeks to decouple itself from Europe. Some believe the United States is planning to abandon its security commitments to its NATO allies. For others, the more frightening concern is that the United States is contemplating fighting a nuclear war with the Soviet Union in which Europe would be the nuclear battleground while the superpowers would remain sanctuaries.

In this political setting, U.S. strategic concepts about maintaining "escalation control" in the event of war and in "extending deterrence" to America's European allies are found by many Europeans to be provocative rather than comforting. Therefore, modification of the ABM Treaty in the near term would likely be seen by many in Europe as further proof of U.S. belligerence or disengagement. Renegotiation of the treaty would only exacerbate the centrifugal forces that are already threatening to alter, if not destroy, the fabric of political relations within the NATO alliance.

On balance, given political complexities and technological realities, renegotiation or abrogation of the ABM treaty is not in the U.S. interest at this time. The United States could consider renegotiation at or prior to the 1987 SCC review session, if sufficient progress in BMD system development had been made. For the time being, the balance sheets that induced American and Soviet acceptance of the ABM Treaty in 1972 still convey the same message to both parties: The advantages of the treaty outweigh its disadvantages.

It would be of enormous benefit to both societies if the transition to a defense-dominated world could be made easily. The uncertainties and ambiguities of a superpower rivalry that relies for nuclear deterrence on the threat of retaliation would give way to a competition in which both rivals would be confident they could defend their homelands effectively against nuclear attack. Perceived vulnerability to a surprise first-strike, to unauthorized use of nuclear weapons, or to an attack by a third party would decline dramatically in both Washington and Moscow.

Defenses can dominate, however, only if offenses are strictly controlled or if a fundamental technological breakthrough materializes. Neither of these conditions seems likely in the near future. In the real world of superpower rivalry, a defensive arms race would stimulate further the already intense offensive arms competition. The attainment of a world dominated by defenses would then be seen as the illusion it is.

NOTES

1.   The main provisions of the ABM Treaty, as modified by a 1974 protocol, are: (1) Each side may deploy one ABM system either at its national capital or at an intercontinental ballistic missile (ICBM) silo launcher site; (2) an "ABM system" is defined to consist of ABM interceptor missiles, ABM launchers, and ABM radars, and the constraints on their deployment are specified by the treaty in quantitative, qualitative, and geographic terms; (3) development, testing, and deployment of sea-based, air-based, space-based, or mobile land-based ABM systems are banned; and (4) an agreed statement regarding the treaty specifies "that in the event ABM systems based on

other physical principles . . . are created in the future, specific limitations on such systems and their components would be subject to discussion in accordance with the articles of the treaty." The treaty is of unlimited duration and is to be reviewed by the parties at five-year intervals. Each party may seek amendments at any time through discussions at the Soviet-American Standing Consultative Commission or withdraw from the treaty after six months' notice "if it decides that extraordinary events related to the subject matter of the treaty have jeopardized its supreme interests."

2. It should be noted, however, that, unlike U.S. declaratory policy, actual U.S. targeting plans have not been limited solely to civilian and industrial sites and have long included military targets.

3. See the summary of discussion by Steven E. Miller in *U.S. Arms Control Objectives and the Implications for Ballistic Missile Defense* (Proceedings of a Symposium held at the Center for Science and International Affairs, Harvard University, November 1-2, 1979), especially pp. 5-11.

4. Note that when the ABM Treaty was signed the United States had begun to deploy MIRVs on its advanced Minuteman missiles, whereas the Soviet Union had yet to test a MIRV.

5. Cited in the first unilateral statement amended to the ABM Treaty text. See U.S. Arms Control and Disarmament Agency, *Arms Control and Disarmament Agreements* (1980), p. 146. At this writing both the United States and the Soviet Union are adhering to the terms of both the Interim Offensive Agreement and the SALT II Treaty, although the former has expired and the latter never legally entered into force.

6. Indeed, "abrogation" has been replaced by "termination" in current parlance at the Department of State. The last treaty the United States terminated was its formal security relationship with Taiwan in 1979.

7. See the articles on ballistic missile defense by E.C. Aldridge, Jr., and William A. Davis, Jr., in *U.S. Arms Control Objectives and the Implications for Ballistic Missile Defense* (Proceedings of a Symposium held at the Center for Science and International Affairs, Harvard University, November 1-2, 1979), pp. 29-68.

8. What is particularly crucial about the effectiveness of LoADS deployed in conjunction with MX/MPS is the preservation of location uncertainty (PLU) of both the missile and the BMD system. Maintenance of PLU involves a complex set of measures and countermeasures. Some of the important considerations are addressed lucidly in Office of Technology Assessment *MX Missile Basing: Report of the Office of Technology Assessment to the Congress of the United States* (U.S. Government Printing Office, 1981), pp. 117-25.

9. As illustrated in the study by the Office of Technology Assessment, "100 single-shot low-altitude defense units defending 100 silos containing MX missiles would only be able to claim 100 RVs from a Soviet arsenal of thousands." *MX Missile Basing, op. cit.,* p. 117. Indeed, prior to President Reagan's October 1981 decision to scrap the MX/MPS system, the Air Force was on record as dismissing the capability of LoADS to defend Minuteman silos. See, for example, *Aerospace Daily* (August 28, 1981):329.

10. Precise schedule information on LoADS development is classified. But E.C. Aldridge, Jr., formerly associated with a defense contracting firm tied to the U.S. Ballistic Missile Defense Systems Command and, at this writing, Under Secretary of the Air Force, has estimated that "the U.S. LoADS could achieve IOC (Initial Operational Capability) towards the end of the 1982–1987 [time] frame." See E.C. Aldridge, Jr., "SALT Implications of BMD Options," in *U.S. Arms Control Objectives and the Implications for Ballistic Missile Defense, op. cit.,* p. 60.

11. This seemingly obvious point is worth elaboration. Two misconceptions have grown up around the treaty: First, that the treaty "expires in 1982" and, second, that the treaty can be renegotiated only at five-year intervals from the date of signature—1982, 1987, and so forth. Both are false. The treaty is of unlimited duration but calls for periodic review at five-year intervals. Either party can seek to renegotiate the terms of the treaty at any time.

12. The reader is referred to Articles V and VI of the treaty and to Agreed Statements D, E, and F for constraints imposed by the treaty on advanced BMD technologies. See *Arms Control and Disarmament Agreements, op. cit.,* pp. 140–141, 143–144.

9 SHOULD THE UNITED STATES CONTINUE TO ADHERE TO THE SALT II TREATY?

Michael M. May

The SALT II Treaty was signed on June 18, 1979, but since no instruments of ratification have been exchanged, it has yet not taken effect. According to the general counsel of the Arms Control and Disarmament Agency (ACDA) under the Carter Administration, however, although there is no legal obligation to abide by the treaty, "certain provisions of the SALT II Treaty can be said to have legal status of a certain nature."[1]

This status derives from customary international law, which "obligates States that sign treaties to refrain from acts which would defeat [the treaty's] object and purpose prior to entry into force, until such time as the signatory State has made clear its intention not to become a Party [to the treaty]."[2] Acts that would defeat a treaty's intent and purpose are acts that would make it impossible for the treaty regime ever to come into force. This customary law was codified in Article 18 of the 1969 Vienna Convention on the Law of Treaties, which was signed but not ratified by the United States and not signed by the Soviet Union, although "both the United States and the Soviet Union took part in the negotiation of the Vienna Convention and Article 18 was included in the Convention by a vote of 102 to zero."[3]

With this background, Ralph Earle II, the Director of ACDA and chief U.S. SALT negotiator under the Carter Administration, told the Senate Foreign Relations Committee on April 22, 1980 that "[the

U.S. Government is] prepared, pursuant to common international law, as articulated in the Vienna Convention, to take no action which would defeat the object and purpose of that treaty while it is pending ratification, and we expect the Soviet Union to do the same and we will continue to do so until they act in a different fashion." To the date of this writing, the Reagan Administration has continued this position and stated it would adhere to existing strategic arms limitation agreements with the Soviet Union so long as the Russians did the same.[4]

The Soviet position has been more ambiguous. Soviet actions apparently have not been such as to defeat the "object and purpose of the Treaty." Brezhnev has called for "continue[d] relevant negotiations with the United States, preserving all the positive elements that have so far been achieved,"[5] though no Soviet spokesman has stated the Soviet Union would adhere to the treaty. On the other hand, V.M. Vasev, the Minister-Counselor to the Soviet embassy in Washington, said on a U.S. television program on February 14, 1981, that since the Soviet Union had not ratified the Vienna Convention, it had no obligation to observe any of the provisions of the SALT II Treaty.

Not all actions forbidden by the SALT II Treaty would defeat its object and purpose. Soviet failure to dismantle excess intercontinental ballistic missile (ICBM) launchers, for instance—in order to comply with the reduction from 2,400 to 2,250 total strategic nuclear delivery systems, which the treaty would have called for as of January 1, 1981—could be remedied at such date as the treaty enters into force. The reduction can then be verified by "national technical means," that is, by satellites and the like. Flight-testing of a missile with more than the permitted number of reentry vehicles, on the other hand, would make later verification of the pertinent bans impossible and therefore would defeat the object and purpose of the treaty. Since the number of reentry vehicles (RVs) on a missile, as well as other characteristics limited under SALT II, must be verified at the time the missile is tested, verification by national technical means may be impossible after the missile is deployed.

The 1972 Interim Agreement on Offensive Weapons, which expired in 1977, has no legal status at all. Continued adherence to it is a matter of policy, enunciated by both the United States and the Soviet Union in 1977 and confirmed in 1981 by the State Department.[6] Since most of the meaningful provisions of the Interim Agreement are incorporated or enlarged upon in the SALT II Treaty, certain specific submarine and submarine-launched ballistic missile (SLBM) limitations aside, and since the principal political debate here and abroad has centered on SALT II, the discussion here is restricted to SALT II.

It seems clear from the foregoing that ratification of SALT II remains a legally and diplomatically possible course of action for the United States; the question is whether it is desirable. In what follows, the major provisions of the SALT II Treaty are first summarized, with brief comments on some of them. The military and technical impacts of these provisions are then discussed, from the point of view of what it is that the treaty permits, does not permit, and interferes with in the way of strategic nuclear offensive and defensive activities. Some of the arguments usually given for and against seeking adherence are then discussed, and a course of action is recommended.

MAJOR PROVISIONS OF SALT II

The SALT II treaty provides for broad limitations on strategic nuclear delivery systems, specific limitations on ballistic missile and aircraft systems, bans on certain other systems, and methods of verifying compliance with treaty provisions. Its other provisions are important also, but they have not been central to the debate over ratification and will not be examined here.

The broadest limitation is on the total number of ICBM launchers, SLBM launchers (i.e., launch tubes in submarines), air-to-surface ballistic missiles with range exceeding 600 kilometers (ASBMs), and heavy bombers. The limit was initially to be 2,400 and then 2,250 after January 1, 1981. Unlike the Interim Agreement, which was a freeze of unequal ballistic missile forces, the limit is the same for both sides and includes bombers. Like the Interim Agreement, SALT II limits launchers of missiles rather than missiles themselves, except for ASBMs, which do not have easily identifiable launchers. With the means of verification used to date, the number of ICBM and SLBM launchers is thought to be verifiable with some precision while the total number of missiles in inventory is not. Both sides are therefore free under the treaty to produce and stockpile extra missiles so long as these missiles are not in the launcher deployment areas.

Within this total, there are several sublimits further restricting the systems that one side or the other thought particularly dangerous, specifically, missiles equipped with multiple, independently targetable reentry vehicles (MIRVs) (on the United States' part) and air-launched cruise missiles (ALCMs) with a range exceeding 600 kilometers (on the USSR's part). The total of heavy bombers carrying ALCMs (any aircraft carrying ALCMs would be considered a heavy bomber) and launchers for missiles (ICBMs and SLBMs) equipped with MIRVs is limited to 1,320. The MIRVed missiles may comprise no more than 1,200 of the total, no more than 820 of which may be launchers of ICBMs equipped with MIRVs.

The more stringent limitations on MIRVed ICBM launchers reflect the U.S. concern with their destabilizing potential, that is, their ability to increase the advantage that would accrue to the instigator of a nuclear strike who used only one ICBM to destroy many. The concern arises because an ICBM RV can be aimed more accurately than an SLBM or an ASBM RV, and accuracy is needed to destroy the hardened ICBM silos. With developing technology using stars and satellites, however, all RVs are likely eventually to have roughly the same accuracy. Cruise missiles, though much slower and more easily intercepted, may be even more accurate.

The treaty includes important further limitations on ballistic missiles and ballistic missile launchers. Fixed ICBM launchers cannot be relocated nor can any more be built. Launchers for light ICBMs (no larger than the Soviet SS-17 or SS-19) or older heavy ICBMs cannot be converted into launchers for modern heavy ICBMs (the Soviet SS-18). There can be no mobile heavy ICBMs, heavy SLBMs, or heavy ASBMs. Upper limits are given on the launch-weight and throw-weight of light and heavy missiles: The maximum light ICBM can have over three times the throw-weight of the Minuteman, as do the SS-17, SS-19, and the MX. The maximum heavy ICBM has about ten times the throw-weight of Minuteman.[7]

Each side is permitted to develop only one new ICBM, which must be light. Existing missiles can have no more than the maximum number of RVs they had been tested with as of May 1, 1979. New ICBMs can have no more than the maximum any ICBM had as of that date (ten); new SLBMs no more than the maximum any SLBM had (fourteen). A new ICBM is defined in terms of number of stages, dimensions, weights, and whether the propellant is solid or liquid.

Only the Soviet Union can have heavy ICBMs under these provisions, but either side could have as many as 8,200 MIRVed ICBM RVs. The Soviet RVs can be larger on the average than the U.S. RVs (and are) and therefore can carry higher-yield weapons, be better defended against a possible future ballistic missile defense (BMD), or both. The United States can have RVs as large as it wishes, practically speaking, by reducing its total number of RVs below the maximum number allowed.

In addition to the 8,200 MIRVed ICBM RVs, each side can have 5,320 MIRVed SLBM RVs, for a total of 13,520 MIRVed ballistic missile RVs. Either side can have more total MIRVed RVs if it deploys fewer ICBM RVs and more SLBM RVs. There can be no more than 28 ALCMs per heavy bomber on the average. Consequently, if the maximum permitted 1,200 MIRVed ballistic missile launchers are deployed, then an additional 120 heavy bombers carrying 3,360 long-range cruise missiles could be deployed. Depending on the number of other (non-ALCM-carrying) heavy bombers it has, each side can also have up to 930 other unMIRVed missile RVs. Other combinations are possible, since the treaty provides for freedom to mix within the limits.

These are high limits, but only a fraction of the weapons would survive an attack. That fraction can be made higher by good design for survivability, a prerequisite to significant reductions (see section II).

The heavy ICBMs are the most salient asymmetry favoring the Soviet Union in the treaty and are limited in several ways. The bans on heavy mobiles, heavy SLBMs, and heavy ASBMs are not very meaningful because such systems are probably impractical. The maximum permitted number of ten RVs per ICBM, on the other hand, is probably most restrictive for heavy ICBMs, since they could carry substantially more. Its introduction may have reflected in part a U.S. concern for the survivability of the multiple protective shelter (MPS) system, under development during the last stages of the SALT II negotiations.

The aircraft affected by the limits are the U.S. B-52 and B-1, the older Soviet Bear and Bison, any future bomber capable of carrying out the mission of a heavy bomber in a manner similar or superior to the above, and any bomber equipped for ALCMs or ASBMs. For bomber aircraft carrying one or more ASBMs, the missiles are counted but not the bomber unless it can also carry bombs. The range of the ALCMs is not restricted, a crucial feature since ALCMs are deployed in large part because the bomber itself is thought to be vulnerable when it approaches or overflies hostile territory. As noted above, there can be no more than an average of twenty-eight ALCMs per bomber. Although existing types of heavy bombers are limited to no more than twenty per bomber, new bombers could have more, consistent with an average of twenty-eight for the whole fleet.

The Soviet aircraft Backfire was, as is well known, the subject of acrimonious debate. Under certain conditions and with a much smaller payload than the heavy bombers listed above, this aircraft can have intercontinental capability. A significant U.S. contingent wanted Backfire to count within the limitations. The Soviet Union successfully argued that it should not, but it did accept limitations on its capabilities and rate of production, limitations which President Carter then called "essential to the obligations assumed under the Treaty."[8] The treaty also bans MIRVed ALCMs and the development, testing, and deployment of ballistic missiles and launchers on surface ships, the beds of seas and inland waters, and earth-orbit. (Some of these bans also occur in other treaties.)

The treaty carries over from SALT I provisions stating that verification of compliance shall be by national technical means, that these means shall not be interfered with (i.e., no antisatellite or other action shall be taken against those systems that are used to verify compliance), and that there shall be no deliberate concealment of activities related to restrictions in the treaty (including no encryption of relevant test data). Systems with certain tested characteristics (number of RVs per MIRVed ballistic missile, for example) are considered to have those characteristics when deployed so that identifications made in the course of test programs govern the assignment of systems to the relevant categories. There is an agreement to update the data base upon which verification rests, a departure from the Soviet Union's refusal in SALT I to provide any data of its own to assist in verification.

SOME MILITARY AND TECHNICAL
IMPLICATIONS OF SALT II PROVISIONS

The strategic implications of the SALT II Treaty cannot be assessed apart from other factors affecting the strategic situation. This section discusses the effect that adherence to SALT II would have on some often used scenarios for nuclear conflict. The scenarios may or may not have much to do with any nuclear conflict that might occur; they do influence perceptions (in the West at least) of adequacy and deterrence. This discussion can therefore provide a guide for correlating one's judgments concerning the consequences of SALT with one's judgments concerning these scenarios.

Nuclear weapons could be used in a first strike attempt at disarming the nuclear forces of an enemy. Targets for such a first strike would include silos (i.e., each side's 1,000 to 1,500 reinforced underground ICBM launchers), which could be destroyed by weapons with hundreds of kilotons to megaton yields and with accuracies within the state of the art.[9] Discussions of first strikes usually assume that the targeted ICBMs would still be in their silos at the time of these explosions, although it is no less likely that the attacked side would have warning of the attack in time to launch these ICBMs before the explosions occur. The situation is complicated by the possibility of attacks on the warning systems and on the command and communication systems, as well as by precursor nuclear bursts that might make the retaliatory launch difficult.

Despite the prominent part they play in the public debate, silos would most likely not be the most valuable targets for a first strike, not only because the ICBMs might not be there but also because they contain at most one ICBM each. Strategic air bases with aircraft still on them and naval bases with submarines in port contain many more weapons—and more easily destroyable weapons—and should be the prime targets of a first strike. Key elements of the warning, command, and communication systems, insofar as they can be targeted, would be necessary for any response and would therefore be very valuable targets. Alternate air and naval bases as well as some other nuclear facilities should also be on a first-striker's list. In all, there would be several thousand targets, perhaps half of which would require large, accurately aimed weapons. The number of weapons required would be significantly increased if the attacker were to use two weapons on each silo or other hard targets in order to reduce the likelihood that the target would not be hit.

Another widely discussed possible use for nuclear weapons is the countervalue second strike, which has often been presumed to be the prime deterrent against either an attempted first strike or some other potentially catastrophic aggression. The targets in this case are the enemy's major industries, transportation centers, and energy sources—in short, all that makes possible the continued operation of an industrialized country. These targets are not hard. Their number depends on how thorough the destruction is to be, with the first several hundred targets the most valuable.

The third scenario also presumes that nuclear weapons should be a deterrent to attack and therefore would not be used first, but its proposed targets are different from those of a countervalue second strike. The response would have two purposes: (1) to deny the first-striker any military or strategic advantage from the attack, by making further military operations (both nuclear and conventional) impossible or extremely difficult and (2) to maintain in a long-lasting reserve some portion of the nuclear weapon systems for deterrence of further enemy attacks and for further targeting of military assets.

This scenario is one of the choices referred to when it is said that the president must have some other option beside mutual suicide if the United States is attacked.[10] The targets for prompt response would include the airfields, naval and other military bases, and command and communication centers and depots that are also first-strike targets. Also included would be the communication, storage, and industrial centers necessary to pursue a conventional or theater nuclear war—for instance, a Soviet invasion of Europe. Most silos presumably would have been emptied in the initial attack, but their reuse would have to be denied. A scenario of this kind would require fewer total weapons and, in particular, fewer accurate weapons than a first-strike scenario, though more than required by most countervalue scenarios. It would also place a premium on maintaining a survivable capability to communicate with and to control forces.

None of these attacks would be surgical; all would wreak major devastation. Depending on a host of variables—some of which would be under the control of the attacker, some not—fatalities after carrying out the first or third scenario would range from perhaps three million to ten or more million people. Fatalities after carrying out the second kind of scenario might range from tens to a hundred or more million people.[11] Present knowledge cannot determine what the difference would mean to the governments concerned or what would be left of those governments. There have been governments in the past that have attempted to deal with such levels of devastation, albeit not with such prompt devastation.

We noted that in the third scenario, and others for that matter, a reserve of nuclear weapon systems would have to be maintained. The knowledge that such a reserve could be maintained may affect not only the outcome of a nuclear war but the deterrence of nuclear war, especially in times of crisis. Some systems are more suited to a reserve role than others. Submarines are probably the main candidate for such a role in the United States today, despite drawbacks. Another effective method of constituting a reserve is to possess weapons and launchers that are hidden in peacetime and cannot be targeted. The Soviet Union can constitute such a reserve; the United States would have difficulty, especially under SALT.

What would SALT II do to the capability of either side to carry out these scenarios? To answer this question, one must first distinguish between the inventories of weapons in the permitted totals, as listed in the preceding section, and the weapons that would survive an attack and be usable and reliable afterwards. Bombers off-alert and submarines in port could not survive attack. Yet, for reasons of logistics and economy, not all bombers can be on alert nor all submarines at sea. Moreover, alert bombers would not all escape their bases safely nor be communicated with successfully, nor would all bombers and cruise missiles penetrate to their targets. ICBMs would increasingly have to be launched under attack or be rebased if they were to survive attack. Roughly estimated, perhaps half of the U.S. strategic inventory would be available for any kind of counterattack, provided the ICBMs were launched under attack or had been suitably rebased, and provided most of the alert bombers or their cruise missiles reached their targets. A heightened state of alert could not only increase that fraction but, more importantly, increase the assurance of survival and of effective communication and control. Somewhat similar considerations apply to the Soviet Union, though the assessment is clouded with uncertainties.

Concerning first-strike capabilities against presently deployed systems on either side, the Soviet Union is deemed capable under SALT II of destroying U.S. ICBM launchers in the near future. The United States could do the same to Soviet ICBM launchers under SALT II in the more distant future, if it procured enough accurate, high-yield RVs that could be carried by any of several present and proposed missiles. The ability of either side to carry out the rest of a disarming first strike, however, is considerably more doubtful and is not affected one way or the other by SALT limitations. Whether there would be ICBMs in the ICBM launchers at the time of the first strike would depend on the warning system, the communication and command system, and certain human intangibles. Whether aircraft on alert would survive a first strike would depend mainly on their ability to get far enough away from their bases after receiving warning and to operate afterwards despite long-range nuclear effects, such as the electromagnetic pulse. Submarines are at present believed able to survive because they can remain hidden in a large enough ocean area. Greater numbers of them (forbidden by the Interim Agreement of 1972 but not by SALT II) would make it more difficult to track or find them.

Countervalue second strikes could be carried out by either side after an attack, even if a smaller fraction of their strategic systems survived than was postulated: The first few hundred weapons would do the greater part of the damage to the civilian economy. Thus, the position that the ability to destroy a large part of the other side's civilian economy constitutes a sufficient deterrent to war by itself is consistent with a position in favor of drastic weapons reductions, unilateral if necessary.

The third scenario requires that most of the ICBMs survive or be launched under attack, that most alert bombers and cruise missiles reach their targets, and that a reserve remain. The countervailing strategy outlined by former Secretary of Defense Harold Brown[12] describes this scenario among others and requires much the same kind of survivability.

SALT II affects these capabilities mostly by affecting the survivability of ICBM launchers and the ability to establish and maintain reserves. Its impact on the former is mixed, on the latter mostly negative. The negative impact on reserves is due both to specific provisions of SALT II and to the political climate created by SALT. The specific provisions are the bans on relocating silos (which prevents the emplacement of ICBM launchers into deep underground sites) and on emplacing hardened missile-containing launchers on the bottom of lakes, oceans, and other water bodies. The negative political climate would arise in the United States if attempts were made to produce and stockpile in hidden locations extra missiles and parts for simple launch systems. For lack of agreed, effective verification procedures, SALT does not ban such extra production and stockpiling, except in the vicinity of the recognized and counted launchers. U.S. attempts to take advantage of this loophole would surely meet with failure. The Soviet Union, on the other hand, with its lack of public accounting and ineffective public opinion (at least in military matters) can choose this route to provide itself with reserves.

SALT II affects ICBM launcher survivability through the overall limits, the freedom-to-mix provision, and the provisions concerning specific systems. The overall limits are high, as we have seen—too high to provide relief from the vulnerability of ICBMs as they are now deployed. They do prevent force levels from going even higher and the task of devising survivable ICBM deployment modes from being even harder than it is. They are imposed both on the numbers of launchers and on the number of RVs and throw-weight. Since the latter limits were sized to the much larger Soviet numbers, they provide a political incentive for U.S. growth in these parameters (via, e.g., the MX) that is difficult to resist. It would be more effective to have a single and tighter limit on overall missile capability—for instance, on the product of missile size appropriately defined and the number of missiles.

Freedom to mix among permitted systems allow deployment of ICBMs on aircraft and submarines, both of which are expected to have substantial survivability for some time to come, if properly designed and operated. Relying solely on these two types of systems would reduce significantly the complexity of the first-strike scenarios, however, particularly so if large reductions in numbers of systems were to be carried out. For that reason, the provisions that limit the possibilities for rebasing ICBMs other than on aircraft and submarines are of concern.

Such rebasing methods as have been considered rely on hardness, mobility, or deception, or some combination of these. Relying simply on hardness would require deep underground basing, which would be prohibited by the ban on silo relocation, as noted above. In the U.S. view, at least,[13] the most widely discussed rebasing system is permited by SALT II. The multiple protective shelter system (MPS) has the ICBMs and essential launch equipment hidden among a greater number of hardened shelters, spaced far enough apart so that each one must be attacked with a separate RV. This system relies on a combination of hardness and deception. (A variant includes mobility also, via the ability to dash on warning to a shelter, in case the location of the missile is compromised.)

SALT II would both help and hurt the survivability of the MPS system. It would help by limiting the number of RVs available for an attack from the counted and limited launchers, though the limit is high. It would hurt because, as we have seen, there can be other RVs, uncounted and unlimited. In particular, the existence of a U.S. system that can be destroyed by attacking a definite and known number of targets may provide an incentive to the Soviet Union to add to its reserve RVs and assign some of them to the destruction of the MPS system.

Other land-mobile systems could be developed and deployed under SALT II, after the protocol period expires. Those without hardened shelters would require more deception and more access to highways or railroads than is likely to be practicable in the U.S. Some land- and some air-mobile systems would require that small missiles be used. These would be seriously handicapped by the SALT II limit on number of launchers, even though the total system need not carry more throw-weight or destructive power than a system using large missiles. Small missile systems also cost more for a given throw-weight than large missile systems.

SALT II also bans the deployment of ICBMs on sea and lake beds, on ships, and on orbital vehicles. Arguments have been given for and against the utility of all of these systems; few, if any, can be ruled out. Which system that turns out to be advantageous from the standpoints of survivability, cost, environment, verification, safety, and so forth depends on technical and political factors that are not reliably predictable. This unpredictability constitutes a strong argument against incorporating into SALT, in the name of limiting a qualitative arms race, prohibitions against poorly understood possible modes of deployment. In the long run, such prohibitions will work against the acceptability of reductions. A better policy would incorporate all systems under overall limitations on offensive power, with provisions for rejecting systems if adequate verification procedures cannot be negotiated.

In summary, it may be said that SALT II has little effect on first-strike capabilities, such as they are or might be and almost no effect on countervalue second-strike capabilities. It has a mixed and possibly important effect on the countervailing capabilities that appear to have governed to a significant extent the size and makeup of both U.S. and Soviet strategic forces.

SALT II AND THE ARMS COMPETITION

This section advances arguments usually given for and against adherence to SALT II. Most of these arguments center on the questions of whether or not SALT II is biased, is needed to prevent a major Soviet buildup, and is an effective limitation on arms competition.

1. Is SALT II Biased?

While evenhanded in the language of its provisions, the treaty is rife with asymmetries in its implications. Only the Soviet Union can have heavy missiles and a Backfire exemption, for instance. Only the United States has forward-based systems that can reach the Soviet Union, and these are not limited. Only the United States derives a significant advantage from ALCMs today and for some time to come, but that is in part because only the Soviet Union has significant strategic air defenses. Only the Soviet Union has to cut back on the total number of strategic systems, but that is because it has built more of them than the United States.

Given the different geopolitical situations and histories of the two sides, asymmetries are inevitable. Looking for complete symmetry would not only foreclose the possibility of meaningful agreement, it would lead to proposals that would be rejected by the defense establishments of both sides. The United States chose smaller missiles, major reliance on submarines, and significant investments in European-based systems for what it considered good reasons. Presumably the Soviet Union made its different choices in a similarly deliberate way.

The task of negotiation at SALT is to balance, limit, and eventually reduce these "apples and oranges," these different systems selected by both sides. In this instance, the force structures were left very much as they had been planned before the treaty. Perhaps the plans were wrong. But it is difficult to argue that a SALT agreement that grants each side almost everything it has plus, for the United States at least, considerable room to grow is biased because of one or another asymmetry viewed in isolation.

2. Is SALT Needed to Prevent a Major Gap from Opening up in Favor of the Soviet Union?

The Soviet capability to add significantly to its strategic forces can be forecast reasonably well from available intelligence data. Although there is uncertainty in specific numbers and therefore uncertainty in the Soviet capability to attack any specific U.S. system, the overall Soviet resources that can be applied and the patterns of Soviet development and deployment are sufficiently well understood as to provide the basis for reasonably secure estimates of overall capabilities. The Soviet pattern for acquisition of strategic forces has been characterized by regularity: regular progression in technological quality, retention of older equipment along with the new, phasing of arms control positions with the successive five-year plans, and a continuing high level of investment as a proportion of total national resources, by U.S. standards.

On the basis of these observations, it is quite likely that the United States will see major new weapon systems replace some of the old in the Soviet inventory, SALT or no SALT. If SALT is adhered to, older systems would be retired so that the total accords with the limits of the treaty. If SALT is not adhered to, some of the older systems might be retained, in the shorter run, and the production of new ones might be extended beyond what was planned for the SALT II regime, in the longer run.

It seems unlikely, however, that the Soviet Union has the unused design and construction capability needed to deploy over the short run much larger numbers of new systems than it had planned. Maintaining such excess capability is extremely expensive for any country, and it is especially so for the Soviet Union, where technologically sophisticated design and production capabilities are at a premium. Taking resources away from other defense objectives may be possible and may be done if the Soviet policymakers conclude that the U.S. strategic challenge warrants it, but it would be a difficult decision to make, and the net result so far as the overall balance of power is concerned would be ambiguous.

The U.S. capability to build strategic systems in excess of what would be done under SALT II is better understood. The limitation here would not be technologically sophisticated design and production capability but the willingness of the American electorate to furnish the extra dollars and manpower needed to build and staff an expanded strategic force. There is little question that the MX design could be completed, for instance, and an increased MX production rate could result in replacing every Minuteman with MXs during the latter half of this decade. The displaced Minuteman missiles could, for instance, be modified for launch from C-5As on much the same time scale. The design for an accurate D-5 missile for Trident submarines could be completed in time to have these at sea in significant numbers by the end of the decade. Meanwhile, the United States could stop retiring old Polaris boats, as it has been doing. More

B-52s could be fitted with cruise missiles, and more could be placed on alert.

Whether or not these things would be done on a time-scale that would match the time-scale of a Soviet buildup is uncertain. It is clear that sufficient money and military manpower would avoid a gap of any more major proportion than the one already developing concerning ICBM launcher vulnerability. Most probably in fact, in the event of an all-out race with adequate political support in the United States, this gap would close sooner than might be expected under SALT II. If the will is there, the U.S. capability is significantly greater than that of the Soviet Union, on a time-scale as short as five years.

The will, of course, would not be there, except under major provocation. An all-out strategic arms race, absent such provocation, would be an expensive, dangerous, and possibly disastrous misallocation of national resources, one that no one in any responsible position has advocated. The only possible provocation would be an equally dangerous and possibly disastrous initiative on the part of the Soviet Union, either in the strategic nuclear area or in some other. On the basis of its track record, it is unlikely that the Brezhnev Administration would provide that provocation. Even an invasion of Poland, while it may make reaching a SALT agreement politically impossible and also cause a strengthening of forces in Europe, would seem unlikely to be either intended by the Soviet Union or read by the United States as a provocation to an all-out strategic arms race. There is abundant evidence that both sides perceive (correctly, in this writer's opinion) the costs and dangers of such an arms race to be too great.

It seems unlikely, therefore, that the U.S. relative strategic position need deteriorate if SALT II is not signed. Whether it would in fact so deteriorate depends on political factors that cannot be reliably predicted, without some knowledge of what the rest of the relevant world would look like. What is clear is that some properly framed agreement—whether formal treaty or informal or even tacit accord—would be useful as a guide and a limitation on further strategic expenditures and as a help in insuring that the strategic forces remain primarily deterrents to adventurous actions rather than provocations to such actions. That insurance—and not the threat of some gap opening up or some putative Soviet capability ready to be unleashed and containable only by a SALT treaty—is a strong incentive for reaching accord on strategic forces, granted that such accord is otherwise desirable.

3. Is SALT II an Effective Limitation on Arms Competition?

This question lies, of course, at the heart of our inquiry. Numerically, SALT holds the line on arms at a very high level. To those who believe that a counterindustrial and counterpopulation capability is a sufficient deterrent, the numbers are obscenely high. Even to those who believe that the possibility of mutual suicide is not enough and that a potential attacker must be denied any hope of military advantage, the numbers could still be cut considerably if two conditions were met. There must be freedom to build survivable systems and to change them as technology and other factors change, and there must be verification procedures that remain adequate at the lower levels of armaments.

Qualitatively, there is no doubt that the limits in SALT II could be more comprehensive and more relevant to what is to be limited—namely, offensive nuclear power. Provisions could be found that would permit the development and deployment of most survivable systems and allow adequate verification. With Soviet cooperation, more meaningful verification procedures for the present SALT provisions could be designed.

The effectiveness of SALT II, however, like the effectiveness of any political measure, must be evaluated relative to the effectiveness of other possible courses of action. The alternatives, at a minimum include the possibility of some improvements, the possibility that a worse agreement could be negotiated, and the possibility of no agreement. They probably do not include the possibility of a drastically different agreement. The compromises within the Soviet government that made SALT II possible are not likely to be built anew on short notice, barring major change in the political or the strategic situation. Further negotiations could produce some very welcome improvements but no major changes in the newly promulgated five-year plan or in the consequent future Soviet deployments, for instance.

In order to decide on the effectiveness of SALT II, therefore, we must decide important questions of timing and specific provisions. We must also decide whether it is better to manage jointly the processes of mutual nuclear deterrence and hope thereby gradually to dampen their cost and risks or to give up on joint management and return to unilateral U.S. defense decisionmaking—or at least to decisionmaking not formally coordinated with the Soviet Union. To discuss this question, we must address the nature of relations between the United States and the Soviet Union and its basis in the politics and attitudes of the two countries.

EVALUATION AND RECOMMENDATION

The styles of Soviet leaders have differed, but the foreign and defense policies of the Soviet Union have changed little in the years since World War II. Although the foreign and defense policies of major nations usually change slowly, those of the Soviet Union have changed more slowly than most. Its main features have been and continue to be: conventional diplomacy in the service of a changeable mixture of pragmatism and communist militancy; steady and costly buildup of military strength; willingness to use that strength along its boundaries, when deemed safe, for the purpose of installing and maintaining acceptable political regimes; and political aggressiveness mixed with military caution elsewhere. The Soviet attitude toward the Western polity is complex. It involves respect of its strength; contempt of its overriding priority on consumer satisfaction and its deference to many conflicting political forces; and envy of its success in providing its peoples and others with material goods, technological advances, and perhaps other, less tangible cultural advantages.

The roots of these policies and attitudes in the history of Russia and in the present circumstances of the Soviet government have been abundantly studied. While analyses differ somewhat, no one expects the policies to change rapidly, so long as the Soviet government is not faced with or does not lead itself into situations with which it cannot deal by its usual methods. Such situations may occur and one must be alert to their possibility, but they cannot provide the basis for American policy.

In particular, the Soviet Union has defined in words and demonstrated in deeds what it believes its strategic relationship with the United States should be: coexistence with competiton. "Coexistence" means avoiding what might lead to nuclear war, including direct confrontation and confrontation in areas that the United States cannot (or thinks it cannot) do without. "Competition" means not avoiding much of anything else: not avoiding armed aggression in other areas, for instance, and attempting to destroy politically the foundations for U.S. alliances and domestic U.S. support for effective defenses. There is little reason to believe that this policy will change rapidly.

The Soviet approach to SALT seems to fit within this policy. The emphasis on forward-based systems stems both from military concerns and a desire to split NATO. The SALT process, aided by considerable Soviet propaganda initiatives,[14] helps focus the disarmament constituency in the United States and Europe on opposition to U.S. strategic arms rather than Soviet arms, opposition to which would be obviously ineffective. The Soviet Union has opposed at SALT every U.S. weapon system initiative, though, there as with the forward-based systems, it has been willing to settle when the United States has stood firm.

On the other hand, the Soviet Union has respected the letter of the agreements in the overwhelming majority of the cases.[15] While not accepting any responsibility not to put U.S. forces or U.S. alliances at risk, it has accepted the fact that the United States can and would take steps to preserve both the forces and the alliances. In sum, it has behaved as a government that wants to avoid risks of war and serious confrontation—whether these risks come from a dangerous strategic arms race or from some other point of the compass—but that otherwise does not take the relaxation of tensions as a primary purpose.

Thus, to the extent the United States believes that SALT can be useful on its own, without necessarily having beneficial effects on other aspects of the competition, a durable agreement should be possible. To the extent the United States does not believe this, agreement is bound to be fragile.

This brings us to the matter of judging political attitudes toward SALT in the United States. Extremes in American political life have usually argued against SALT as a delusion and a moral fraud, whether the threat is viewed as the Soviet Union, the American social and political way of life, or the international system. The great majority of the electorate has disagreed with these extreme views, however, and disagreed in the language that matters most for policy—namely, who was voted into office. Both President Reagan and President Carter campaigned on the platform of meaningful arms control, as has every other president of recent times. Presidential candidates who have departed from the formula of meaningful defenses together with meaningful arms control have been massively defeated (e.g., McGovern and Goldwater). The electorate apparently wants a serious effort at both defense and arms control and has voted for this combination since World War II. The great majority of both houses of Congress has reflected the same view.

It seems unlikely, based on popular and congressional sentiments expressed over the period, that this stance is based on an unduly rosy view of Soviet goals and methods. Quite the contrary, the electorate and its representatives seem—on the basis of the body of laws passed regarding not only defense but internal security and trade agreements —to be more robustly suspicious of the Soviet Union (pocketbook issues apart) than are most concerned intellectuals. The ascription of motives to electoral mandates must be speculative, but it seems reasonable to ascribe the popular stance to the pragmatic view that the United States has an adversary—an enemy, perhaps—but that one does business with adversaries all the time and with enemies when necessary. Keeping U.S. defenses up while minimizing the cost and risk associated with those defenses seems to be the message.

A significant group within this general U.S. consensus ascribes special importance to SALT and other arms control negotiations and would take them out of the normal framework of the U.S.-USSR relations or at least give them overriding priority within this framework. In this group's view, the nuclear weapons themselves and the competition in nuclear weapons are the major dangers, and limiting them is by itself a major amelioration of the risk of nuclear war, notwithstanding Soviet behavior in other areas.

Another significant group is unwilling to accept SALT on Soviet terms, SALT without beneficial effects on other aspects of Soviet behavior, or SALT without linkage. This group's membership swells in the wake of such actions as the invasion of Czechoslovakia in 1968 and of Afghanistan in 1979, but, after a time, it is hard to see the impact of its views on governmental actions. Perhaps some concessions of detail have been won, but, on the whole, Soviet patterns of behavior have not been changed by SALT.

Most of the time, U.S. administrations observe in practice the electorate's injunction to work seriously on both effective strategic forces and arms control negotiations, and for good reasons. First, we do not know enough arms theory to keep the peace. The race to arm has obvious great dangers, but a race to disarm, or unilateral steps to disarmament, could leave one side or the other in a position where it could not (or thought it could not) take steps to remedy a dangerous situation. It might then rearm or try other risky remedies in a time of crisis. Keeping up both secure armaments and the efforts to limit them allows the governments on both sides to proceed cautiously in times of danger.

Second, there are overriding practical arguments for the electoral message being the policy. Not only is it likely to be the only policy supported at the polls, but the existence of strong electoral views on the desirability of combining defense and arms control efforts makes this policy the most likely to succeed internationally as well. Domestic support for policies is perhaps the most important coin of the international realm.

Tactically, the present circumstances are unique, or nearly so, in SALT history. President Reagan has expressed both support of arms control in principle and dissatisfaction with the results to date, at a time when approval of the SALT II Treaty hangs in the balance. He also has called for improvements in U.S. strategic forces at a time when several important new programs are up for decision: the MX missile and basing system, a new bomber, and more accurate missiles for the Trident submarine. He thus finds himself, in the short run at least, with considerable flexibility to take initiatives regarding both SALT and strategic forces, to coordinate these initiatives, and to follow through with political support at home and therefore with clout abroad. The United States thereby has an unusual opportunity to pursue initiatives in its new strategic weapon deployments and at SALT that can help the cause of stable relations.[16]

Granting then that both secure deterrent forces and effective arms limitations will continue to be pursued, the United States appears likely in the next few years to set important precedents regarding the new strategic weapon systems it chooses to pursue and to argue for—whether MPS or other mobile system, large missile or small, ballistic missile defense or not, and silo relocation or not. As a result, the systems should be evaluated carefully for their long-run implications. The considerations bearing on the choice include:

- Does the system promise lasting survivability in the face of likely technological evolution? There is no survivability panacea, of course, but some systems will probably be much more difficult to attack as time goes on than others (e.g., submarines, certain aircraft, and deeply buried missiles).
- Is the system synergistic with other deployed systems, so that the whole is more difficult to attack than each part? Bombers and hard ICBM launchers are the usual examples.
- Does the system offer a reserve capability? Not all systems need it, but some do in order to maximize crisis deterrence.

- Does the system offer the possibility of lasting and redundant communication and control means? No aspect of survivability is as important for deterrence as that of communication and control.
- Can limits on the system be verified, particularly taking into account likely improvements in national technical means? It is necessary to look beyond current and past capabilities in making this judgment. How intrusive are the likely methods of verification?
- Does the system possess versatile targeting capabilities that are amenable to changes in doctrine and to reductions? Most systems can probably be made accurate in the future, but a variety of other considerations (time to target, number of weapons) affect versatility.

Turning to strategic arms limitations it should be remembered that many features of the SALT II treaty came about as a result of and reinforced some improvements in the American-Soviet dialogue (i.e., the agreement that both sides would provide facts relevant to their strategic system deployments; the willingness to extend nonconcealment provisions to relevant test programs; acceptance of limits on size of missiles and on total number of deployed weapons). These provisions, such as acceptance of limits on size of missiles and on total number of deployed weapons, have lasting value. To discard them because they do not go far enough seems unlikely to lead to any progress in U.S.-Soviet relations.

Such SALT II provisions might well be retained, together with the introduction of modifications that would allay concerns expressed in this chapter. The modifications might:

1. Broaden freedom to mix to include new and not specifically defined systems, subject to the verification and overall limits provisions;
2. Tighten the limits on total throw-weight and total number of weapons (RVs, ALCMs, bombs), while recognizing the possibility that more small delivery vehicles might be needed later if not now;
3. Deal with verifiability on a system-by-system basis. In general, verification of the numbers and characteristics of large mobile systems (airplanes, submarines, mobile missiles) that require manpower, exercises, and maintenance facilities to make them effective is easier and surer (to the accuracy needed to assure that the strategic balance is being maintained, if not that needed

to satisfy all observers that no one is cheating) than verification of the number of items (missiles, bomb) produced and warehoused. This gives flexibility in some directions and not others, and specific verification rules might be negotiated accordingly.

The present administration is politically well-positioned to preserve valuable accomplishments in the treaty as well as to make suitable modifications along the lines described. The President's speech in Eureka and Brezhnev's response suggest that the talks could be resumed soon. Negotiations must be accompanied by strategic initiatives to protect the U.S. deterrent. Improvements should be expected to come gradually. Since it is unlikely that a SALT agreement will affect Soviet behavior elsewhere or that it is needed to prevent a Soviet strategic advantage, there is every reason to take the time to work toward a satisfactory agreement. A compromise policy of this type probably has the best chance of enlisting popular support and therefore the best chance of being successful.

NOTES

1. Thomas Graham, former general counsel, Arms Control and Disarmament Agency, private communication (March 18, 1981).
2. *Ibid.*
3. *Ibid.*
4. *The New York Times* (March 4, 1981).
5. *The New York Times* (February 4, 1981).
6. *The New York Times* (March 4, 1981).
7. (a) Selected Documents No. 12B, SALT II Agreement, Vienna June 18, 1979 (Department of State Publication No. 8986, released July 1979).

    (b) The International Institute for Strategic Studies, *The Military Balance 1980–1981* (IISS, 1980).

    Document 7(a) provides the treaty definitions of "light" and "heavy" ICBMs and, in an annex, an analysis of the treaty by Secretary of State Vance. On page 17 a unilateral U.S. definition of the parameters of the SS-19, the heaviest light ICBM, is given.

    Document 7(b), in tables on pages 88–89 provides estimates of throw-weights for Minuteman, SS-19, and SS-18.

8. See Note 7(a) which includes the Soviet Backfire Statement on page 58. This reference is to a written Soviet statement on Backfire, a clarifying remark by President Brezhnev, and a statement by President Carter.
9. (a) Harold L. Brode, "A Review of Nuclear Weapons Effects," *Annual Review of Nuclear Science 18* (1968):153–202.

(b) Robert R. Soule, "Counterforce Issues for the U.S. Strategic Nuclear Forces," The Congress of the United States, Congressional Budget Office (Washington, D.C.: Government Printing Office, January 1978).
Document 9(a) gives the relationships between blast overpressure, nuclear weapon yield, and distance from the explosion. See especially page 180.
Document 9(b) provides unclassified analyses of strategic force vulnerabilities and some reasonable estimates of how "hard" Minuteman silos are. See pages 10 and 60.

10. Harold Brown, *Annual Report of the Secretary of Defense: Fiscal Year 1980* (Government Printing Office, January 25, 1979):75–79.

11. Office of Technology Assessment, "The Effects of Nuclear War" (Government Printing Office, May 1979).

12. Harold Brown, *Annual Report of the Secretary of Defense: Fiscal Year 1980* (Government Printing Office, January 25, 1979), pp. 74–81.

13. (a) Ralph Earle II, Statement of September 12, 1979 before Senate Foreign Relations Committee, *Congressional Record* 125, no. 121 (September 19, 1979):S13067–68.
(b) Statement Submitted to the Congress by the President Pursuant to Section 36 of the Arms Control and Disarmament Act, Fiscal Year 1982 Arms Control Impact Statements (February 1981).

14. Typical of recent high-level Soviet statements on forward-based systems and arms control are the following:

President Brezhnev, *The New York Times* (June 10, 1981):10; (June 13, 1981):3; (June 24, 1981):3.

Foreign Minister Gromyko, *The New York Times* (June 16, 1981):6.

15. (a) Robert W. Buchheim, in Hearings Before the Committee on Foreign Relations of the U.S. Senate, 96th Congress, 1st Session, "Briefing on SALT I Compliance by Robert W. Buchheim, U.S. Commissioner on the Standing Consultative Commission, and Sidney Graybeal, Former Commissioner" (September 25, 1979; secret hearings declassified November 7, 1979).
(b) See also a speech by Ambassador Buchheim on this topic published in the *Congressional Record* (May 11, 1979):S4729–32.

16. The administration has made certain strategic weapons decisions since this chapter was written. There remains opportunity to coordinate the U.S. SALT position with these decisions.

10 THE FUTURE OF STRATEGIC ARMS CONTROL

Joseph S. Nye

For more than a decade, the Strategic Arms Limitation Treaty (SALT) talks played a central role in U.S.-Soviet relations. The U.S. failure to ratify the SALT II treaty after seven years of negotiation by three administrations left both arms control and U.S.-Soviet relations in considerable disarray in the early 1980s. The Reagan Administration has called for a tougher posture toward the Soviet Union. It has also spoken, with several voices, in favor of renewed arms control talks, but the internal preferences of administration officials range from no arms control to deep cuts in strategic weapons. Despite the rhetoric of linkage, the connection of arms control negotiations with the overall U.S.-Soviet political relationship remains unclear.

It has become commonplace to observe that arms control is a political, not a technical, process. As such, arms control policy cannot be formulated or implemented in a vacuum but must be fully integrated with defense and foreign policy. One cannot think of arms control policy without specifying its role in overall U.S.-Soviet relations. In the 1970s, SALT was the focal point of arms control policy, and it was embedded in the concept of detente or relaxation of tensions in U.S.-Soviet relations. SALT became the centerpiece of detente. As one participant described the early 1970s, "the strong feeling was that SALT should be regarded as part of a 'process.' . . .

223

SALT, therefore, was of less interest for its technical achievement than for its political impact in the U.S.S.R."[1]

With the demise of detente in U.S.-Soviet relations (though not in European-Soviet relations, as will be discussed below), arms control policy must be readjusted to fit a period of difficult relations. Hostility does not make arms control impossible. Arms control antedated detente and could, in principle, survive it. Indeed, arms control may be unduly constrained if it is tied too closely to detente and to the processes of the 1970s. As two early theorists of arms control warned in 1961,

> the least favorable prognosis is probably for an agreement that one party expects to symbolize the burying of the hatchet, a new era of good feeling, and a resolution to live up to new standards of international friendship, while the other takes for granted that "realistic" diplomacy will prevail, subject only to the concrete measures agreed on. In this case, acute disappointment and recrimination might result, and the greatest of misunderstandings.[2]

This chapter discusses some of the problems of and prospects for adjusting the arms control process to fit the post-detente period.

U.S.-SOVIET RELATIONS

Americans tend to view international politics from a liberal historical perspective in which peaceful and harmonious relations are the normal condition. Thus, U.S.-Soviet relations should eventually return to this norm. Such expectations may be frustrated, however. There are several deep-seated reasons to believe that tension is likely to be a continual feature in U.S.-Soviet relations. First, as Tocqueville saw in the nineteenth century, the enormous size and resources of the Russian and American nations foreshadowed a future bipolar rivalry. Then in 1917, the Bolshevik revolution added a layer of deep ideological incompatibility. When the Second World War destroyed the multination balance of power existing before 1939, it left a bipolar structure of world power centered on the U.S.-Soviet rivalry. The accumulation of vast nuclear arsenals overshadowing those of all other nations has consolidated that special relationship. From a power politics point of view, the probability of tension is built into the very structure of the relationship.[3]

Nonetheless, at different times there have been different degrees of tension and hostility. In fact, there have been six major phases in U.S. policy toward the Soviet Union. Our first policies toward the Soviet Union stressed ostracism. In the 1930s, we turned to recognition and trade, and in the 1940s, of course, came the wartime alliance. Since the war, there have been three major phases: Cold War from the late 1940s to the early 1960s; deepening detente in the 1960s and early 1970s; and renewed tension since the mid-1970s. In no period, however, was the relationship warm or easy.[4]

While there have been changes in the Soviet polity—Brezhnev's Russia is certainly not the same as Stalin's—and in Soviet foreign policy, Soviet objectives have probably changed less than American perceptions of them. Both Russian history and Communist ideology have given a conflictual, expansionist, and military cast to the Soviets' declared policy goals.[5] While there are differences of view among experts regarding the defensive versus offensive roots of expansion, its planned or opportunistic nature, and the degree of risk that Soviet leaders would bear to achieve these goals in the face of constraints, most tend to agree that there has been a degree of consistency in Soviet objectives, albeit considerable variety in Soviet tactics.

At the same time, American attitudes, responding in part to Soviet moves and in part to the requirements of democratic politics, have tended to alternate between overemphasis and underemphasis on the threatening nature of Soviet objectives and between different approaches to containing Soviet power. The result has been an inconsistency in policy and missed opportunities. During the Cold War, our exaggeration of Soviet capabilities prevented us from negotiating at a time when our position was strong. As Adam Ulam has written, "long-range solutions can be reached in this sinful world only through short-range and partial accommodations. The tragedy of 1949–50 was that no such negotiations took place. Moreover, the net effect of our nuclear superiority debilitated rather than helped American foreign policy."[6] Subsequently, the ideological interpretation of policy and domestic political constraints prevented American policy from exploiting the diplomatic opportunities in the Sino-Soviet split for more than a decade after it occurred in the late 1950s. Conversely, the enthusiasm for detente in the 1960s and early 1970s led some American officials to underestimate the Soviet military buildup, delay an appropriate response, and encourage false domestic expectations of future restraint in Soviet international behavior.[7]

Certainly, changing Soviet tactics have helped trigger American policy changes, but the exaggeration in American attitudes may develop as much in domestic political pressures and reactions toward previous swings of the policy pendulum as from the actual changes in Soviet behavior.[8] Ironically, low but realistic expectations about Soviet behavior serve to dampen the degrees of exaggeration that have characterized previous alterations in American policy toward the Soviet Union. Arms control embedded in a rational expectation of continuing tension may prove more durable than arms control that becomes associated with exaggerated expectations of improved relations. Balance of power concepts and controlled wariness may prove a firmer foundation than hopes of revived detente.

BALANCE OF POWER
AND PRUDENT PRACTICE

An understanding of the balance of power and maintenance of a perceived stable balance is the bedrock of successful foreign policy as well as arms control. There are several distinctive features of the U.S.-Soviet balance of power since 1945. First, it is bipolar. Many theorists have argued that the reduced flexibility and focused hostility of a two-country balance leads it either to erode or explode. One reason this has not occurred is that it is the first nuclear balance of power. Indeed, this second feature has led it to be called a balance of terror. The destructiveness of nuclear weapons introduces a disproportion between most ends that the superpowers seek and the major military means at their disposal. The result is that general wars cannot play their traditional role as "moments of truth" in calibrating the balance in world politics. In this sense, nuclear crises are the functional equivalent of war, but such crises involve huge risks. The balance of nuclear terror introduces an element of prudence or foresight of potential consequences. It is as if the statesmen of 1914 who expected a short general war had been handed a crystal ball with a vision of the disastrous 1918 outcome.

This leads to a third feature of the balance, the evolution by a process of trial and error of some primitive rules for avoiding crises. The rules are so primitive that they might more correctly be called prudent practices. As described by Stanley Hoffmann, one such informal rule was the non-resort to atomic weapons. . . . A second rule was the avoidance of direct military clashes between the armed forces. This meant that their games of chicken had to end with the retreat of one of the players rather than with a fight. . . . A third element was the slow (and for America) painful learning of limited wars . . . calculated so as to limit the risks of escalation, even if those constraints made a clearcut victory or a rapid settlement impossible. Later came the beginnings of nuclear arms control between Washington and Moscow.[9]

In addition, there was observance of rough spheres of influence in contiguous areas. Rudimentary as these rules or prudent practices are, they are significant if one believes that maintenance of peace requires a degree of moderation in the actors' behavior, as well as military balance.

When there is a degree of common interest in stability, maintaining the balance of power can become a joint benefit game in which neither side loses. Indeed, an international "regime"—a set of tacit or explicit rules and procedures—may be developed to encourage a stabilizing perspective of long-range rather than short-range self-interest. The nineteenth century balance of power system and the contrast between Bismarck's restraint and the failure of his successors is often cited as an example.

To say that the postwar U.S.-Soviet balance of power has been embedded in such a regime would be to stretch the point.[10] The rules are ambiguous and not openly accepted by both sides. In 1972 and 1973, Nixon and Brezhnev signed agreements that seemed to codify the rules, but the ambiguities (such as exceptions for wars of national liberation) later led to a sense of cheating and deception after the Middle East war of 1973 and the events in Angola in 1975 and 1976. Moreover, an agreed regime implies reciprocity and flexibility in bargaining behavior as the opponents seek to avoid jeopardizing the regime. In U.S.-Soviet relations, however, reciprocity has proven to be limited in time and on issues. It is difficult to "bank good-will" from one time or issue to another in the relationship. While both sides have a degree of interest in preserving a limited stability in the form of preserving the basic nuclear bipolarity and the avoidance of nuclear war, their competition makes it impossible to agree on a broader political status quo. Thus while a common interest exists, it is limited largely to the avoidance of nuclear war and is severely strained by the competitive political dimension.

Over the past two decades, the military dimensions of the U.S.-Soviet balance shifted. The CIA estimates that from 1971 to 1980, the Soviets consistently added 3 percent a year to their total defense efforts, while real U.S. defense spending in 1980 was the same as it was in 1960 (discounting inflation). Such figures fail to reflect the fact that the Soviet Union also faces a threat from China and that when alliances are compared, NATO actually slightly outspends the Warsaw Pact. Moreover, defense spending is a crude measure of inputs, rather than outputs. Nonetheless, as a Carnegie panel concluded, "we can say with some confidence that Soviet increases in defense expenditures, especially in the area of investment, have led and will continue to lead to improved military capability relative to the United States."[8] Specific improvements in Soviet nuclear and conventional military capabilities have created anxiety in the West. On the other side, in the early part of the decade, American power was limited by introspective moral and social concerns in the aftermath of Vietnam and Watergate. The United States spent less in real terms on defense, foreign aid, embassies, and foreign broadcasting than it did in 1960. Moreover, there was no political consensus on how to bring the non-military aspects of American power (such as our almost 2 to 1 advantage in GNP; our grain reserves, and our advanced technology) to bear upon U.S.-Soviet relations. Different groups resisted or insisted on their preferred linkages. In these circumstances of shifting power, domestic dissent, and ambiguous rules, it was not surprising that Soviet tactics proved adventuresome. Nor is it surprising that efforts to develop the prudent practices into a regime failed. By the end of the decade and well before the 1980 election, American attitudes had changed, and this change affected the SALT process even before the Soviet invasion of Afghanistan.[12]

FUTURE DIRECTIONS OF
STRATEGIC ARMS CONTROL

The current disarray in strategic arms control may be traced to the failure of the Senate to ratify SALT II in 1979 and the subsequent electoral politics in 1980. Well before the 1980 election, however, even sympathetic critics expressed various concerns about the lengthy and cumbersome nature of the SALT process. As one former participant put it, "most arms control negotiations have taken so long to complete, that each time the wave of political opposition and new negotiating problems has become truly formidable."[13]

Critics on the right charged that placing limits on strategic launchers rather than throw-weight failed to remove the threat posed by the Soviets' MIRVed missiles. Critics on the left also complained about inadequate reductions and the failure to make real savings in defense possible. Moreover, both the negotiation and ratification aspects of the treaty process raised to an undue prominence the details of how the treaty would be verified. Verification is never perfect, and the effort to maximize verifiability may actually have limited some of the security benefits that could be attained. At the same time, undue emphasis on verification would raise political problems by focusing debate on whether we could ever trust the Russians. Thus, the formal treaty process proved to be expensive in terms of political capital. Not only did the Senate's two-thirds ratification requirement set a high threshold in domestic politics, but the negotiating process was lengthy and cumbersome to coordinate within the government and with our allies.

More important than the specific details of the treaty, however, was the high visibility and centrality of the formal treaty process, which meant that even if political leaders had avoided tactical linkage, there would have been a strong inherent linkage to the overall state of U.S.-Soviet relations. As shall be discussed below, a certain degree of linkage is inevitable and may at times be desirable, but SALT in the visible centerpiece role was not sufficient to transform U.S.-Soviet relations.

> In effect, the SALT talks became a weathervane of U.S.-Soviet relations, the centerpiece and primary symbol of a certain model of that relationship. As such, the talks were criticized by, indeed contributed to, the creation of a coalition of dedicated opponents who fought both the treaties and the process which led to them, as much for what they implied for U.S.-Soviet relations as for whatever specific limitations they did or did not impose on American and Soviet nuclear weapons.[14]

Even before the 1980 election, therefore, there were concerns about whether the gains from the formal SALT treaty process were commensurate with the political costs and whether the balance between costs and gains could be improved if the strategic arms control process were altered in the future. Ironically, the *de facto* observance of critical aspects of the unratified treaty by the new administration is already a departure in process, which avoids some political costs and indicates an interest in reaping the security benefits. How long that can continue is an open question.

Given the political problems that engulfed SALT in 1980, the future of strategic arms control is uncertain. At least five major paths have been suggested, and will be examined in turn: revival of SALT II, no arms control, deep cuts, informal arms control, and multitrack nuclear stabilization talks that would encompass SALT but make it less central in U.S.-Soviet relations.

REVIVAL OF SALT II

A simple but unlikely path would be to pretend that 1980 never happened: no linkage to the Soviet invasion of Afghanistan, no election in which the winning candidate declared the SALT II Treaty to be fatally flawed. The fact that the new administration has lived within the bounds of a de facto SALT II world is cited as evidence that the revival and ratification of SALT II is not impossible. It is not difficult to imagine a renegotiation of elements of the treaty, either cosmetic or far-reaching, that would allow President Reagan to put forward SALT II or II-A as his own.[15] It is more difficult to see the politics working out. Renegotiations that are largely cosmetic may be acceptable to Moscow but not enough for the current administration. Renegotiations that are profound enough to satisfy the administration may prove unacceptable in Moscow. The political leeway is narrow, perhaps large enough only to support de facto observance of the unratified treaty until some political shock or new weapons program or a new arms control proposal overtakes it.

NO ARMS CONTROL

A sharply contrasting path but one with some adherents within the administration is to hold back on serious arms control initiatives. In this view, strategic arms control is exhausted and should be avoided because it is technologically unrealistic, has a distorting effect on Western defense efforts, and is bound to hurt the West more than the Soviet Union.

Opponents argue that since weapons technology is inherently unpredictable in the long run, efforts to constrain it within formal frameworks are bound to be frustrating and frustrated. Efforts to constrain technology are compared by these individuals to squeezing in a balloon: It gives in one place only to protrude in another area, one that may be more dangerous. Moreover, some new technologies may be stabilizing—witness the effect of strategic submarines in the early 1960s. It is difficult to know the ultimate effect of a technology in its early stages, particularly as it continues to evolve under the normal process of creeping improvements.[16] These are not empty arguments. They serve as important caveats against premature rigidity and overformalism, but they do not prove the impossibility or undesirability of *all* arms control—as shall be explained below.

A second point made by the opponents is that arms control has a distorting effect on Western defense efforts by developing a momentum of its own and integrating poorly with defense planning. Moreover, they maintain arms control has a lulling effect in the West, relaxing public support for defense expenditures. The same is not true for the Soviet Union; thus, their constant willingness to engage in the process. Specifically, it is alleged, the SALT process caused the United States to fail to respond to the Soviet military buildup in the 1970s.

As a matter of history, arms control may not have cured the imbalance between Soviet and American defense spending that developed in the 1970s, but neither was it the cause. In the early part of the decade, the impetus to cut defense budgets grew from reaction against the Vietnam war and from domestic social changes. As Kissinger has noted, in 1969, " 'reordering national priorities' was the slogan of the period." Critics even "drew from the approaching nuclear parity the amazing conclusion that one should cut our conventional forces in which we were already vastly inferior."[17] All this was well before SALT was negotiated. If anything, the debate surrounding SALT heightened attention to strategic issues and defense budgets in the late 1970s.

In the long run, arms control can benefit defense efforts, not only in allowing defense planners to use their resources more effectively than if they had to use the most conservative assumptions for every contingency but also by creating public confidence that the nuclear balance of power is being prudently managed. Given the horrors of nuclear war, public opinion in this and allied countries wants assurance that national security managers are exercising prudence in their development and possible use of nuclear arsenals. In the longer term of postwar history, the alliance between the United States and Europe and Japan has been of profound importance in the world balance of power. Maintenance of alliance cohesion is more important than the fine points of nuclear hardware. Because Europeans are continually worried that the United States will do too little or too much in their nuclear defense, arms control contributes to the sense of management. In fact, it has been part of NATO doctrine since 1967. The alternative is likely to be wider oscillations in public opinion, as have occurred in Europe during the past decade. In short, like the opponents' first argument, this objection is better viewed as a caution against unrealistic arms control than against all arms control.

A third major concern of arms control opponents stems from their perception of the nature of the Soviet Union. The critics charge that arms control rests on abstract theorizing about stability rather than Russian reality. Arms control theory shows that it is rational for two antagonists to cooperate despite their enmity, but the abstract players of game theory don't exist in the real world. We may be A, but the Soviets have never learned to play B. The nature of the Soviet society, political objectives, and military posture make stable arms control agreements impossible.

The crude version of the societal argument portrays the Soviets as liars and cheats. The more sophisticated version stresses the tradition of secrecy and concealment as instruments of defense in Russian history and the restrictive perception of agreements with bourgeois states that characterizes communist ideology. Various negotiators have reported instances where the Soviets have treated agreements as contests, concealing rather than volunteering information and always pressing against the loopholes and legal limits.[18] Russian secrecy would be an even greater problem for defense planners without the bonus of additional transparency that comes from arms control (such as agreement not to interfere with national technical means of surveillance). While it is true that the Soviets have pressed to find loopholes, there have not been unambiguous violations of the SALT I agreements.[19]

The argument that the Soviets' political objectives are revisionist and expansionist can be valid without undermining the soundness of arms control. Given the turmoil in the third world and the likelihood that in many situations the United States will wind up on the side of the status quo while the Soviets support a revolutionary cause, there will be frequent opportunities for conflicts over political change in third world countries to interrupt arms control. The fact that Soviet objectives will generally be revisionist tells little about their actual actions unless one also knows about costs and risks. Nuclear deterrence, the balance with China, and local political resistance all can raise the costs and risks for the Soviet Union. Expansionist political objectives alone have not prevented a degree of prudence and a degree of arms control in the past. They do remind us, however, that arms control depends upon effective defense and foreign policy and that if those conditions are allowed to change, arms control bargains may not hold.

The same can be said about the opponents' argument that arms control is impossible because of military asymmetries. As a traditional land power on the Eurasian continent close to areas of vital U.S. interests, the Soviet Union has a conventional military advantage. It is argued that in the past the United States used nuclear superiority to offset this advantage and that negotiated parity in strategic nuclear weapons thus fails to preserve the overall balance. In this view, deterrence of Soviet conventional attacks depended on U.S. ability to credibly threaten to escalate the conflict and emerge victorious; this is known as escalation dominance.

History is not so clear.[20] It is true that the United States has refused to forego the threat of first use of nuclear weapons in order to deter Soviet conventional attacks, but the United States also raised conventional defense capabilities in Europe in the 1960s to a level that would make such an attack very costly. Deterrence may have been a result of the combination of a high enough conventional threshold to signal that any use of force would be costly, plus Soviet uncertainty about nuclear escalation, rather than clear American escalation dominance. After all, a state of nuclear parity has existed for more than a decade.

Nor is it likely that nuclear superiority can be obtained. Parity symbolizes a major achievement for the Soviets, and the ability to further increase defense spending may be easier in an authoritarian than in a democratic political system. While the West's comparative advantage may be technology rather than military manpower, that technology can also be applied to rectify the conventional balance in the form of precision guided weapons, improved surveillance, and other means of raising the conventional threshold. Of course, technology alone is not sufficient, but it can help to improve conventional defenses. What the skeptics' argument does tell us, however, is that strategic arms control measures cannot be divorced from measures to keep theater nuclear and conventional forces in balance.

Finally, opponents sometimes argue that the asymmetry of nuclear doctrines makes arms control impossible. In this view, the United States stressed stability through mutual assured destruction (MAD) even after a first-strike; thus, neither side would have an incentive to strike first. In contrast, the Soviets' doctrine and force structure allegedly stressed counterforce and war-fighting capabilities.[21] With such different doctrines, say the skeptics, arms control agreements have totally different meanings to the two parties. While they exist, the doctrinal differences should not be exaggerated.[23] Whatever its declaratory policy, the United States has always had some degree of counterforce options in its operational nuclear targeting plans, and to the Soviets it may have looked like a first-strike capability. Moreover, each side inescapably has assured destruction capabilities to withstand a first-strike and retaliate with devastating power. High level Soviet leaders have talked increasingly about the impossibility of winning nuclear war and of stability as a condition where neither side can hope to win from a first strike. Moreover, while their past emphasis on heavy ICBMs is worrisome, their major investment in conventional forces and submarine forces is consistent with this view. It is true that Soviet military doctrine speaks of the importance of preparing to fight and striking first once war is imminent, but this is not a historically surprising view. Similar views have existed since Thucydides and even have been expressed by U.S. military figures from time to time. Moreover, any doctrine of prolonged nuclear war fighting would raise similar problems of command, control, communications, and avoiding countervalue spasm attacks for them as it does for us. It remains to be demonstrated that the doctrinal differences are so great as to make arms control impossible.

What the opponents tell us is not that arms control is impossible because of Soviet society, political objectives, and military posture but that it will not be easy and that it is not sufficient if military and foreign policy conditions are allowed to change. Their arguments are useful cautions against overly facile arms control arguments and useful reminders of the need to preserve the overall military balance while attempting to control strategic nuclear weapons.

DEEP REDUCTIONS

While past SALT approaches have included modest force reductions, a number of proposals have been made for a very different approach—a formal treaty to make deep cuts in strategic arms. George Kennan has suggested a 50 percent cut in all nuclear weapons by each side. President Reagan has suggested renaming the process "START," to stress that they are strategic arms *reduction* talks. The approach may be politically appealing. Rather than the intangible goal of "crisis stability" stressed by arms control, it promises tangible reductions easily grasped by the public mind. Not only is there a promise of major savings of money, but the deep cuts would also promise a significant change in the momentum of the strategic competition. Nonetheless, such proposals contain a number of problems and ambiguities. [23]

First, deep reductions may not be desirable, depending upon which weapons were affected and how they were phased. The dangerous consequences of nuclear weapons lie in their use, rather than their existence. While high numbers may increase some statistical probability of use in an accidental or mechanical sense, they do not necessarily increase the probability that their use would be initiated deliberately. On the contrary, low numbers may invite preemption or raise uncertainty about the perceived stability of the military balance and thus have a negative effect on the probability of weapons actually being used. While overall numbers of weapons in both arsenals are very high, the ratio of weapons on each side does affect political perceptions as the recent concern over vulnerability of land-based missiles has shown. Moreover, certain types of proportional cuts could be destabilizing. For example, cutting the number of strategic submarines in half, given the fact that half of the remainder would then be in port, would mean that fewer than ten submarines would have to be tracked and destroyed for a successful preemptive attack.

Another version of deep cuts would focus on land-based missiles. The problem here would be negotiability, as the March 1977 experience demonstrated. [24] The Soviet Union has roughly 75 percent of its strategic capabilities in land-based missiles, compared to the United States' 25 percent. While the Soviets have been investing heavily in submarines and will face a worsening problem of the vulnerability of their ICBMs later in the decade, it is hard to see them giving up the political advantages they associate with large land-based missiles. History and geography reinforce this reluctance. If the United States has been unwilling to give up the land leg of its triad, it is even harder to see the Soviet Union doing so. If that is the only proposal, it may lie on the table for a very long time.

This leads to the third problem with the deep cuts approach—its focus. If all efforts were concentrated on the deep cuts proposal, would other aspects of arms control be neglected? In principle, one could imagine also making progress on other specific and more limited items but not if they were linked politically or in bureaucratic practice to a nonnegotiable deep cuts proposal.

This is not to argue that all deep cuts are undesirable or impossible. The overall number of weapons is so high that major reductions of certain types can be made without damage to deterrence. Various formulas can be constructed. It may be possible to devise a verifiable measure of equal destructive power, allowing each side to choose a force structure within a common limit that can be significantly reduced,[25] but it will not be easy, and it is unlikely to be quick. If the search for the perfect becomes the enemy of the good, all arms control may become stalled or discredited. As a long-term measure but not the sole focus of strategic arms control efforts, the right kind of deep cuts treaty may be possible. Indeed, its negotiability may depend on being related to other arms control measures, including theater forces and other talks, as described below. However, as the sole focus to replace SALT, a formal deep-cuts treaty could have substantial problems. Ironically, these very problems may explain its appeal to some who prefer no arms control.

BACK TO BASICS: INFORMAL ARMS CONTROL

Another possible direction would be for arms control to refocus on the sort of informal measures discussed in the early 1960s. As Thomas Schelling has written, "the institutionalizing of arms control as a formal diplomatic process, over the past dozen years, has caused some of us to forget that the essence of arms control is conditional restraint, however induced and enforced, not only formal treaties. . . . SALT has become self-limiting rather than weapons-limiting."[26] Schelling would not scrap what has been achieved but suggests a path that emphasizes a number of central features of the 1960 vintage writings about arms control.[27] That writing was skeptical of the disarmament approach and Wilsonian liberal formalism. Arms control was conservative in its concern with stabilizing, rather than radically altering, the international system.

Treaties certainly were viewed as acceptable sources of arms control, but reciprocated unilateral decisions were considered as possibly more effective than formal treaties since they could create less incentive to find loopholes and limits and place less emphasis on the details of verification. The central concern was crisis stability rather than numbers of weapons. The character of weapons was considered more important than their number. The possibility of unintended use of nuclear weapons was believed to have more to do with characteristics of weapons than with their numbers and ratios. In some instances, it was suggested, arms control might be better served by increasing rather than decreasing numbers of weapons. Weapon decisions should be steered toward crisis stability by emphasizing such characteristics as continual control and invulnerability to a first strike. Redundancy and invulnerability achieved through the deployment of many small missiles rather than fewer large ones could reduce concern about exact numbers and reduce significance of verification.

Arms control typically is said to have three objectives: (1) crisis stability or reduction of the probability of war; (2) damage limitation if war breaks out; and (3) cost reduction from creating stability in the arms competition. Force reductions may help toward the third objective (though it is worth remembering that strategic forces are a small portion of the defense budget) but probably not for the second, given the large numbers of weapons that would still exist. They are not necessarily significant for the first objective.

But the first objective, crisis stability, remains central to the arms control approach. While negotiated reductions are one way to seek crisis stability, they are not the only way. What is crucial for crisis stability is to avoid force structures that give a decisive advantage to striking first. It also requires an improved degree of transparency, communication, and predictability in order to allow defense planners to adjust doctrine and weapons procurement decisions to maximize security (which includes both deterrence, crisis stability, and damage limitation) within resource constraints. Transparency, communication, and predictability can be enhanced by an informal arms control process even if there are no formal treaties or reductions. It is sometimes said that the very process of arms control discussions produces benefits of good will in U.S.-Soviet relations; this is debatable. It is certainly not the history of the 1970s. But the process can help increase transparency and communication (TAC). If SALT talks are impossible or impossibly slow, it still makes sense to have TAC talks.

Some early proponents of arms control, such as Schelling, argue that it would be wise to use the current pause in strategic arms control to restructure the process more along the informal lines suggested in the 1960s literature rather than merely trying to revive SALT. While the flexibility of the informal approach is attractive, it also raises a number of problems. The blackboard is not clean, and it would be politically costly to erase it. The ABM Treaty is in force, and SALT II exists de facto. Public opinion at home and in Europe would react badly to an actual termination of the SALT process. Moreover, the treaty and negotiating history of SALT include a number of transparency and communication features that may be as important as the clauses limiting numbers of launchers, warheads per launcher, and the introduction of new missiles. Such features include definitions, noninterference with national surveillance, and the Standing Consultative Commission (SCC) for discussions about possible violations.

In addition, informal arms control procedures may be difficult to explain to the public, to Congress, and to the Soviets. It is hard to find unambiguous evidence of informally reciprocated restraint in central strategic systems. Ironically, one of the prime examples is the current de facto observance of the unratified SALT II Treaty. Too much indeterminancy lends itself to worst-case analyses and support in public opinion for extreme interpretations of Soviet behavior and necessary U.S. reactions.[28] Moreover, Congress likes treaties for the leverage they provide to the legislature over the executive branch. Finally, the Soviet Union appears committed to SALT. In short, whatever the merits of trying to return to basics and informal arms control, there are obstacles in trying to get there from here.

NUCLEAR STABILIZATION TALKS

A fifth approach to strategic arms control incorporates the importance of maintaining transparency, communications, and predictability even in the absence of formal agreements but takes the history and existence of the formal comprehensive treaty approach into account. In this view, SALT or START would remain part of the process but less centrally. This approach places less of a political burden on SALT/START to maintain good overall U.S.-Soviet relations, while also ensuring that the TAC dimensions of arms control could be pursued even if SALT/START became bogged down. In theory, it is wise to have as many policy instruments as one has policy objectives. The fifth approach proposes a broad framework of nuclear stabilization talks (NST) with different instruments incorporated within it designed to meet different arms control objectives.[29] In effect, the NST process would mean simultaneous pursuit of four major tracks: TAC talks, force structure discussions, limited agreements, and SALT/START.

First, crisis stability would be served by establishing a regular pattern of TAC talks designed to enhance transparency and communications. Such talks could be held at several levels. One aspect might include meetings between the Chairman of the Joint Chiefs of Staff and his Soviet counterpart. These discussions would not seek formal agreement but could explore ambiguities in posture and doctrine as well as military perspectives on possible specific measures and agreements. The TAC talks might also explore confidence-building measures and limited agreements on selected problems. Whatever the fate of the SALT process, efforts would be made to continue the transparency and communications features already attained, such as the noninterference with surveillance agreement and regular SCC meetings. It might also be useful to discuss topics like strategic doctrine or targeting of command centers, even if no formal agreement were feasible (or desirable). Existing confidence-building measures—such as discussion of naval incidents, notification of exercises in Europe, and the hot line—could be supplemented by new measures, such as a ban on testing depressed trajectory launches of submarine missiles or of fractional orbit bombardment systems. The talks might discuss cooperative measures to deal with nonproliferation or Senator Nunn's idea of a crisis center to identify and deal with nuclear explosions by third countries.[30]

Such measures would not profoundly affect the central strategic balance, but they would help to enhance stability in its management. Transparency and communication will not change the nature of the strategic balance, but various experiments have shown that the classic game of "prisoner's dilemma," in which each side can cooperate but is tempted to sell out the other, is played differently when there is communication and many rounds. TAC talks cannot transform the relationship to one of trust, but they can help to set some limits on the worst case analyses that might otherwise occur in both capitals.

A second initiative would be regular force structure discussions among high-level Soviet and American civilian and military officials. Such discussions would be designed to encourage the informal arms control process. They would not seek to reach negotiated agreements but would explore areas of potential informal reciprocity. For example, one modality might be three list discussions. Civilian and military officials would describe their respective defense programs in three categories: (1) those that are unalterable and nonnegotiable; (2) those that are firm in principle but that could be altered, depending on which of a set of specified actions the other side takes; (3) those with long lead times and joint gains if each side exercises restraint or if preclusive arrangements can be worked out. There need be no formal commitment, but the effects of their procurement decisions could be made clear to the other side. Some of our decisions would depend on their behavior; others would not. Verification would be simplified since our behavior would respond to their observed behavior. While this is obviously a simplification, the important point is to develop a way to encourage informal arms control procedures to supplement the formal treaty negotiating process and not be hostage to it. Obviously, such informal approaches would require congressional consultation and possibly congressional involvement in delegations. Such an involvement may be difficult but is a necessary condition in our democracy.

A third track to the nuclear stabilization talks would be negotiations to reach limited agreements where they are possible. The stability of the arms competition (and possibly crisis stability) could be served by seeking preclusive agreements that fenced off certain areas or technologies from arms races. Indeed, one of the lessons of past arms control efforts is that when there is adequate lead time it is easier to preclude arms races than to agree on reduction of existing systems. The ABM Treaty is a case related to technology, and the Antarctic Treaty, Outer Space Treaty, and Seabed Treaty are spatial examples. Current candidates for such discussion may include space-based laser technologies and the testing of systems intended to destroy satellites in geosynchronous orbits (satellites that provide critical early warning and communications capabilities are located in such orbits). Neither side can achieve a decisive advantage in these areas, since the other inevitably would respond in kind, and the technology is not so advanced that preclusive arrangements would be impossible.

The fourth track, obviously, is SALT/START. Negotiated comprehensive limitations and reductions in strategic forces, where these are possible, can contribute to crisis stability and potentially to reduction in the costs of the arms competition. This latter concern may become more important if both the Soviet and American economies perform at low growth rates in the 1980s. Proposals in this area may remain difficult and lengthy to negotiate, particularly if they involve deep cuts or difficult verification problems. Patience will be necessary. If they are not the central or sole focus of the arms control process, however, it may be possible to carry out such prolonged negotiations without their falling victim to the inevitable political vicissitudes of U.S.-Soviet relations. If they are pursued as one track in a broader framework of nuclear stabilization talks, there will be less danger of the whole process of arms control being limited to what may be the excruciating slow pace of the SALT/START talks. An effective SALT/START process should not preclude pursuit of the TAC and other limited dimensions of arms control. On the contrary, it may well benefit from being embedded in such a broader context.

LINKAGE AND FEASIBILITY

Even if the desirability of a nuclear stabilization talks framework were granted, would it be feasible given the current climate of U.S.-Soviet relations? Since arms control must be seen in the context of the overall relationship and linkage is inevitable in the political process, won't new initiatives have to wait for a fourth turn in the postwar alternations of American attitudes toward the Soviet Union?

Not necessarily. Linkage can be tactical or de facto. The former is a matter of choice. Its wisdom will depend on circumstances. Generally speaking, it would be unwise to assume such an asymmetry of strategic interest that tactical linkage will often be to our advantage, but in some cases it may be inherent. Linkage is a matter of degree, and the NST framework is designed to take that into account by placing less of a central role and political burden on the SALT effort to limit and reduce strategic forces. TAC talks among civilian officials and military staffs, force structure discussions, and limited agreements on depressed trajectories or antisatellite warfare may be sufficiently useful to our defense planning and yet limited in their effect on overall relations so that public opinion would accept their negotiation without, for example, a drastic change in Soviet behavior in the third world. In other words, there will be situations where linkage need not enter the negotiating process if we so choose. Of course, there are degrees of Soviet behavior and in some cases we will choose linkage. A bloody Soviet invasion of Poland, for example, would be likely to interrupt even such limited measures for a substantial time.

One can imagine a range of Soviet behavior in the third world that would also delay progress but without necessarily leading to a breakdown in all items within the NST framework. The specific outcomes would depend on the administration's response to and public perceptions of the Soviet behavior in question, on the reaction of allies, and on the existence of other policy instruments for response to the Soviet behavior. To the extent that arms control is the only strand in the relationship, it will be bound to bear more of the tactical burden of response. On the other hand, to the extent that public opinion and military planners want the sense of predictability and management in the nuclear competition that an NST framework would imply, it would limit the tactical manipulation of arms control procedures as signals and sanctions. This would be further reinforced if U.S. tactical linkage permitted the Soviet Union to divide the alliance and pursue detente in the European context in a manner that isolated the United States. In short, some inherent linkage would be inevitable, but within limits the tightness of the link with different aspects of the NST framework would depend upon U.S. tactical policy choices.

What about the other side of the relationship? Are there incentives for the Soviet Union to take an NST framework seriously, particularly if the SALT/START component involved a demand for such a deep reduction of their ICBMs that they refused and American defense spending continued to increase? Probably yes. Defense programs can help rather than hinder a favorable Soviet reaction if they create incentives to bargain and maintain a balance. To the extent, however, that the United States couched its programs as an effort to regain nuclear superiority, it would tend to stimulate Russian determination to respond in kind. The ambiguities of rough parity and equal security may prove more useful symbols for a dual policy of defense modernization plus nuclear stabilization talks.

Soviet incentives would also be affected by internal and external political factors, notably their adverse economic and demographic trends and the combination of threats and opportunities they perceive related to China, Europe, and the third world. In general, however, there is no conclusive reason why the Soviets should not accept a nuclear stabilization talks framework; their initial flexibility on the de facto existence of SALT II may be a positive indicator of this.

With time, some of the more modest measures in the NST framework may affect the more ambitious aspects, like the SALT/START component. They may even have a positive effect on efforts to develop the rudimentary codes of behavior of the postwar balance into something closer to the stabilizing prudential rules of the nineteenth century balance of power. Since everything is related to everything else to some degree in U.S.-Soviet relations, linkage could have a positive as well as negative effect. In the long run, one could hope that arms control negotiations might gradually help to alter the relationship by contact and by providing incentives for more moderate behavior. Even in the short run, if the tactics of linkage are not blatant, the existence of arms control negotiations may create such incentives. If so, the mode of constant negotiation and small agreements may be the most subtle and effective form of linkage. Arms control efforts can be judged by their political effect on the relationship as well as by their intrinsic merit.

If such effects occur, they should be seen as welcome secondary effects rather than a primary goal of the arms control process. It would be a mistake to relate arms control measures too closely to hopes for a revival of detente. It is unlikely that we have seen the last turn in the alternation of U.S. attitudes toward the Soviet Union; both improvements and worsenings will probably occur again. The more arms control tries to become the centerpiece of managing both the military balance and the overall relationship, the more vulnerable it becomes to interruption, the less able to contribute to specific achievements en route to its own three objectives of crisis stability, arms race stability, and cost and damage reduction, and, ironically, the less able it will be to contribute at the margin to an improved relationship.

Arms control cannot change the Soviet view of history. It cannot make them accept what they consider threatening change in their sphere of influence or forego significant opportunities to support what they see as historical progress in the third world. It can affect their military programs (witness the ABM Treaty), provide communication that enhances crisis stability, and, at the margin, sometimes encourage moderation in behavior. Arms control by itself, however, cannot transform the relationship. Strategic arms control can never be isolated from the overall relationship; neither can it bear the entire burden of the relationship. It will work best to the degree it plays a limited, if critical, role.

NOTES

1. William G. Hyland, *Soviet-American Relations: A New Cold War?* (Santa Monica: The Rand Corporation, 1981), p. 55.

2. Thomas C. Schelling and Morton H. Halperin, *Strategy and Arms Control* (New York: Twentieth Century Fund, 1961), p. 132.

3. See Thomas Larson, *Soviet-American Rivalry* (New York: Norton, 1978).

4. See, for example, Peter G. Filene, *Americans and the Soviet Experiment, 1917-1933* (Princeton: Princeton University Press, 1967); or Charles Bohlen, *Witness to History: 1929-1969* (New York: Norton, 1973).

5. See William Taubman, *Stalin's American Policy* (New York: Norton, 1982).

6. Adam Ulam, *The Rivals* (New York: Viking, 1971), pp. 19, 156, 102.

7. See, for example, the evidence assembled in Hyland. See also the debate over Albert Wohlstetter, "Is There a Strategic Arms Race," *Foreign Policy 15* and *16* (Summer and Fall, 1974).

8. See John L. Gaddis, *Strategies of Containment* (New York: Oxford University Press, 1982).

9. Stanley Hoffmann, *Primacy or World Order* (New York: McGraw Hill, 1978), p. 11; see also Michael Mandelbaum, *The Nuclear Revolution* (New York: Cambridge University Press, 1981), ch. 3.

10. See Robert Jervis, "Security Regimes," *International Organization* (Cambridge, Mass.: MIT Press, forthcoming).

11. Carnegie Panel on U.S. Security and the Future of Arms Control, *Challenges for U.S. National Security: Assessing the Balance, Part II* (Washington, D.C.: Carnegie Endowment, 1981), p. 49.

12. See Daniel Yankelovich and Larry Kaagan, "America and the World," *Foreign Affairs 59*, no. 3 (1981):696-713.

13. Leslie Gelb, "A Glass Half Full," *Foreign Policy 36* (Fall 1979):24.

14. Barry M. Blechman, "Do Negotiated Arms Control Limitations Have a Future," *Foreign Affairs 59* (Fall 1980):109.

15. See, for example, the discussion in Carnegie Panel on U.S. Security and the Future of Arms Control, *Challenges for U.S. National Security, Part I* (Washington, D.C.: Carnegie Endowment, 1981). See also Lloyd Cutler and Roger Molander, "Is There Life After Death for SALT?," *International Security 6* (Fall 1981):3-200.

16. Deborah Shapley, "Arms Control as a Regulator of Military Technology," *Daedalus* (Winter 1980):145-57.

17. Henry Kissinger, *The White House Years* (Boston: Little, Brown and Company, 1979), pp. 197-200.

18. See, for example, House of Representatives, Committee on Foreign Affairs, *Soviet Diplomacy and Negotiating Behavior* (Washington, D.C.: Government Printing Office, 1979).

19. During the SALT II debate, there were various accusations of Soviet violations of SALT I, but Sidney Graybeal, who was U.S. Commission of the Standing Consultative Commission (where such issues were

discussed), testified that he was "unaware of any case where the Soviets have been in violation of the provisions of the SALT I agreements." Senate Committee on Foreign Relations, *Briefings on SALT I Compliance* (Washington, D.C.: Government Printing Office, 1979), p. 25. Recently, however, serious unanswered questions have been raised about Soviet observance of the (unratified) Threshold Test Ban Treaty and Biological Warfare Convention. See Robert Einhorn, "Treaty Compliance," *Foreign Policy,* no. 45 (Winter 1981–82):29–47. See also Leslie Gelb, "Keeping An Eye on Russia," *The New York Times Magazine* (November 29, 1981).

20. See McGeorge Bundy, "Strategic Deterrence Thirty Years Later: What Has Changed?," *The Future of Strategic Deterrence,* Adephi Paper 160 (London: International Institute for Strategic Studies, 1980).

21. Richard Pipes, "Why the Soviet Union Thinks It Could Fight and Win a Nuclear War," *Commentary* (July 1977):21–34; and Fritz Ermath, "Contrasts in American and Soviet Strategic Thought," *International Security* (Fall 1978):138–155.

22. Dmitri Simes, "Deterrence and Coercion in Soviet Policy," *International Security 5* (Winter 1980–81). Derek Leebaert, ed., *Soviet Military Thinking* (London: Grange, Allen and Unwin, 1981).

23. See Leon V. Sigal, "Kennan's Cuts," *Foreign Policy 44* (Fall 1981). See also Colin Gray and Keith B. Payne, *SALT: Deep Force Reductions* (Groton-on-Hudson: Hudson Institute, 1981).

24. For details of the U.S. proposal to cut Soviet heavy missiles in half, see Strobe Talbott, *Endgame: The Inside Story of SALT II* (New York: Harper and Row, 1979), ch. 3.

25. For example, see Sidney Drell and Kent Wisner, "A New Formula for Nuclear Arms Control," *International Security* (Winter 1980–81): 186–94.

26. Thomas Schelling, Preface to Hebrew edition of *Arms and Influence* (Mimeo of English translation).

27. In addition to Schelling and Halperin (1961), a representative volume is Donald Brennan, ed., *Arms Control Disarmament, and National Security* (New York: George Braziller, 1961).

28. For example, contrast George Quester, "Arms Control: Toward Informal Solutions," with William Kincade, "Arms Control: Negotiated Solutions," in Richard Betts, ed., *Cruise Missiles* (Washington, D.C.: Brookings Institution, 1981).

29. For those who believe that the medium is the message in this acronym bedevilled field, NST could be called "NuStab."

30. Sam Nunn, "Arms Control: What Should We Do?" *Washington Post* (November 12, 1981). See also J.S. Nye, "The U.S. and Soviet Stakes in Nuclear Non-Proliferation," *PS XV (Winter 1982):32–9.*

11 AN EFFECTIVE STRATEGIC POSTURE

The Study Group

In the next few years, American and Soviet policymakers will separately and together resolve a number of critical strategic issues. The decisions they make will determine the character of the strategic balance, strongly affect the future course of U.S.-Soviet relations, and influence the risk of nuclear war well into the next century. It is important, therefore, that these questions are being examined in a time of rapid technological change and in a political-military context considerably altered from that existing only a few years ago. Both these aspects must be kept firmly in mind in designing the new U.S. strategic posture.

POLITICAL AND MILITARY CHANGE

The Reagan Administration's approach to strategic issues is evolving as various political, economic, and military constraints and opportunities come into sharper focus. As with other administrations, this one has shown many elements of continuity in its strategic policy: The decade-long trend toward more flexible and diverse targeting options has continued; the Carter Administration's attempt to address problems of command, control, and communication has been intensified; recurring concerns about the overall survivability of America's

247

strategic forces have dictated various modernization programs. No administration can completely escape an inheritance of weapon programs and doctrinal issues.

Nevertheless, some of the strategic emphases of the Reagan Administration are significantly different from those of the several preceding administrations. U.S. officials now seem to place greater stress on the roles that nuclear weapons can play in both U.S. and Soviet defense plans and foreign policy. Evidence of this new orientation can be found in campaign rhetoric calling for regaining strategic superiority, in greater budgetary support for strategic weapon programs in order to achieve "a margin of safety," in efforts to orient strategic doctrine more rigorously around concepts of nuclear war-fighting, and in increased emphasis on assuring the credibility of American nuclear threats in order to secure interests in Europe and in other regions of importance, notably the Persian Gulf. Generally, the Reagan Administration has stressed substantial improvements in U.S. strategic forces while deemphasizing the effort to control the strategic competition through arms negotiations.

For the most part, these shifts in emphasis fell largely on receptive ears in the Congress and the country. A powerful antinuclear/pro-arms control movement emerged in 1982, but its electoral clout remains to be demonstrated. American perceptions of U.S.-Soviet relations clearly have shifted from the expansive optimism of the early 1970s—which saw ambitious plans for mutually beneficial economic ties and continuing progress toward arms control—to the tensions that have characterized the early 1980s. Two factors seem to have caused this change.

First, Americans have been disturbed profoundly by the assertiveness of Soviet foreign policy, particularly as it affects the third world. Tactically successful Soviet involvements in a series of crises in the third world—notably Angola (1975), the Horn of Africa (1978), and Afghanistan (1979)—contrasted vividly with the evidence of America's declining fortunes in the same regions—the fall of South Vietnam (1975) and the Iranian hostage crisis (1979–80). These contrasts had sharp impact on American perceptions of Soviet intentions and the potential benefits of detente. They also played a significant role in shaping the foreign policy debate in the United States. In the future, U.S.-Soviet relations may be even more prone to crises because these past events clearly have led to diminished American tolerance for new Soviet adventures, as suggested by reactions to Soviet involvement in the military repression in Poland. This alteration in the character of U.S.-Soviet relations set the stage for important changes in American attitudes toward strategic doctrine and policy.

Second, and having a more direct impact, increases in Soviet military forces have altered U.S. perceptions of appropriate strategic policies. The buildup in Soviet capabilities has included a substantial improvement in conventional forces, which seems to reflect global aspirations. Moreover, there has been a sustained accumulation and modernization of Soviet nuclear forces, as well as some measures, actively and passively, to deny targets to U.S. nuclear forces. All of this suggests that Soviet policymakers may have a higher estimate of the role and the utility of nuclear weapons than many Americans previously assumed. Not surprisingly, this has given pause to American policymakers and the American public.

The effect of Soviet weapon programs on the quantitative balance of strategic power over nearly two decades has been dramatic and widely advertised. In 1965, for example, the United States possessed roughly three times as many long-range bombers and intercontinental ballistic missiles (ICBMs), four times as many submarine-launched ballistic missiles (SLBMs), and five times as many deliverable nuclear warheads as the Soviet Union. By 1982, however, the USSR had deployed more ICBMs and SLBMs than the United States and was rapidly closing the American lead in deliverable warheads. In addition, newer Soviet military systems represent technologically advanced, sophisticated, and versatile weapons that provide the USSR with an impressive array of military capabilities.

The strategic balance in 1982 is thus much different from that existing nearly twenty years earlier. The United States continues to have the edge in some types of strategic capabilities: Among others, it is superior in antisubmarine warfare capabilities; its bomber force remains far larger, more capable, and more modern than that of the Soviet Union; it has a significant lead in cruise missile technology; and it still has more than one thousand more nuclear weapons in its strategic arsenal than does the USSR. In addition, it is certainly not the case that American strategic forces have stood still over the last decade. During the 1970s, the number of warheads in the American strategic arsenal more than doubled; a number of new and more capable missiles, such as the Minuteman III ICBM and the Poseidon C-3 SLBM, were introduced; and the B-52 force was modernized steadily. Moreover, the United States began to deploy several major new systems during the last decade, including the Trident submarine and missile (C-4) and the air-launched cruise missile, and developed several others, including the MX ICBM and B-1 bomber, which are planned to begin entering the force structure in this decade.

But the Soviet Union has pushed forward in all strategic components, deploying new generations of land-based and submarine-launched missiles, stressing the deployment of air defenses and the development of missile defense technology, and closing substantially what had been a significant gap in qualitative features of the two sides' strategic forces. As a result, in a number of measures of strategic capabilities, the lead has passed from American to Soviet hands. Most importantly, the Soviet Union presently has at its disposal more land-based missile throw-weight and deliverable megatonnage than does the United States, giving it far greater capabilities to destroy hard targets, like missile silos, promptly. Because of developments like this one, whether one feels that the Soviets have achieved superiority or parity, the strategic balance is clearly less favorable from an American perspective than it once was.

These are the unavoidable and undisputable facts of recent strategic weapons deployments. The changes in the strategic balance, however, can be viewed from very different perspectives; there is little agreement about the meaning and implications of these facts. These disputes have to do largely with what may be inferred from the Soviet strategic buildup about the nature of the Soviet Union as an adversary and what may be inferred from a shifting strategic balance for international politics. Alternate perspectives on these and related questions were explained in preceding chapters. While not of one mind, the study group believes that the following may be a reasonable way to approach these issues.

It is evident that the widespread public optimism that accompanied the first round of strategic arms limitation talks in the late 1960s and early 1970s proved to be unrealistic. The Soviet Union's willingness to participate in serious negotiations about central nuclear forces— a sharp departure in Soviet policy that surprised many—did not indicate fundamental changes in Soviet perspectives on world politics. Their willingness to talk about nuclear arms, and their acceptance— indeed, eagerness—for the political superstructure of detente, should not have been taken to indicate that the Soviets had abandoned either expansionist aims or their desire, if possible, to attain military superiority. Soviet leaders continue to see the dynamic behind world politics as a struggle between irreconcilable social systems, a struggle in which military instruments of policy—even nuclear weapons—at times can play necessary and legitimate roles. The continuing buildup of Soviet military power, particularly in strategic forces, makes clear that they are willing to sink considerable resources into a quest for ever greater military capabilities.

Nor should Soviet agreement to the 1972 ABM Treaty and Interim Agreement on Offensive Weapons have been taken, as was suggested by some, to indicate a significant modification of Soviet perspectives on nuclear weapons. As the repository of ultimate destructive potential and—when included in strategic missile systems—an expression of the most advanced contemporary military technology, Soviet leaders clearly see nuclear weapons as an important, if not vital, manifestation of national strength and thus a key factor in determining a nation's position in world affairs. Soviet leaders do not believe that nuclear war is impossible; they clearly recognize that, deliberately or not, nuclear war might begin someday, and they have taken some steps to assure the least unfavorable outcome feasible for the Soviet Union in such an eventuality.

Neither do Soviet leaders underestimate the potential costs of nuclear war for either themselves or their nation, nor, some would say, do they misjudge the corrosive effects of the strategic arms competition on political relations between East and West and, thus, on their ability to secure a variety of near- and mid-term objectives. Consequently, Soviet leaders are willing to participate in arms negotiations: cynically, for the overall effect that negotiations may have on Western attitudes about military spending and on ties between the United States and Europe, but also more sincerely, in an attempt to limit the threat posed to them by U.S. nuclear forces. Obviously, Soviet representatives at any talks will attempt to secure the agreement most advantageous to themselves. Equally obviously, they will not accept any agreement that provides them significantly less than equal security. Nonetheless, they clearly have been willing at times to compromise on previously hard-fought points when either the aggregate advantages of agreement or their perception of the value of U.S. concessions seemed to override the cost of whatever they were forced to give up.

With this in mind, most members of the study group have concluded that it is essential to end adverse trends in relative strategic capabilities and restore a more equitable strategic balance—both

to make clear to the Soviet Union that its quest for military dominance is futile and to avoid what may be the negative political consequences of these trends in relative strategic capabilities. Though the
study group is far from unanimous about the political implications of
these trends, many of its members believe that Soviet advantages in
highly visible indicators of strategic power (e.g., the number and size
of delivery systems) as well as in calculations of particular capabilities
(e.g., capabilities to destroy opposing missile silos) could convince
Soviet leaders that they had greater freedom of action in crises. Furthermore, they feel that these trends have an important influence on
the perceptions of third parties, with important effects on day-to-day
relations among nations.

Some study group members believe that the very existence of adverse military trends casts these shadows on political relations.
Others believe that the effect is more indirect, in that continued expressions of U.S. concern about these military trends may cause Soviet leaders, as well as officials in third nations, to do exactly what is
forecast. Either way, the effect is the same. Consequently, the majority of the study group concluded that, real or perceived, adverse
trends in the strategic balance are making it more difficult to protect
U.S. interests and that steps therefore should be taken promptly to
rectify the past disadvantageous shifts in the strategic balance.[1]

This is not to say, however, that a majority of the study group
believes that it is possible for either superpower to achieve meaningful—in the sense of "militarily useful"—strategic superiority nor
that it is helpful politically to articulate such a goal. With the strategic arsenals of each side soon to include more than 10,000 bombs
and missile warheads, it is difficult to imagine numerical advantages
in particular categories of weapons being translated into real military

---

1. The minority view suggests that trends in the strategic balance play only a small, if any,
role in contemporary international politics. This viewpoint holds that the nuclear arsenals of
the two superpowers neutralize each other politically, since each has the potential to virtually
destroy the other, even after having received a nuclear strike. This viewpoint maintains that far
more important than relative strategic capabilities in determining the behavior of leaders in the
Soviet Union and third nations are (1) the basic uncertainty that would attend any nuclear confrontation and (2) factors related to the source of the crisis, such as the interests at stake and
the balance of relevant conventional military capabilities. As a result, proponents of this view
believe that it is relatively unimportant to reverse recent trends in the strategic balance, so long
as the United States retains survivable strategic forces with the capability to retaliate appropriately after any Soviet nuclear attack, and so long as adequate attention is paid to U.S.
conventional military capabilities.

options. When it comes to real military actions, the decisions of both sides seem likely to be dominated by the awesome prospect of events escalating uncontrollably, just as they have in previous confrontations. Moreover, both sides have demonstrated their willingness to take whatever steps are necessary to end the other's dominance of near-term trends in military capabilities. While each superpower clearly pursues its own purposes and concepts of the utility of nuclear weapons in determining the proper size and composition of its own strategic forces, there is an equally clear competition between them, in that each responds—in some fashion—to the other's decisions. To some extent, deployments of strategic weapons have been interactive.

Consequently, the articulation of strategic superiority as a policy objective tends to result in greater external and internal pressures on the opposing side to match or offset any new weapon deployments that appear. It also casts the nation explicitly seeking superiority in a negative light in the eyes of those, particularly in Europe, who have great fears about the ultimate consequences of the strategic arms competition because of its implications for the risk of nuclear war. Articulating strategic superiority as a policy objective, even setting aside questions of its feasibility, thus appears unattractive.[2]

TECHNOLOGICAL CHANGE

Obviously, a major consideration in assessing strategic choices must be the opportunities offered by technological developments to alter the strategic balance. The results of technological change in the 1980s are already clear, for all practical purposes, even though their exact

---

2. A minority of the study group believes that the United States should not reject the goal of strategic superiority out of hand. While recognizing the difficulty of defining, let alone achieving, a margin of superiority that might have political or military utility, this minority feels that it may be necessary to attempt to achieve some measure of superiority in strategic forces to offset what is likely to remain Soviet superiority in general purpose forces (based on substantially larger forces of increasingly competitive quality). In any event, this minority is clear as to the importance of preventing the Soviet Union from achieving strategic superiority—real or widely perceived—a situation that could be a real possibility given the momentum of Soviet programs and the relatively less attention given by the United States to strategic modernization for at least a decade. In this view, the present Soviet theoretical capability to destroy most of the U.S. ICBM force, while utilizing only a portion of their ICBM force, means the Soviet Union could gain a substantial advantage by striking first. This is viewed by some as seriously weakening crisis stability and may already be having a political impact on perceptions of the U.S.-Soviet strategic balance.

pace, direction, and extent will depend considerably upon how many resources are allocated to various possibilities. Longer-term technological prospects are more conjectural. Evaluations of alternative strategic policies, weapon programs, and arms negotiating postures, however, must be informed by judgments about how these long-term technological possibilities could either improve U.S. strategic forces or augment the threats posed to those forces by the Soviet Union.

A key conclusion about technological trends reached by the study group is that ballistic missiles can be so accurate by the end of the 1980s that the error in placing land-based ICBMs would be smaller than the destructive radius of their warheads against hard targets. The accuracy of submarine-launched ballistic missiles also could be improved markedly, probably eventually matching ICBM accuracies. These improvements in accuracy are guaranteed by technologies already in hand, such as terrain-matching terminal guidance and mid-course corrections based on information supplied by navigation satellites.

The greater accuracy of future missiles would permit the use of smaller warheads to achieve the same destructive effect as existing warheads, in turn allowing more warheads per given missile payload. In addition, future missiles of a given size will probably be able to lift somewhat larger payloads. Together, these trends could produce ICBMs with payloads so destructive that, for all practical purposes, numbers of missiles would cease to be an effective constraint on capabilities.

These developments would mean that the probability of destroying any immobile, undefended point target would approach unity, and yet, if deployed in immobile silos and not effectively defended, the survivability of missiles would approach zero. Superhardening silos to increase their resistance to nuclear blasts would not assure the survivability of ICBMs against missiles with the accuracies predicted for the end of the decade. If land-based missiles are to remain a survivable component of U.S. (or Soviet) strategic forces, they will have to be based deceptively, deployed on mobile launchers, or defended by antiballistic missile systems, or steps would have to be taken in arms negotiations to constrain the forces that could be used against them. Of course, various combinations of such measures would be possible.

Because of the growing difficulty of assuring the safety of land-based ICBMs, it is all the more important to safeguard the survivability of the other components of U.S. strategic forces, as well as their ability to penetrate prospective defenses. Fortunately, our assessment of technological trends suggests that both bombers and strategic submarines (SSBNs) are likely to remain effective at least into the 1990s, and SSBNs well beyond that.

Bombers on the ground, of course, are extremely vulnerable to nuclear attack. Similarly, if bombers could be detected in a timely fashion at great distances while in flight, they theoretically could be destroyed by a barrage of nuclear weapons directed at their escape routes. This is not a serious threat in this decade, but over-the-horizon radars and sensors deployed on satellites could place airborne bombers in potential jeopardy in the early 1990s. Even so, such countermeasures as jamming over-the-horizon radars appear feasible, inexpensive, and readily available, and it therefore does not seem likely that this threat to bombers would be great.

Strategic submarines will retain their invulnerability while at sea well beyond this decade, since neither the United States nor the USSR has solved the problems of detecting, tracking, and destroying submarines in the open ocean. Moreover, the longer range of modern submarine-launched ballistic missiles has substantially increased the size of the ocean areas in which strategic submarines can operate, thereby increasing the magnitude of the problem faced by opposing antisubmarine warfare forces. When confined to narrow areas, such as choke points between their ports and operating areas, some submarines may already be vulnerable to detection by sonar arrays. Once at sea, however, strategic submarines can operate with relative impunity. A successful attack against them is particularly difficult to imagine when scenarios in which any appreciable number of submarines must be destroyed simultaneously are considered.

Certain technologies are being developed that over the long term may diminish some of the difficulties now faced by antisubmarine forces. For example, extremely sensitive acoustic arrays are able under certain conditions to detect and identify the sounds made by submarines at distances of hundreds of miles. The netting of data from several such arrays and from other sources eventually may make possible more effective surveillance of strategic submarines. Additionally, it is possible that in the future systems will emerge that have the ability to detect and classify the wakes of submarines.

Even if they matured toward the end of the century, the ability of these technologies to threaten the survivability of strategic submarines remains problematic: There appear to be effective countermeasures to each of them, and the countermeasures are likely to be easier to design and implement than the systems they are meant to negate. Strategic submarines are therefore likely to remain highly survivable for the indefinite future. Since the accuracy of SLBMs also will improve substantially during the 1980s, the study group felt that the submarine component of U.S. strategic forces could be assigned an even more critical role in U.S. plans and policies than it has played in the past.

The study group concluded that technological developments were also unlikely to pose a major threat to the ability of strategic bombers and ballistic missiles to penetrate enemy defenses in the near future. Bombers, it is true, are facing important changes in air defenses with the emergence of radars and interceptor aircraft capable of detecting and destroying low-flying aircraft (sometimes called "look-down, shoot-down capabilities"). But the deployment of large numbers of small cruise missiles, which will probably be invisible to these systems, will in any event permit the saturation of defenses in particular sectors. Moreover, the advanced technology bomber, incorporating Stealth technologies, is being designed to elude look-down, shoot-down defenses by dramatic advances that would dampen its radar signature and other emissions. This advanced bomber, representing a response proportionate to prospective dramatic advances in air defenses, should be available in the early 1990s. Stealth technologies also could be applied to cruise missiles, of course, improving their prospective capabilities to penetrate defenses even further.

Indeed, substantial advances in recent years in technologies associated with the cruise missile (along with additional improvements possible in the future) have increased the range and accuracy of this system while reducing its size and vulnerability to detection by radar. Because it is also relatively cheap, the cruise missile has become an attractive procurement option and will be deployed in large numbers during the 1980s as nuclear delivery vehicles. This is a new and important feature of the strategic balance.[3]

Current American plans call for several thousand cruise missiles to be deployed in the next few years, primarily on B-52 aircraft but also at sea on nuclear-powered submarines and on land in Europe. This

3. The cruise missile also has considerable potential as a conventional weapon, and the widespread deployment of it in both conventional and nuclear versions could blur the distinction between nuclear and non-nuclear systems; this could complicate the verification of compliance with nuclear arms control agreements.

means that the magnitude of the threat facing Soviet air defenses will grow enormously and seriously tax its capabilities—just as growth in the number of warheads magnified the problems of ballistic missile defense. This trend reinforces the conclusion that despite improvements, and although they will place substantial demands on U.S. forces, Soviet air defenses will remain penetrable.

There also have been considerable improvements in the technologies of ballistic missile defenses (BMD) since the 1960s. Nevertheless, the ability of ballistic missiles to penetrate potential defenses is even less in doubt, at least for the near and mid-term. The deployment in the 1970s of multiple independently targetable reentry vehicles (MIRVs) complicated the problem faced by defensive systems by greatly increasing the number of missile warheads that would have to be detected, tracked, and intercepted successfully. This means that BMD systems must have enough launchers or rapid refire capabilities to defeat saturation tactics (i.e., tactics in which the attacker tries to overwhelm the defense's ability to track and intercept targets simultaneously and attempts to exhaust the defense by firing more warheads than the defender has interceptors). This problem aside, other difficulties—such as the potential vulnerability of BMD radars to a variety of offensive tactics—also would limit the effectiveness of missile defenses in this decade. However, improvements in BMD technologies have raised the possibility that a missile defense system, if designed appropriately for the specific purpose, could help to make the ICBM force somewhat more survivable.

BMD technologies with greater promise may be within reach in the 1990s. For example, optical sensing systems capable of being rapidly launched into space upon warning of an attack are being studied as a possible means of tracking warheads and discriminating between warheads and decoys before they reentered the atmosphere. If developed successfully, these systems might make possible the use of very accurate defensive missiles, each with multiple warheads, to intercept attacking reentry vehicles in space. It is by no means certain, however, that continued development of such technologies would eventually result in an effective, deployable system, and, like ASW technologies, advances in BMD technologies would be susceptible to countermeasures. Thus, the advantage seems likely to remain with the offense for the foreseeable future. The deployment of ballistic missile defenses based on technologies available before the end of the century would raise the cost of threatening particular targets in the

United States, such as ICBM sites, and would make it possible to destroy some percentage of the incoming warheads should an attack take place. It would not call into question, however, the ultimate ability of most ballistic missiles to penetrate to their target, especially to targets not hardened by steel and concrete.

Over the longer term, it is conceivable that missile defenses utilizing directed energy technologies (lasers or particle beams) could be deployed on satellites with great effectiveness. This would require relatively large numbers of unmanned space stations. Although precise tracking of large numbers of missiles would be extraordinarily difficult, it is not impossible, since its problems are those of engineering and economics, not of basic physics. It is conceivable that such a system could be deployed early in the next century, though only at enormous cost—perhaps in the range of hundreds of billions of dollars. Moreover, such a system could be vulnerable to countermeasures. For example, to counter a space-based laser BMD, offensive missiles could be hardened to resist the laser's energy, or the space vehicles containing the laser mechanism could themselves be attacked by such antisatellite weapons as space mines. Given these great uncertainties about the potential effectiveness of these exotic BMD technologies, it is premature to contemplate investment of the huge sums that would be necessary to move toward deployment.

Finally, in considering the effects of technological trends on offensive capabilities, it should be kept in mind that improvements in sensor, communications, and computer technologies (often, though not exclusively, incorporated into military satellites) combined with the growing accuracy of ballistic missiles raises the prospect of greater flexibility in the employment of strategic forces. Although many command and control systems possess inherent and worrying vulnerabilities and could not survive large-scale attacks dedicated to their destruction, their enhanced capabilities make possible a number of limited nuclear options. Obviously, both the United States and the USSR would have such possibilities, something that must be considered when devising doctrines to cover the potential use of strategic forces.

HOW TO THINK ABOUT THE
STRATEGIC POSTURE

Based on these military, political, and technological considerations, the study group urges that the United States adopt a strategy that pushes ahead with efforts to modernize U.S. strategic forces and that also pursues arms negotiations. This combined effort would try to (1) rectify past trends in relative U.S. and Soviet strategic capabilities; (2) develop a strategic balance that is likely to be more stable in crises—and thereby to reduce the chance of nuclear war; and (3) achieve negotiated reductions of the nuclear forces of both sides.

Clearly, U.S. strategic forces must be adequate to deter attacks on this nation under any circumstances and to prevent the coercion of the United States by the threat of such attacks. U.S. strategic forces also must be adequate to extend this nuclear umbrella to U.S. allies, particularly Japan and the members of NATO. Because our own survival and the survival of Europe and Japan are evident as vital American interests, American threats to risk nuclear war on their behalf have a certain amount of inherent credibility. Even here however, trends in the strategic balance have been cited, in some circles, as raising questions about the U.S. commitment. Doubts about the credibility of the U.S. nuclear posture arise more pointedly in situations in which the nation's resolve to use its nuclear forces would be more questionable—situations in which the U.S. stake may not seem comparable to the dangers of nuclear war.

Whatever the stakes, however, it is far from clear how to measure the adequacy of U.S. strategic forces for deterrence. At a minimum, there is a need for secure retaliatory capabilities that can respond even after a massive Soviet attack. As a result, care must be taken to preserve the overall survivability of U.S. strategic forces. When whole components of the force become seriously vulnerable, programs to remedy them should be initiated and sustained. At the current time, this would entail—and pointedly so—a response to the vulnerability of land-based missiles; that response could take many forms. It is neither necessary nor possible to eliminate every perceived vulnerability; indeed, U.S. strategic forces have always included some considerable vulnerabilities, such as bombers not on alert and submarines in port. In general, however, the extension of vulnerable strategic components can have adverse political effects over the long term and, in crises, could raise the incentives for an opponent to initiate nuclear war.

Programs that seek to provide more ambitious strategic capabilities—particularly those suggesting capabilities to fight nuclear wars at various levels of escalation—are more controversial. Most members of the study group would neither reject all countermilitary capabilities, on the one hand, nor place great confidence in the possibility of controlling nuclear war, on the other. They would differ, however, on the degree of flexibility and countermilitary capabilities required to maintain an effective deterrent. This debate raises several tangled issues.

First, there is the question of whether the character of retaliatory capabilities affects the United States' ability to credibly deter the Soviet Union. While some maintain that it is simply the possibility of some form of retaliation that ensures deterrence, most believe that some flexible retaliatory options—including options to attack opposing nuclear forces—are necessary, because certain kinds of retaliation may not be credible in certain circumstances. In particular, it is argued, the ability to launch large-scale attacks against Soviet cities may not be a credible threatened response to a Soviet attack limited to military targets that resulted in relatively few civilian casualties or destruction. While present American forces do provide some flexibility, there remain serious differences within the study group about the extent to which the United States can and should improve and modernize its nuclear delivery systems and its strategic command, control, communications, and intellience (C^3I) capabilities in order to provide greater retaliatory flexibility. An important element of this controversy concerns the degree to which these retaliatory counterforce capabilities must include the potential to be used promptly against hardened targets.

A second, related concern has to do with the requirements of extending deterrence to America's industrial allies. Since the mutual incineration of Soviet and American societies is not a rational response to a Soviet conventional attack against Western Europe, it is argued by many that the United States must possess a range of credible nuclear options in order to dissuade the Soviet Union from attacking and, equally important, to persuade the European members of NATO that America's nuclear guarantee is reliable. By this reasoning, the United States requires flexible and limited counterforce options to make credible the first-use of nuclear weapons in the event that NATO were losing a conventional war. A few members of the study group, however, believe that the risk of escalation to all-out nuclear war is sufficient to deter Soviet conventional attacks and to reassure America's NATO allies. Indeed, they note, discussion of the possibility of limited nuclear war has caused political problems within the alliance but has not reassured the allies about U.S. commitments. A dispute remains over the kinds of nuclear capabilities required by America's alliance commitments.

These issues raise yet a third dimension of the controversy over U.S. strategic force requirements: the complicated relationships among conventional forces and battlefield, intermediate-range, and strategic nuclear capabilities. Emphasis on the adequacy of conventional forces could reduce the role of nuclear weapons in American strategy, but over nearly thirty years, persistent conventional deficiencies have been made up at least in part by NATO's European-based nuclear systems. These systems are themselves a cause of doctrinal confusion, because although most see them as the bridge connecting conventional and strategic nuclear forces, some maintain that they could serve as an intermediate escalatory option that would decouple the United States and U.S. central strategic forces from the defense of Europe.

Moreover, the improvement of Soviet conventional and strategic nuclear forces—including particular attention to command and control systems—combined with the modernization of its theater nuclear forces, has raised doubts about the adequacy of American forces at every level. This development has triggered the concern about "escalation dominance." To summarize, some maintain that an ability to fight successfully (or at least not be clearly inferior) at various levels of nuclear escalation is necessary to make U.S. nuclear threats credible, and therefore effective, in protecting U.S. interests in a variety of situations. Some would go so far as to argue that even the basic commitment to deter nuclear attack against Europe would no longer be credible without such capabilities. Others, on the other hand, argue that deterrence is based fundamentally on the certainty of retaliation and the uncertainties surrounding any outbreak of nuclear war, not the specific character of the forces possessed by each side. From this perspective, so long as neither side is vulnerable to a disarming first-strike, capabilities to fight nuclear wars are not only unnecessary but destabilizing, because they raise the danger of preemptive strikes by the opponent in a crisis.

These divergent perspectives pervade the strategic community; they were faithfully reflected in the study group. Although it is not possible to present a single position, there is some common ground between these two very different approaches to strategic policy. The recommendations about the procurement of strategic forces that follow generally inspired widespread support *despite* these disagreements.

Moreover, all the study group's members believed that, along with weapon programs, arms negotiations can make a contribution to American security policy; the attainment of some strategic goals—achieving a more stable strategic balance and reducing nuclear force levels—can be more easily and more safely accomplished if arms negotiations play a constructive role than if they do not. Consequently, it is worth taking steps to preserve what has been accomplished in previous arms negotiations and to move forward with the arms control process.

A number of political factors, however, will have a role in determining the position of arms control in U.S. policy. It has become an important symbolic issue, for example, in American domestic politics. Though arms control negotiations were never intended to solve all America's strategic problems or to alter Soviet foreign policy behavior, they have been judged by these criteria. So long as arms negotiations are expected to accomplish such unrealistic goals, arms control will experience domestic political difficulties, particularly when it becomes a partisan electoral issue.

Arms negotiations will always constitute only one dimension of the broader Soviet-American relationship, and they are bound to be affected by the others, including such controversial issues as human rights and economic relations. Arms negotiations will both influence and be influenced by the character of overall U.S.-Soviet relations, and it would be difficult for either the tone or the pace of negotiations to be out of phase with the rest of the relationship. Arms control, therefore, is linked inherently to Soviet behavior in spheres unrelated to nuclear weapons, whether or not it is also policy to deliberately manipulate arms negotiations in this way. Events over the past fifteen years have demonstrated amply that, welcomed or not, some linkage is unavoidable. In a democratic political system, government can influence but cannot determine the popular response to world events. If there is to be real progress in arms control, there will have to be significant improvements in the tone and substance of U.S.-Soviet relations.

Events of the past several years have also highlighted another kind of linkage—the linkage of arms control negotiations to relations within the Western alliance. Nuclear weapons issues have become particularly sensitive in Europe, and NATO nuclear modernization programs have had significant domestic political repercussions there. In turn, these events have led to considerable pressures for accelerated progress in arms negotiations. The apparent strength of the antinuclear movement in Europe has been sufficient to virtually compel negotiations on intermediate-range nuclear systems based there, for example.

Given this complicated political matrix for arms control—with some political pressures constraining it while others are urging it forward—it is not easy to define a coherent, constructive, and politically sustainable arms control policy. The problem is complicated by the messy institutional infrastructure of arms control: There are multilateral talks in Madrid on the possibility of negotiating "confidence and security-building measures" to reduce the risk of war; interalliance negotiations in Vienna on mutual force reductions covering conventional and possibly some nuclear forces in Europe; bilateral U.S.-Soviet talks in Geneva on intermediate-range nuclear forces (INF) in Europe; as well as the legacy of the SALT talks in the form of the still unratified SALT II treaty and the possibility of new Soviet-American strategic arms reduction talks (START). The connections between these various fora are ill-defined, and the overall framework to justify all this is not well thought out. When combined with political factors, this can result in policies that do not make much sense (for example, INF negotiations at a time when there are neither formal limitations on, nor active negotiations about, central nuclear forces).

Still, there is no doubt that arms control can make a constructive contribution to U.S. security policy. The potential benefits, moreover, make it urgent to attempt to resolve these difficulties of pursuing arms negotiations as soon as possible.

WEAPON PROGRAMS

Despite the recent and prospective growth in American defense spending, difficult choices lie ahead in weapons procurement. Even if the five-year defense budget proposed by the Reagan administration in 1982 were enacted fully, there would not be sufficient funds to pay for the proposed improvements in strategic capabilities, expansion of conventional forces, and step-ups in the readiness of U.S. armed forces. Despite the economic problems facing the United States, which themselves constrain the government's ability to spend on defense, the major difficulties in maintaining higher levels of defense spending are political. Recession and substantial cutbacks in spending on domestic programs—to say nothing of prospective annual deficits in excess of $100 billion—do not provide an atmosphere conducive to sustaining a consensus in favor of significantly higher defense spending. There is tension between the administration's effort to increase the defense budget and both the traditional objectives of the Republican party's economic policies and the programs favored by the Democratic party's traditional constituencies.

The United States can certainly afford to devote a larger share of its resources to defense, as it has done in the past. But this would require deferrals or cancellations of planned tax cuts, high deficits, further reductions in major social programs, or all three. In the current political-economic reality, it seems probable that steps like these can be taken only if the defense program also is trimmed back as the administration and the Congress come to terms with fiscal limitations. Under these circumstances, serious thought must be given to how the defense posture should be changed to accommodate possible budgetary shortfalls. Moreover, it is crucial to establish priorities among defense programs to assure that this nation's investment in defense is not spent unwisely.

In this context, the study group noted particularly that the need to improve conventional forces has important implications for strategic nuclear policy. Although strategic forces presently account for a relatively small share of the defense budget, each of the several strategic modernization programs now under consideration would require tens of billions of dollars over the next few years. Such sums are significant relative to expenditures on modernization programs for conventional weapons. Indeed, given the large share of the defense budget that is used for manpower and related expenses, strategic modernization, as now planned, could constitute a major portion of the total funding for weapons acquisition which is available to the Defense Department.[4]

4. During the next five years, strategic modernization programs conceivably could include the continued deployment of *Ohio*-class submarines and procurement of Trident I and Trident II submarine-launched ballistic missiles; acquisition of the MX ICBM and eventually, perhaps, a new basing system in which it would be deployed; substantial purchases of air-launched, ground-launched, and submarine-launched cruise missiles; acquisition of the B-1B bomber and extensive research and development on the advanced technology bomber; accelerated development, and possibly deployment, of a ballistic missile defense system; the acquisition of several components of an air defense system; accelerated spending on civil defense; and major improvements in the national command and control system. In October 1981, Secretary Weinberger estimated the five-year cost of these programs as $180 billion, a figure thought to be low by most observers.

In short, the longer-term budgetary implications of major strategic modernization programs should be examined in detail. It is possible, of course, to improve both conventional and nuclear forces simultaneously, especially in the context of rising defense budgets. And, if the United States does not maintain an adequate strategic force posture, it may find it increasingly difficult or risky to employ conventional forces in situations in which the USSR might become involved. Nonetheless, explicit consideration should be given to the opportunity cost of spending on strategic forces in terms of the size and readiness of the conventional forces in the mid- to late-1980s. In particular, should several major strategic procurement programs reach peak funding years simultaneously, such a development could have severe consequences for conventional forces. Avoiding this problem requires that priorities be established among candidate strategic programs.

Command and Control

The study group is of one mind that the highest priority among strategic programs should be increasing the survivability of command, control, communications, and intelligence capabilities. The strategic command and control system has long suffered from relative inattention and underfunding, despite its essential role in enabling American policymakers to actually employ nuclear forces, if necessary, and, thereby, its contribution to the credibility of the basic retaliatory threat. Unfortunately, strategic command and control is usually treated as an afterthought in public debate, which seems to be preoccupied with doctrines and weapons. Command and control is a very complicated subject and necessarily more highly classified than most other aspects of strategic questions. Moreover, command and control does not fall in the domain of any single military service and does not involve the procurement of major, and thus politically salient, systems—two additional reasons why public attention has been paid to it only recently.

The command and control system is beset with serious vulnerabilities; indeed, the United States probably has never had a system that could survive an attack dedicated to its destruction in any coherent sense. Although this vulnerability would not prevent some form of American retaliation, it would severely restrict the president's flexibility in deciding how to respond and could limit the effectiveness of whatever retaliation were chosen. The vulnerability of the system raises the risk that a president may mistakenly believe that he possessed many options, when in fact he possessed few. Alternatively, the vulnerability of command and control systems may lead the president to respond massively to an attack soon after a war were initiated, though he might have preferred to respond in a more deliberate and discriminating way. Moreover, an attack on U.S. command and control assets would not be very demanding for Soviet forces; it has been well within their grasp for many years.

Despite these existing vulnerabilities, the demands placed on the command and control systems are increasing. The trend in American strategic doctrine toward more flexible options and a broader set of targets creates new requirements for an effective and survivable command and control system. The deployment of ballistic missile defenses and antisatellite weapons would place even greater demands on the command and control system. The imbalance between the requirements of current targeting doctrine and existing C^3I capabilities is a serious problem, one that calls into question the reality of such doctrines.

The vulnerability of command and control has several dimensions. Even prior to a nuclear attack against the United States, early warning and communications satellites would be vulnerable to several kinds of antisatellite weapons. During a nuclear strike, communications could be disrupted by electromagnetic pulses (EMP) resulting from nuclear explosions and by the physical destruction of equipment. Command and control facilities also could be sabotaged by agents of the hostile power. Finally, the National Command Authority—that is, the political chain of command headed by the president that these communications systems are meant to serve—could be attrited. In short, with existing systems, in the event of nuclear war, the president and his designated successors might not survive, communications with and thus command of the units tasked with strategic missions could be fragile, and decisions of extreme importance may have to be made on the basis of inadequate and ambiguous information.

For all these reasons the study group urges that a concerted effort be made to reduce the vulnerability and increase the capabilities of the command and control system and that these efforts be given high budgetary priority. Such an effort would make an important contribution to the deterrence of nuclear war by ensuring that the president had a flexible array of retaliatory options at his disposal and by denying to Soviet leaders any possibility of believing that they could disarm the United States by striking at the command and control system. Significantly improving the command and control system will not be easy, however, requiring ten to fifteen years and tens of billions of dollars to complete. Moreover, there are many uncertainties about the technological possibilities for improving C^3I; simply throwing money at this problem would not necessarily result in significant improvements.

Nevertheless, improvements are desirable, and those measures aimed at improving the short-term survivability of the command and control system and at reducing the chance of premature or false response to warning receive the endorsement of the entire study group. Such measures would reduce the danger that only spasmodic responses to nuclear attack would be possible and would diminish the attractiveness of command and control assets as targets for preemptive attack. In general, programs that introduce further redundancy, proliferation of C^3I assets, and diversity should be pursued in order to reduce the current vulnerabilities of the system. Efforts also should be made to increase the interoperability and connectivity between the diverse components of the system, and additional steps should be taken to assure that the development of both commercial and government communications assets proceeds in a way that would support the nation's security in an emergency. There is also a specific need to harden communications systems against EMP effects.[5]

The desirability of attempting to develop long-term endurance for the command and control system as part of a war-fighting posture, on the other hand, is very controversial. For one thing, there are doubts about the technical feasibility of achieving a truly enduring system, one that could survive an initial attack and be reconstituted to perform its functions effectively in a continuously hostile environment during a protracted nuclear war. Survival, of course, would be a function of the scale of conflict: Survival for weeks or even months might be possible in exchanges limited to tens of weapons; in exchanges of hundreds of weapons, survival might be limited to hours

5. Programs that warrant consideration include additional airborne command posts and launch centers; larger numbers of communications and intelligence satellites, some of which could be kept as reserves; provision of antijamming capabilities and attack-detection sensors for satellites; the development of self-contained, mobile command centers; and possibly the burial of key communications nodes deep under ground.

or perhaps days. It is unreasonable to expect the C^3I system to survive beyond an initial response when confronted with an attack involving thousands of weapons. Of course, no matter how prolonged or intense the nuclear exchange might be, it may be possible to restore command and control capabilities over a period of time. This would be difficult and uncertain but not necessarily impossible.

Setting aside these technical problems, some members of the study group believe that steps toward the development of an enduring C^3I system capable of fighting nuclear wars are important to improve the credibility of the U.S. deterrent. Others, however, believe that attempts to develop capabilities to use nuclear weapons in limited wars would increase the risk that nuclear war would occur, by creating the illusion, but not the real means, of being able to control a nuclear war once it began.

Sea-Based Forces

A large majority of the study group urged that a high priority also be accorded to continued modernization of the sea-based component of U.S. strategic forces with *Ohio*-class submarines and Trident missiles, including development of the Trident II missile (which could have greater range, higher accuracy, and more warheads of larger yields than the Trident I SLBM). Submarines are clearly the most survivable component of the force posture for the foreseeable future. They can thus serve as the major component of the United States' nuclear retaliatory potential well into the next century. Moreover, the greater capabilities of Trident submarines and missiles make it possible to consider adding new missions to those already assigned to sea-based forces.

The extended range of both Trident I and Trident II missiles will increase the expanse of ocean in which U.S. strategic submarines can operate and still strike targets in the Soviet Union; this will complicate the problems faced by Soviet antisubmarine warfare forces and thus reduce the potential vulnerability of U.S. submarines. Other characteristics of the *Ohio*-class ballistic missile submarine, such as reduced acoustic and other emissions, would make it even more difficult to detect and localize U.S. strategic submarines.

The increased lethality of the Trident II missile would have two effects. First, it would give American strategic forces an effective capability to destroy hardened Soviet targets, such as missile silos, thus eliminating the prospect that the Soviet Union could launch a very damaging first-strike against U.S. ICBMs, using only a small portion of its own ICBMs, and be assured that the remainder of its strategic forces would be virtually invulnerable. Thus, militarily, Trident II might provide additional assurance that the Soviet Union would not be tempted to strike at U.S. ICBMs under extreme circumstances. Second, politically, Trident II could offset whatever adverse consequences might be associated with the emergence of unmatched Soviet capabilities to destroy missile silos.[6]

Trident II could serve these purposes either as a supplement to, or substitute for the MX missile deployed on land. Sea-based missiles for these purposes could be deployed either in additional *Ohio*-class submarines or in smaller and less expensive submarines.

Bombers

There also was agreement among virtually all the members of the study group that the force of strategic bombers should be maintained and modernized. The existence of bombers makes it even more unlikely that the Soviet Union could come to believe that it might be able to attack the United States and suffer relatively little damage in retaliation, since both effective missile and aircraft defenses would be necessary to stop the U.S. retaliatory strike. Bombers are thus a hedge against a catastrophic failure of ballistic missiles. Since bombers also rely on unique means of surviving a Soviet first strike, their existence greatly complicates any Soviet plans to initiate nuclear war. Bombers also can be launched but delayed from striking their targets, as well as be recalled, thus providing greater flexibility and more time than ICBMs to decisionmakers considering responses to less than all-out attacks. Finally, bombers can be useful in a variety of missions unrelated to nuclear war planning.

The question of how to modernize the bomber force, on the other hand, was the subject of lively debate. The trade-offs among the aircraft and cruise missiles that are considered candidates to replace existing B-52s are complicated and partly dependent upon subjective

---

6. As suggested previously, not all members of the study group believe that these military and political risks are significant.

factors. Resolution of the issue is made more difficult by the fact that only limited information is publicly available about the Stealth program, resulting in uncertainty about its current status and future prospects.

Most members of the study group believe that the existing bomber force is formidable and are confident that, for at least the remainder of this decade, B-52s and FB-111s flying at low altitudes will be able to penetrate Soviet air defenses. Whatever improvements in Soviet air defenses may occur, they believe, will be more than compensated for by the program already underway to equip 170 of the existing 250 later model B-52s with 3,000 long-range cruise missiles. Consequently, they maintain that it is not necessary to decide for several years which new type of aircraft should be acquired. Postponement of procurement funding for the B-1B bomber would permit the advanced technology bomber to be developed to the point where a better informed choice might be made, as well as easing somewhat the expected squeeze on procurement monies in the mid-1980s.

Indeed, some people believe that it may be possible to avoid acquiring new aircraft designed to penetrate Soviet air defenses indefinitely, relying instead on a less costly aircraft that would stand off from Soviet airspace and fire cruise missiles that would penetrate to the targets. Cruise missiles and aircraft without the design characteristics necessary to penetrate air defenses are relatively inexpensive and thus could be purchased in large enough quantities to rely on saturation tactics to offset improvements in Soviet air defenses. Moreover, the modern cruise missile is a relatively new weapon, and its performance can be substantially improved over time with respect to greater range and speed, lesser detectability (employing Stealth technology), and the provision of electronic countermeasures, decoys, and multiple warheads.

The case for the B-1B rests in the first instance on uncertainties about the eventual effectiveness, date of availability, and cost of the advanced technology bomber. In theory, an aircraft incorporating Stealth technologies would be the most effective counter to prospective improvements in Soviet air defenses. The question is whether these concepts and laboratory designs can be converted into an effective aircraft, and, if so, when, at what cost, and with what risks.

Additionally, the B-1B has some advantages over the B-52, which might be important in assuring the effectiveness of the bomber force through the 1980s. Because it could take off more quickly, accelerate more rapidly, and would be more resistant to the effects of nuclear explosions, B-1Bs would be better able than B-52s to survive a Soviet first strike. Additionally, it could be deployed in time to help offset perceptions of a strategic imbalance favoring the Soviet Union in the mid- and late-1980s. This might help to avert any political consequences that might be associated with a sense that the USSR had all the momentum in the strategic arms competition.

On the other hand, it seems likely that the B-1B, like the B-52, would be vulnerable to the deployment by the Soviet Union of look-down, shoot-down capabilities in the early 1990s. While the B-1B's smaller radar cross-section is an improvement over that of the B-52 in this respect, it may not be small enough to permit it—like the cruise missile—to be indistinguishable from radar returns from the ground and thus to remain undetectable. If this were the case, then the very large expenditures planned to buy the B-1B ($20 to $40 billion) would have been used for an aircraft whose usefulness in strategic planning would be very short-lived. Although B-1Bs could then still be used in conventional warfare, there are less expensive ways of acquiring those capabilities. From this perspective, the B-1B thus appears to be a poor bargain, biting deeply into available procurement monies for limited purposes and perhaps delaying development of Stealth technologies. Those who hold this view maintain that it would be more efficient to forego the B-1B, instead spending as much as could be spent effectively on development of the advanced technology bomber.

Three factors combined to persuade the majority of the study group that the B-1B should not be procured: the substantial capability of the existing B-52/cruise missile force; the prospective effectiveness of the advanced technology bomber; and, most importantly, concern about the cost of the B-1B. Given the likelihood of severe budgetary difficulties over the next three to five years, most members of the study group believe that the B-1B program has to give way to higher priorities, such as improving command and control systems and modernizing the sea-based forces. In this context, it makes sense to delay procuring a new bomber while Stealth technology is developed further.

Land-Based Missiles

The members of the study group agreed that unless they were launched on warning of, or during an attack, the present U.S. force of ICBMs would have to be considered vulnerable to a Soviet first strike. While operational factors might degrade the effectiveness of an attack as compared to theoretical calculations, the members of the study group did not believe that these factors were serious enough to reassert confidence in the survivability of missiles based in silos.

Unfortunately, it has by now become clear that there are no solutions to the problem of ICBM vulnerability without significant drawbacks; after years of study, the best we can hope to find is the "least-bad" alternative. It is the contrast between the clearcut strategic imperative to preserve survivable forces and the absence of a clearcut solution to ICBM vulnerability that makes this question so difficult.

Concern about the vulnerability of ICBMs derives in part from a larger concern to preserve the diversity of U.S. strategic forces. The maintenance of diversified forces contributes to overall force survivability by complicating Soviet attack planning: Because different strategic components rely on different means of protection, it would be extremely difficult for the Soviet Union to destroy each of the several types of systems simultaneously. Diversified forces also hedge against the sudden emergence of presently unknown vulnerabilities. By confronting the Soviets with several technical and military problems to solve in order to place the entire U.S. strategic force in jeopardy, the United States maximizes both the cost and difficulty of the Soviets' acquiring a first-strike capability, thereby providing incentives for the USSR to negotiate measures to stabilize the strategic balance and reduce the size of strategic forces.

While the need for diversity is compelling, the forces that are necessary to satisfy the requirement are less well defined. There are many ways that diversity can be built into the strategic arsenal, and the existing configuration of forces need not be treated as sacrosanct. In the current context, this means that land-based missiles could be replaced with other than land-based missiles and still preserve diversity.

The study group noted that the issue of ICBM vulnerability has raised a whole series of policy questions, which are often mixed together in a confused and undifferentiated way in the public debate. Some focus on the question of whether much effort should be devoted to maintaining the ICBM leg of the triad, given the great difficulty in preserving its survivability. Others assume that ICBMs should be maintained and are preoccupied with finding the best means of modernizing the force so as to reduce its vulnerability. The problem of ICBM modernization also is bound up with the dispute over

U.S. requirements for capabilities to promptly destroy hardened targets; the new ICBM—the MX—would have much greater capabilities in that regard than most alternatives that have been proposed. A related issue is whether ICBM modernization ought to emphasize flexibility of employment or survivability. Is it necessary to reproduce the capabilities of the current Minuteman force (in terms of command and control, target coverage, flexibility, etc.), or is the main point simply to preserve some kind of relatively survivable land-based strategic component?

Some approach the specific issue of Minuteman vulnerability as an immediate policy problem requiring short-term remedies in order to avert the danger that the Soviet Union might exploit this vulnerability politically and perhaps even militarily. Others see it in terms of ensuring the survivability of the U.S. strategic arsenal over the long run; from this perspective the issue is really one of providing a hedge against a future Soviet breakthrough in ASW technologies rather than simply a matter of fixing the ICBM vulnerability problem as such. Still others feel that Minuteman vulnerability should neither raise the specter of Soviet intimidation nor be related to the unlikely prospect of a Soviet ASW breakthrough, and that perceptions of this issue have been overblown by the inflated rhetoric of public debate. In short, there is not even agreement on what the problem is, much less on how to solve it.

Perhaps because of this lack of clarity, proposed solutions produce controversy and disagreement. Pointedly, some members of the study group question the need for the proposed MX ICBM. They point out that the MX has been advanced as the solution for a whole series of strategic problems, including not only ICBM vulnerability but the need to recapture momentum in the strategic competition to counter the political effects of the Soviet strategic buildup, the desire to stress Soviet defense planning as much as possible by making Soviet ICBMs vulnerable, and the necessity of hedging against longer-term concerns about possible breakthroughs in antisubmarine warfare capabilities. But, they argue, the MX in a mobile, land-based mode is not a necessary solution to any of these concerns, including the problem of reducing ICBM vulnerability. There are alternative ways of achieving these objectives. The relevant question is really how to minimize the risk of a Soviet first-strike, not simply how to make ICBMs less vulnerable.

Those who hold to this view suggest that the United States has long lived with, and accommodated in its strategic thinking, substantial degrees of vulnerability in its strategic force. There is no need for all three legs of the triad to be completely invulnerable, it is argued; and although the vulnerability of the ICBM force ought to be reduced in the long run, the current bomber force—and, especially, the strategic submarine force—provide the United States with sizable and relatively flexible retaliatory capabilities. Moreover, there are a number of scenarios involving limited nuclear exchanges in which the Minuteman force, despite its vulnerability, would be valuable. In addition, some of the benefits of a diverse force, in particular, the complication of Soviet attack planning,. are attained as a consequence of the mere existence of the Minuteman force, regardless of its vulnerability. Given that the survivability of the overall strategic force is not now in question and that at least some of the benefits of diversity are provided by even a vulnerable Minuteman force, the proponents of this point of view conclude that it is unnecessary to move rapidly toward deployment of the land-based MX.

Nor are they persuaded by the argument that the MX is urgently needed because the United States requires capabilities to destroy Soviet hard targets. Some, as noted, do not believe the United States needs such capabilities at all, but others suggest that even if capabilities to destroy hard targets are desired, MX is not the only nor the best system that could provide it. By the early 1990s, or even sooner, submarine-launched ballistic missiles could be accurate enough to perform that mission as well.

Additionally, considerable skepticism is expressed about the extent to which the MX would really solve the ICBM vulnerability problem. Hardening silos is rejected as an effective means of protecting ICBMs in the late 1980s and beyond. The proposal to base at least some MXs in existing Minuteman silos simply ignores the ICBM vulnerability problem. Ideas like burying the MX deep underground or deploying it on special aircraft designed to remain aloft for protracted periods of time require further development before they could be fully evaluated. The air mobile system, for example, may be vulnerable to a degree while in the air, as was suggested above for bombers, thus reducing its benefits for diversity. Basing the MX deep underground raises problems of its own. While most members of the study group stressed the desirability of continuing to explore these ideas, they were also skeptical of their ultimate practicality.

Some form of a system to move the MX among a number of protective shelters (like the Carter Administration's MPS system) certainly would raise the cost of a Soviet attack, but in addition to its environmental and political problems, the expected survivability of such a system would depend on the size of the threat posed against it. Thus, for example, just adding additional reentry vehicles to the existing number of SS-18 and SS-19 ICBMs would give the Soviet Union more than enough warheads to cover the 4,600 targets provided by the Carter proposal. Any such scheme thus would depend heavily on negotiated limits on Soviet forces for its survival, of which there would be no guarantee. Recognizing this problem, the Carter Administration envisioned maintaining a ballistic missile defense system in development that could credibly threaten to invoke a high price on any Soviet attack against the MPS system and threatening to deploy such defenses if the Soviets balked at limiting the warheads that could be targeted against MX/MPS. This, however, would raise problems of its own, as will be discussed shortly.

Those who subscribe to these arguments support various alternatives to the land-based MX. Some favor doing nothing new and relying more heavily on the other two components of the strategic force— perhaps expanding both the planned bomber/cruise missile force and the planned purchase of *Ohio*-class submarines so as to offset any political consequences of the continued vulnerability of U.S. ICBMs. Others favor deploying an intercontinental-range missile such as the MX or the Trident II on new types of smaller submarines. Largely because of their size, but also for other reasons, submarines of this type would be much less expensive than *Ohio*-class submarines and thus could be purchased in larger numbers. (At the same time, again because of their size, each would carry fewer missiles, and thus it is not clear what the difference might be, if any, in the cost per deployed missile or warhead.) The deployment of this new type of submarine would greatly aggravate the problems already faced by Soviet ASW forces, because they would have to deal with a much larger number of potential targets; moreover, the value of each submarine they were able to destroy would be reduced. In particular, ASW techniques depending on tracking individual targets would be made more difficult.

One proposal of this type, known as SUM, envisions building large numbers of diesel-powered submarines that would patrol in waters near the United States. Deployments in this zone would make the Soviet ASW problem even more difficult because of the distance from Soviet shores and military bases and also would ease somewhat problems of command and control associated with existing submarine deployment zones. Because these submarines would be small and quiet, they would be difficult to detect, another reason why Soviet ASW efforts would be made more difficult. While some concern was expressed at one point by a few defense officials about the potential vulnerability of these submarines to barrage attacks if deployed along the continental shelf (the so-called Van Doren effect), the deployment zone actually envisioned is large enough to mitigate these worries as well as threats imagining attempts to blanket a large ocean area with weapons that could destroy any submarine located there.

Other proposals also urge diversifying U.S. strategic forces by acquiring larger numbers of smaller and less expensive submarines that would deploy in different areas than *Ohio*-class submarines, but do not necessarily support either the use of diesel power for these submarines nor the proposal to deploy them near U.S. waters. Deployments under the Arctic ice have been suggested, for example, which would require that the new type of submarine be nuclear-powered.

In any case, the choice between additional *Ohio*-class submarines and smaller submarines hinges on economic and technical considerations. The prior and primary policy question is whether an expanded sea-based deterrent could provide a viable alternative, politically and militarily, to a new type of land-based missile.

None of this is to suggest that the MX was without its supporters in the study group. Because the MX would be much larger than existing American ICBMs, it would reduce the Soviet advantage in missile throw-weight, thus providing a political offset to Soviet heavy missiles. Because it would be so accurate, the MX also would enable the United States to match Soviet capabilities to destroy missile silos, again with the salutary political consequence of ameliorating perceptions of strategic imbalance. Preserving the land-based ICBM force, it is suggested, is preferable to having it appear that the Soviet Union, by acquiring substantial countersilo capabilities, was able to compel the United States to abandon ICBMs.

Proponents of the MX make several points concerning its potential vulnerability. Any mobile deployment would have to be targeted by thousands of Soviet warheads that otherwise could be allocated to the destruction of America's strategic bombers and submarines. It thus would contribute significantly to the overall survivability of the strategic force and prevent the USSR from devoting all of its resources to the problems of attacking bombers and submarines. Although it seems very unlikely, no one can be absolutely certain that the Soviets will not come up with effective antisubmarine or air defense weapons based on presently unknown technologies.

Because of these fundamental disagreements between proponents and critics of ICBM modernization, there is widespread support in the study group for only the more general propositions about ICBM vulnerability—notably, that diversified strategic forces should be maintained and that vulnerabilities in the strategic forces should not be permitted to become so great that they threaten the overall survivability of the force. There is no consensus about the specific paths to be followed in implementing these general propositions.

Finally, the ICBM vulnerability problem raises anew the question of ballistic missile defenses. Some maintain that the MPS system or the recently proposed "Dense-Pack" deployment scheme could be combined advantageously with ballistic missile defenses to provide viable options for preserving the survivability of land-based missiles. These issues are discussed in the next section of this chapter.

APPROACHES TO STRATEGIC ARMS CONTROL

Are there ways of realizing the potential benefits of arms control while avoiding its problems? The study group thinks so. It must be understood first, however, why past efforts to negotiate limits on arms have encountered serious problems. While there clearly have been important and tangible gains from the negotiations, they have not succeeded in easing the central problems of managing the strategic balance—namely, creating force postures that would be stable in crises and substantially reducing force levels. Why is this?

The periodic deteriorations in U.S.-Soviet relations represent a basic difficulty in pursuing arms control. Because it has been impossible to establish and sustain a mutually acceptable relationship, it has been hard to put arms control on a firm long-term footing. This is especially true when arms control policies are employed by American or Soviet policymakers as an instrument with which to reward or punish the other's behavior.

It is also true, however, that some linkage of the U.S. approach to arms negotiations with Soviet behavior is an unavoidable fact, whether or not it is also a deliberate policy choice. There is no way to completely isolate arms control from the effects of Soviet foreign and defense policies on American opinion. Arms control can not be completely exempted from other strains on political relations because the domestic political support necessary for the success of negotiations erodes when Soviet-American relations deteriorate. As a result, arms negotiations cannot be pursued effectively when confrontations arise, such as happened following the Soviet intervention in Afghanistan.

Because there are so many potential points of friction in U.S.-Soviet relations, dramatic successes in Soviet-American arms control efforts are unlikely. Yet conversely, and perhaps paradoxically, in the long run, good U.S.-Soviet relations probably require active and successful arms negotiations since they embody most vividly the mutual interests and possibilities for cooperation between the two powers. It is difficult to imagine a modus vivendi ever being reached between the two great nuclear powers, so long as they continue—unrestrained—to arm themselves with weapons intended to obliterate each other. This reverse linkage highlights once again the important relationship between arms control and foreign policy considerations.

That relationship also is evident in yet another kind of linkage, the linkage of arms control to European-American relations. NATO nuclear weapons policy has become, for the time being at least, a highly volatile issue in the domestic politics of a number of West European countries and therefore is a particularly sensitive aspect of Alliance relations. As we have noted, the public clamor in Western Europe for negotiations on intermediate-range nuclear forces proved impossible to ignore. Similar pressures are likely to bear on these talks as they continue, as well as on the prospects for resumption of talks about central forces. American policy toward arms negotiations, as well as NATO decisions on nuclear deployments, cannot be made without taking this political situation into account.

Thus, arms control is linked, in various ways, to Soviet behavior and to American and European domestic politics. The powerful impact of these linkages on the fortunes of arms control is suggested by the fact that the Carter Administration tried but failed to resist the linkage of SALT II to Soviet behavior, while the Reagan Administration tried but failed to resist the linkage of talks on intermediate-range nuclear forces to European politics. It seems clear that political factors constitute a fundamental constraint on arms control policy; any arms control strategy that fails to take this into account will surely run into trouble.

Turning to specific items on the possible agenda for arms control, a major unresolved issue is the status of the SALT II Treaty. Signed by Presidents Carter and Brezhnev in 1979, it has been observed, but not ratified, for nearly three years. How long this situation can continue is unclear.[7]

Renouncing the SALT II Treaty explicitly, without the prior establishment of a viable substitute, would obviously not make sense. Politically, of course, such an abandonment of arms control could cause grave difficulties in U.S.-European relations, as it would scuttle the ongoing Geneva talks on intermediate nuclear forces and, with them, the NATO decision to deploy Pershing II ballistic missiles and ground-launched cruise missiles. Militarily, such a move would mean that the Soviet threat could become more severe. Limits in SALT II on the number of warheads that may be deployed on each type of missile, for example, prevent the Soviet Union from exploiting fully the large throw-weight of their land-based missiles. Ceilings on the number of MIRVed missiles and heavy ICBMs further limit the number of Soviet warheads. Without these provisions, it could be even more difficult to cope with the putative vulnerability of U.S. ICBMs.

The most important point, however, is that the United States has nothing to gain from terminating SALT II because none of the strategic programs now planned are foreclosed by the treaty. In the short run, terminating the treaty would open options for the USSR and none of significance for the United States. It seems likely that, in an unconstrained strategic environment, the Soviet Union might do at least some of the things presently available to it, such as deploying more missiles, putting additional warheads on existing missiles, deploying Backfire bombers at a more rapid rate, and so on.

For these reasons, the study group concluded that American interests are served by the continued viability of the restrictions in SALT II.[8] Clearly, the treaty does not solve the major strategic prob-

---

7. Also, the 1972 SALT I Interim Agreement on Offensive Weapons, which expired formally in 1977, has continued to be observed by both parties.

8. Most members would except the restrictions on cruise missiles included in the Protocol to the Treaty from this judgment; the Protocol was to have remained in effect only until the end of 1981, in any event.

lems facing the United States, nor does it provide a long-term framework for making strategic policy, as its lifetime is short. Still, observance of the SALT II limits can play a constructive, if modest, role in American strategic policy.

At present, of course, it seems unlikely that the existing SALT II Treaty will ever be ratified. After the Soviet occupation of Afghanistan, the necessary political support for the treaty crumbled. President Reagan and many of his top foreign affairs advisors took the position during the 1980 electoral campaign that the treaty was "fatally flawed" and therefore unacceptable. This means that it would be politically awkward for the administration to ask the Senate for ratification, at least without first obtaining Soviet agreement to some changes.

Under the circumstances, both the most likely outcome, and that preferred by a majority of the study group, is continued tacit U.S. adherence to the SALT guidelines so long as the Soviet Union does so also. This is certainly preferable to the abandonment of the arms control process and would provide the constraints of the treaty if not its legal weight.[9] Such an arrangement may not be sustainable over the long run, however, and in any case would not facilitate additional steps toward more meaningful negotiated controls on strategic forces.

One possible next step would be negotiations to modify the SALT II Treaty. While the Soviets might well accept a number of cosmetic changes to make ratification more attractive politically, talks to modify the treaty in a substantive fashion would almost surely be protracted. The Soviets would no doubt match any changes desired by the United States with their own proposals for changes, which would then require a substantial recasting of the treaty. Rather than get mired again in detailed negotiations about SALT II, most study group members agreed that modifications to the treaty should be sought only if it were determined that relatively minor changes would be politically significant and necessary to facilitate ratification of the treaty by the Senate. Of course, the Soviets may insist that action be taken on SALT II before moving on to negotiations about other limits on strategic forces, in which case prolonged talks about the existing treaty could not be avoided without scrapping strategic arms negotiations altogether.

---

9. Some limitations, such as requirements that certain Soviet forces be dismantled by certain dates, obviously would not be observed in the absence of ratification. Similarly, as noted, the limitations contained in the Protocol have already expired.

In moving beyond SALT II, the most immediate and pressing issues concern how to limit intermediate-range nuclear forces in Europe. Progress toward agreement on those forces, or at least the appearance of such progress, seems to be prerequisite for successful implementation of NATO's decision to deploy Pershing II ballistic missiles and ground-launched cruise missiles in several nations; it would also help reduce the present political disarray of the alliance.

The stakes are high. If the deployment decision falters, it would constitute a major crisis in U.S.-European relations by making it appear that the Soviet Union had a veto over NATO weapon decisions. It could have severe domestic political repercussions in Europe, where a number of governments have expended considerable political capital to support the decision. Moreover, collapse of the modernization program would deprive NATO of weapons that for several years have been touted as politically and militarily necessary.

Moved by these concerns, the Reagan Administration agreed in November 1981 to continue U.S.-Soviet negotiations on intermediate-range nuclear forces. The political problem is to make these negotiations credible to NATO governments and particularly to the European public. This may be difficult because the issues are complex and politically sensitive, little thought has been given to them relative to central forces, and rapid progress is unlikely. Moreover, the Soviet Union has incentives to drag out the negotiations. The United States may thus be torn by conflicting pressures: the need to bargain carefully over complicated issues, on the one hand, and the need for tangible progress to mollify European opinion, on the other.

The Geneva talks also raise a number of difficult substantive issues. For one thing, the objective of the talks has not been clarified. Are they being pursued primarily to make NATO's planned long-range theater nuclear force modernization politically acceptable in Western Europe? Is there some required minimum level of these forces upon which NATO must insist? Is the "zero option" (that is, President Reagan's offer to forego NATO's intermediate-range missile deployments if the Soviet Union eliminates its own forces) attainable?

In terms of the possible content of a treaty, there is no agreement on what to count (missiles only, or missiles and aircraft, and, if so, which ones). A means may have to be found to deal with British and French nuclear forces, which the U.S. refuses to include in the negotiations but which the Soviet Union insists must be accounted for, somehow, in any negotiated limits. It is not clear what would happen to missiles that have to be withdrawn from Europe as the result of agreement. If only moved elsewhere, they would pose a threat of sudden abrogation of the treaty, as well as complicate other political relations. Moreover, there are likely to be serious problems of verification, since the SS-20, Pershing ballistic missiles, and cruise missiles are small and mobile as compared to strategic systems, and many types of aircraft can be assigned to either conventional or nuclear missions.

But there is an additional complication: These negotiations make little sense outside the framework of strategic arms control. There is little logic in seeking constraints on intermediate range nuclear systems if they are not accompanied by, and coordinated with, constraints on intercontinental systems. Nor is any agreement dealing strictly with intermediate forces—those weapons whose political implications form the most sensitive junctures of U.S.-European-Soviet relations—likely to be able to withstand the political heat of public scrutiny.

Thus, the members of the study group were nearly unanimous in recognizing that there is a political imperative to continue talks on intermediate-range nuclear forces in Europe, making progress as circumstances permit. Most felt it also was essential, however, to embed those talks as soon as possible in the broader context of negotiations about all strategic forces. Whether these latter talks should concentrate initially on modifying the SALT II treaty or move immediately to discuss deep reductions in strategic forces or some other more ambitious form of strategic arms control should depend on a judgment about the chances for retaining the continued viability of SALT II restrictions without its formal ratification. This judgment, in the opinion of most members of the study group, can be reached only on the basis of at least preliminary discussions with the Soviet Union.

When negotiations on central forces resume, they will confront many difficult issues. The Reagan Administration has stated repeatedly that it wishes to concentrate on bringing about significant reductions in strategic forces. The Soviets, for their part, have indicated a certain empathy with this approach, but the specific implementation of any cuts could well be difficult. An obvious problem would be how to apportion whatever cuts were agreed to. The United States will surely emphasize the desirability of reducing MIRVed land-based missiles—the weapons that threaten the survivability of U.S. ICBMs—but the Soviets, who have invested the largest portion of their forces in these types of weapons, are likely to have rather different priorities for reductions.

A second problem concerns the metric to be used in specifying permissible force levels. Past SALT agreements focused on missile launchers and bombers, but some—including many officials of the present administration—have urged turning to more telling indices of strategic capabilities, indices that could take into account the fact that different missiles are equipped with different numbers of warheads of differing yields and accuracies and thus have different lethalities.

If such a change were made, it would raise a third problem to even greater prominence: How should compliance with future arms control agreements be verified? Already, the U.S. administration has stated its intention of seeking more effective means of verifying compliance with arms agreements, citing serious questions raised recently concerning Soviet compliance with the still unratified Threshold Test Ban Treaty, the 1925 Geneva Protocol on Chemical Warfare, and the 1975 Convention on Biological Weapons. The Soviets, for their part, reject both the charges made against them of noncompliance with previous treaties and the need for other than continuing reliance on national technical means of verification. In past negotiations, however, the Soviets have demonstrated a willingness to entertain various sorts of cooperative measures to facilitate verification of agreements, and thus the possibility of significant changes in this area should not be ruled out.

An additional issue necessarily on the strategic arms control agenda for resolution in the near term concerns the future of the ABM Treaty. Although the treaty is of indefinite duration, and although it can be amended at any time, its provisions also require that it be reviewed at five-year intervals, 1982 being one such year. The salient question is whether the treaty should be amended now to permit the deployment of missile defenses to protect ICBM sites.

Obviously, it would not be sensible to amend the treaty if there is no BMD technology at hand that could be deployed with reasonable expectation of success. During the debate on the Sentinel and Safeguard ABM systems during the late 1960s and early 1970s, the most telling arguments against proceeding with deployment were that the proposed system would not work or that it could be easily countered. Despite tremendous advances in some BMD technologies, most members of this study group agreed that this remains largely true today. Any sort of effective area defense of cities and populations still remains beyond reach, as it does not appear that the capabilities necessary to intercept large numbers of attacking warheads in space, effectively and reliably, could be achieved in the foreseeable future. And defending ICBMs in silos, while less implausible, does not yet appear possible because such defenses could be saturated and because key components would remain vulnerable to attack. Even if there were technologies that inspired greater confidence, it would not be sensible to amend the treaty until the deployment schedule suggested that a provision of the treaty might otherwise be violated.

The best case for a BMD deployment to protect ICBMs can be made in conjunction with a multiple protective shelter system including a large number of potential targets. Such a system would remain relatively survivable even if a considerable fraction of the attacking warheads succeeded in penetrating the defenses. The BMD system need be only moderately effective to serve its purpose, so long as one assumes that the preferential defense of those shelters actually containing ICBMs is feasible. Also, because only the shelters in which the ICBMs actually were located would need to be defended, and because the Soviet Union presumably would not know which these were, each ABM interceptor could require the Soviet Union to expend many warheads to be sure of destroying each shelter in the cluster; in this circumstance, the defense would gain considerable leverage over the offense. Finally, in a multiple protective shelter scheme the BMD system could itself be deployed in a mobile and deceptive way, thereby reducing its own vulnerability.[10]

Even if it were decided to deploy ICBMs among multiple protective shelters, however, it would still be necessary to weigh the putative gain in survivability implied by an accompanying BMD system against the costs of seeking to amend the ABM Treaty. Aside from the political disarray that could result from reopening this one most significant accomplishment of U.S.-Soviet arms negotiations, the major cost would be the deployment of a Soviet BMD system, which could make American targeting plans more difficult and several types of limited options less feasible.

It also could raise concerns about the future capability of ballistic missiles to penetrate Soviet defenses, since American policymakers would have to plan against the possibility that a Soviet BMD system would work better than expected and be expanded suddenly. This, in

10. There are, however, technical questions as to whether all the signatures of the offensive and defensive missiles could be simulated with sufficient accuracy to maintain confidence that their real location would remain unknown.

turn, could lead to pressures for higher levels of offensive forces as well as poisoning the political atmosphere even further. British, French, and Chinese officials could have similar concerns about their own ballistic missiles and thus about the effectiveness of their deterrents. There also would be allegations that it might not be possible to distinguish between ICBM site and area defenses, even if the Soviets agreed—which seems unlikely—to permit the former and not the latter. Because area defense of population centers would stand a much better chance of success against the residual U.S. forces that survived a preemptive attack than against the entire strategic arsenal of an adversary, charges that the Soviets had deployed area defenses could raise worrisome questions about possible Soviet intentions to strike first, particularly in the event of a crisis.

The choice, then, is between a world in which neither side has significant ballistic missile defenses and a world in which both might. The latter must be clearly preferable and achievable for it to be worth seeking to alter the ABM Treaty. In the opinion of nearly all members of the study group, this is not now the case, given the current and prospective capabilities of BMD technologies.

This does not mean that the ABM Treaty should be treated as sacrosanct. At some point it may become desirable to modify the treaty to permit carefully defined defensive missile sites. For now, however, the costs appear to outweigh the benefits, and it would be premature to consider modifying the treaty in 1982. Though the next scheduled review conference would not be until 1987, negotiations could be opened at any time to amend the treaty, at either party's request.

There remains the question of the long-term future of strategic arms control negotiations. Three factors must be examined: the objectives they could fulfill; the means by which those objectives could best be achieved; and the feasibility that these benefits would be obtained.

Clear specification of the objectives of arms control negotiations is important to the proper understanding of the contribution they can make to American security policy. These talks are not the answer to all the problems of U.S. strategic policy, and those who judge them by that standard will inevitably be disappointed. But negotiations can help to shape the strategic environment in ways that are beneficial to American security.

The most important goal of arms control is to reduce the chance that a crisis would erupt into nuclear war. This is really a matter of structuring the strategic environment so that the incentives to use nuclear weapons are low. A second objective of arms control is to dampen the intensity of the arms race, so as to avoid its adverse effects on political relations. This entails prevention of the competitive accumulation of weapons by both sides that result in no net gain in security for either. Achieving this objective also could reduce the financial cost of maintaining an adequate strategic posture.

These, of course, are the classic objectives of arms control. They have informed strategic arms control efforts in the past and are a reasonable and practical guide to future efforts. If the American public comes to expect more—if it expects arms control to play the major role in preserving the survivability of U.S. strategic forces, to change the character of the Soviet Union or to alter Soviet foreign policy behavior, or to enable the United States to avoid costly but necessary weapon programs—then the arms control process is bound to be perceived to have failed.

What means can best be employed in pursuit of these objectives? Here the important point is that there are a number of approaches to arms control, and American policy should not focus exclusively on any one of them. Formal negotiations proceed very slowly and cannot always keep pace with developments in technology. They also produce treaties whose hidden compromises and great complexities are not easy to explain or to defend in the court of American public opinion.

There is room therefore for less formal, less public arrangements, focusing not on treaties but on the cooperative management of the strategic balance. A model for such efforts is the Standing Consultative Commission (SCC), created by the 1972 ABM Treaty to allow for the discussions of concerns about compliance with that treaty and the coincident Interim Agreement on Offensive Weapons. It meets periodically with relatively little fanfare, providing both powers with the opportunity to exchange views on troublesome developments. In the view of most members of the study group, this type of forum could help to ease the sorts of concerns that make crises more dangerous. One possibility would be to expand the functions of the SCC, either formally or simply by persuading the Soviets to permit new types of issues to be taken up in that forum. Regular talks between U.S. and Soviet military commanders could also serve as a mechanism for low-key discussions of strategic developments of mutual concern.

Much else could be done that would be stabilizing. Some members of the study group stressed the possibility of negotiating confidence-building measures to reduce the risks that a crisis would escalate to war because of inadvertence, miscalculation, or misperception of the other's intentions. One candidate for discussion would be the locations and modes in which nuclear weapons are based in Europe. Others might involve the operational patterns of certain strategic forces.

Ultimately, however, the question of how to restructure the strategic environment so as to reduce incentives to use nuclear weapons in the event of a crisis returns to the central theme of the section of this chapter on weapon programs; how to reduce the vulnerability of specific components of the strategic force posture. Here, formal arms negotiations, theoretically at least, could assist unilateral efforts to make strategic forces more survivable. It is not inconceivable, for example, that an agreement specifying deep reductions in strategic force levels could be structured so as to facilitate a shift from vulnerable, immobile, land-based systems to some sort of mobile alternative (and also specify cooperative measures to facilitate the verification of restrictions on mobile systems). Similarly in formal negotiations, the two sides could begin to discuss limitations on systems that present potential long-term threats to strategic components, such as satellite-based directed energy BMD systems. More exotic approaches to air defense and antisubmarine warfare might also provide useful topics for discussions. Experience has demonstrated repeatedly that success in arms negotiations is more likely to occur when the topics of discussion are some years away from realization.

The future of arms control is obviously not hampered primarily by a lack of reasonable goals or of potentially effective means of accomplishing them. The great question clouding the future of arms negotiations is the future course of U.S.-Soviet relations and the consequent political feasibility of such efforts. By this criterion, the historical record is not encouraging. The long history of SALT II exemplified pointedly the vulnerability of the arms control process to adversities in U.S.-Soviet relations.

We return, therefore, to the basic point that arms control is ultimately a problem of foreign policy and that it is to a large degree hostage to the state of U.S.-Soviet relations. For it is primarily dissatisfaction with the latter that has caused the erosion of political support for strategic arms control. This means that the future of arms control is dependent, first, on future Soviet foreign policy behavior and, second, on how the United States fits arms control into the overall pattern of its relations with the Soviet Union. These are the crucial questions for the future.

STATEMENT
by George Rathjens

Although a much-appreciated effort has been made to have chapter 11 reflect the range of views within the study group, my differences place me so far from its center that I wish to add supplementary comments.

I cannot imagine *rational* decisions by political leaders about the use of force that would be affected by the kinds of choices to which Chapter 11 gives such weight, for example, whether the United States should go ahead with the B-1, Trident II, or defense of MX missiles; and since such weapons will not reduce damage to us in the event of "irrational" decisions—nor necessarily make such decisions less likely—there is not much of a case for these weapons. While this perspective is well reflected in footnote 3, most of the chapter, which is understandably based on the majority view, is at variance with it.

I particularly discount scenarios that involve Soviet attacks against U.S. ICBMs. Barring drastic reductions in U.S. strategic capabilities, the Soviet Union could not execute such attacks without having to expect catastrophic consequences. Accordingly, the emphasis in Chapter 11, and in administration policy, on measures to deal with "ICBM vulnerability problems" seems misplaced and diversionary. We risk leading the public and political leaders here and abroad to believe, wrongly in my view, that improved security is to be found through greater investment in strategic weapons, and we acquiesce in the diversion of resources from the civil sector, and from other military programs, where they could make a difference.

Although a "freeze" on development, testing, and deployment of central strategic systems has its problems—it would not, in itself, leave us secure—there is more merit in that concept than in proposals for new strategic systems, and the group could have beneficially given attention to it. It might also have dealt more fully with reductions in strategic arms, considering the emphasis in the Reagan Administration's rhetoric and such proposals as George Kennan's for immediate reductions of 50 percent.

Turning to new weapons for Europe and the issue of their limited use raises problems that are more worrisome than those of the central balance, particularly because nuclear war—and its escalation beyond rational control—is more likely to result from the deployment and use of these "theater" weapons. Discounting "escalation dominance," as I do, as a prudent and feasible approach to European defense, GLCMs and the Pershing IIs, particularly the latter, can serve little purpose except to make escalation of conventional conflict more likely. That is something we do not need. They should not be deployed. Whether or not they are, NATO should adopt a "no-first-use" policy for nuclear weapons.

If these weapons and their Soviet counterparts, the SS-20s, are so worrisome—and also politically troublesome, as they are—I see no reason why negotiations relating to them need be dependent upon efforts on central strategic systems, as the working group suggests. Both in negotiations and in otherwise thinking about nuclear arms, those in Europe should command priority.

I have other problems with Chapter 11's treatment of arms control. *Significant* successes with central systems may be further off than it suggests; and those within early reach, less important. The latter are likely to have little effect on damage should war occur and, if I am right in earlier remarks, little effect on the likelihood of war. They may reduce uncertainties about worrisome adversary programs and may lead to reduced military expenditures—the ABM treaty has been important in both respects—but new negotiations, I fear, will be likely to have adverse consequences rather than favorable ones as we invest in systems we would otherwise not buy, justifying them as needed for negotiating strength.

Also, in emphasizing formal negotiations as *the* approach to arms control and in suggesting that progress must almost inevitably be coupled with good Soviet-American relations, the focus of Chapter 11 seems too narrow. Unilateral initiatives taken in the hope of some kind of reciprocation, such as occurred with the nuclear testing moratorium of 1958, may offer more hope for the future than continuing at a glacial pace with negotiations along SALT lines. Moreover, in the resolution of the Cuban missile crisis we have an existence proof that arms control successes can be achieved more quickly through still other procedures than those implied in Chapter 11, *given* sufficient motivation, *even* when Soviet-American relations are anything but harmonious.

While the working group did a good job in looking at strategic arms problems in detail, our product is disappointing. As Einstein said, "The unleashed power of the atom has changed everything save our modes of thinking, and we thus drift toward unparalleled catastrophes."

STATEMENT
by Leon Sloss and Brent Scowcroft

Strategic policy issues are fraught with controversy. Honest men frequently differ. Although we respect the wisdom and probity of our colleagues on the study group, our perspective differs substantially from the majority's. We believe that the majority view, specifically its overreliance on sea-based forces and the uncertain prospects of arms control, would produce a strategic posture inadequate for deterrence and insufficient to bolster an eroding alliance.

We are in agreement with most members of the study group in believing that the primary purpose of strategic forces is to deter. To do so, strategic forces must pose a credible threat to enemy forces and leadership. This requires flexibility, survivability, endurance, and counterforce capabilities. We also contend that nuclear forces can and should contribute, with other forces, to deterrence of non-nuclear aggression and to escalation control, should a non-nuclear war begin. This somewhat broader view than that of our colleagues affects the conclusions we reach regarding U.S. strategic requirements.

One vital role of strategic forces is to assure allies and underwrite U.S. nuclear commitments. This, in turn, furthers U.S. objectives to curb nuclear proliferation. Assuring our allies depends on their perceptions of U.S. strategic power in relation to that of the Soviets. Allied assessment of *trends* in the U.S.-Soviet strategic balance is a major factor affecting their perceptions.

The majority believes there is no pressing need to modernize the U.S. bomber force and questions the urgency of MX or any new ICBM program in the immediate future. They would place increasing reliance on sea-based forces as the heart of the U.S. deterrent. We share many of their doubts regarding the cost of the B-1 bomber program and the survivability of suggested MX deployments. We cannot share their conclusion that we can safely delay the initiation of these two programs. The overall effect of the majority's recommendations would be to slow the momentum of U.S. strategic programs, causing us to fall further behind the Soviet Union in the above-mentioned trends, and thereby increase perceptions of a growing imbalance between U.S. and Soviet strategic capability. This would have disastrous consequences for our international security relations.

The majority's conclusions on the B-1 are influenced by a view that additional spending on strategic forces will result in inadequate support for non-nuclear forces. They imply that there is a danger of overspending on strategic forces at the expense of non-nuclear forces, but no figures are produced to support this concern. Nowhere does the study suggest that presently planned strategic programs would unduly affect non-nuclear force capabilities, even if Congress reduces the defense budget. In fact, proposed strategic force outlays for the next several years represent under 15 percent of the total defense budget. Ignored is the equally cogent fact that if strategic power is insufficient to deter conflict escalation, the United States will be deterred from employing any forces. We need an appropriate balance, one not defined in this paper.

The majority is optimistic about the continuing penetrability of the bomber force and invulnerability of our submarines in the 1990s. This underlies their conclusion that B-1 and MX deployments can be safely deferred. We agree there is no *immediate* threat to either the survivability of the submarine force or the penetrability of a large portion of the combined bomber-cruise missile force. Nevertheless, we cannot wait until these threats are upon us to initiate new programs. We must hedge against future threats by beginning these programs now, because the strategic weapons acquisition process takes as long as a decade. The majority suggestion to rely heavily on sea-based forces involves unacceptable risk to our future security.

Arms control is an important portion of our overall security posture, but its role is not well captured by the majority's positions. These fail to acknowledge fully the limitations of arms control and give insufficient emphasis to alternative approaches that might better attain the original objectives of arms control—*a more stable military posture that reduces the risk of war.* We would put more emphasis on suggestions only briefly mentioned, stressing confidence-building measures and methods to reduce the risk of war, rather than limiting the number of weapons. On the basis of experience, there is no reason to believe that quantitative arms control schemes (embodied in the present INF negotiations and the approaches to START proposed in this paper) would contribute to these objectives. The paper makes some contributions to a more realistic approach to arms control, but we believe it is much too tentative in pressing for new approaches that would address stability more directly.

STATEMENT
by R. James Woolsey

Chapter 11 is a fair and professional effort to reflect the differing views of a relatively diverse group of individuals. The first three-quarters of the chapter admirably recognize that the Soviet Union has caused the current instability in the strategic equation. I would only point out that I believe it is too early to speak of trimming back the defense increases requested by the administration for FY 1983 and beyond. Some reorientation may prove to be in order, but increases that require moving from about 6 percent of gross national product devoted to defense to around 7 percent will almost certainly be necessary. Furthermore, it is not clear in mid-March of 1982 that the Reagan administration has deemphasized the effort to control the strategic competition through arms negotiations; there has certainly been some delay in making proposals while the new administration has determined its strategic program and set forth its position on theater nuclear forces in Europe. Once we see the nature of its strategic arms proposals, it will be possible to assess whether they are or are not compatible with something that all participants in this debate should strongly desire: a long-run approach toward strategic programs and arms control that can be sustained on a bipartisan basis regardless of changes in administrations.

The last quarter of the chapter, in my view, puts a bit too much weight on the importance of bilateral agreements about strategic forces between the United States and the Soviet Union—both politically and strategically. I believe that nonproliferation should be the first item on the arms control agenda and that renewed efforts in this area are vital if we are not to see the nuclear peace broken by nations other than the United States and the Soviet Union. Second, I believe that cooperative measures between the United States and the Soviet Union to reduce the chance of nuclear war occurring by accident or through attack by a third party—for example, significant improvements in the hotline—may be more important in reducing the risk of nuclear war than bilateral agreements on force structure. Third (and the paper makes this point indirectly), I believe that strong conventional forces are vital if we are to avoid putting a disproportionate emphasis on the role of nuclear weapons. And finally, it seems apparent to me that bilateral strategic arms control agreements between the United States and the Soviet Union can only be negotiated successfully if the Soviets are convinced that we can and will preserve a strong deterrent even if such negotiations are not successful, for whatever reason.

It seems to me important to keep such caveats in mind if our arms control negotiators are to resist the urgings occasionally communicated to them to reach an agreement, whatever the terms of that agreement might be. Such urgings may come from many quarters, including any administration's political advisors. But the only approach that would let us negotiate with the Soviets successfully in this field is one embodying the patience and firmness that were shown, for example, by Ambassador Llewellyn Thompson in his successful negotiations to conclude the Austrian State Treaty in the 1950s. A sense of the limitations in agreements proceeding from SALT or START thus seems to me both substantively and tactically essential.

In general I believe that both the Aspen Consortium and the chairman of this project, Barry Blechman, deserve a vote of thanks for the thoroughness and fairness with which this effort was conducted. For those interested in a reasoned approach to the very difficult problems of national security and arms control, whatever their substantive differences of opinion, it has been a model undertaking.

INDEX

ABMs (antiballistic missiles), 40,
  142, 144-45
  as ICBM defense, 141-42, 144-45
  limits on, 53
  safeguard system, 30
  space-based, 143-44
  technological advances, 141-45
ABM Treaty (1972), 30, 40, 59, 179,
  183, 187, 283
  advantages for Soviet Union,
    184-86, 187, 196
  advantages for United States,
    181-82, 196
  disadvantages for Soviet Union,
    186-87
  disadvantages for United States,
    182-84, 189-90
  future prospects, 179
  Interim Agreement on Strategic
    Offensive Forces, 187, 251
  modifications, 188-89, 284-85
  provisions, 196, 197n
  renegotiations, 189-92, 193, 196
  and SALT, 185
  Standing Consultative Commission,
    193, 196, 238, 286
  U.S. withdrawal from, 187-88
Accuracy of missiles. *See* Inertial
  systems

Afghanistan, 68, 72, 81, 84, 117,
  156, 248
Africa, 81
Air mobile systems, 134
Airborne warning and control systems
  (AWAC), 139
Aircraft, conventional U.S., 18-19
Aircraft, strategic U.S., 134-35
  See also specific aircraft
Angola, 68, 72, 81-82, 83, 227, 248
Antisubmarine warfare, 136
"Arc of crisis," 81
Armed Services Committee hearings
  on SALT II, 164-65, 170
Arms control
  American public opinion of, 2,
    156-59
  arguments against, 230-34
  and crisis stability, 237
  deep cuts treaty, 234-36
  limited nuclear test ban treaty
    (1963), 50, 161
  and LRTNF issue, 112-13, 119,
    124
  and nuclear deterrence, 126
  objectives, 237, 285-86
  priorities for reductions, 282
  and START, 234-36, 238-43
  verification problem, 122-23, 282

295

Central Committee Plenum, 63, 65
Chernenko, Konstantine, 63
China, 60, 68, 85
  arms assistance to, 68
  Nixon trip to, 182
  nuclear weapons of, 186, 191
  and Soviet relations, 72, 92
  and U.S. relations, 171
Circular error probable (CEP), 130,
  132, 134
Clausewitz, Karl Von, 58, 61
Cold war, 18, 19, 20, 73, 225
Command, control, communication
  and intelligence (C³I system),
  146–50, 188
  computer malfunctions in, 134, 146,
  150–51
  effect on crisis stability, 45, 237
  modernization, 38, 44, 45, 149,
  151–53, 265–68
  as target, 205–206, 266
  vulnerability, 38, 146–47, 150,
  265–68
Committee on the Present Danger,
  156, 157, 160
Containment doctrine. See Detente
Convention on Biological Weapons,
  283
Conventional weapons, 25, 41–42, 45,
  90, 261
  vs. nuclear weapons, 20–21, 43, 45,
  98
Counterforce attack. See Scenarios for
  nuclear war
Counterforce capabilities, 11, 22, 71,
  190
Counterforce dominance, 22–23
  See also Nuclear superiority;
  Retaliatory strike
Countervailing strategy, 35–36, 38,
  45. See also Strategic policy, U.S.
Countervalue second strike
  See Scenarios for nuclear war
Cranston Group, 176
Crisis stability, 37, 39–40, 45, 237,
  239
Cruise missiles, Soviet, 71–72
Cruise missiles, U.S., 32, 85, 101, 104
  on B–52 bombers, 127, 132
  ceilings for, 203
  detection of, 140–41
  See also Detection systems
  ground-launched, 33, 104

lethality, 132
modernization, 69, 132, 135,
  256–57
penetrativity, 140–41
terminal guidance system on, 130
Cuba, 82–83
Cuban missile crisis, 23, 29, 79, 86
Cutler, Lloyd, 167, 168, 174

D–5 missile, 212
December 1979 NATO decision
  See LRTNF
Decoys, 142–44, 184, 257
Defense spending, U.S., 263–65, 291,
  292
  effect of ABM Treaty on, 190–91
  on conventional weapons, 264–65
  vs. inflation, 69
  public opinion of, 159
  and SALT, 231
"Dense-Pack" deployment scheme,
  277
Detection systems, Soviet, 137,
  139–40
Detection systems, U.S., 147–50
  for aircraft, 134–49, passim, 255
  decoys in, 142, 184
  for cruise missiles, 140–41
  packet switching in, 149–50
  for reentry vehicles, 142
  for submarines, 136–39, 148
  See also Lasers; Radar; Satellites
Detente, 32, 61, 79, 85, 95, 117
  origins of, 80–81
  public opinion of, 160
  and SALT, 96–97, 223
Deterrence. See Extended deterrence
Dual key arrangements, 46n

Earle, Ralph, 168, 199–200
Einstein, Albert, 289
Eisenhower, Dwight D., 80
Electromagnetic pulse (EMP), 266
Electronic countermeasure systems
  (ECMs), 140–41, 144
  See also Stealth technology
England, 26, 186
Equivalent force relationship
  See Balance of power
Escalation control. See Flexible
  response; Nuclear war
Escalation dominance, 104

ABOUT THE EDITOR

Barry M. Blechman is presently vice president of the Roosevelt Center for American Policy Studies, where he directed its activities concerning foreign and defense policies.

A New York City native, Blechman received a masters degree from New York University then moved to Washington, D.C., where he worked for the U.S. Army and enrolled at Georgetown University, receiving a Ph.D. in international relations in 1971. Professionally, Blechman joined the staff of the Center for Naval Analyses, a government-sponsored research organization, in 1966, remaining there until 1971, when he became affiliated with the Brookings Institution. Among other responsibilities, he was head of Brookings' defense analysis staff and co-author of its annual analysis of the federal budget, *Setting National Priorities*. In 1976, he took leave from Brookings to work on the Carter/Mondale transition planning staff at the Office of Management and Budget. The next year he became assistant director of the U.S. Arms Control and Disarmament Agency. During his two and one-half years with the government, Blechman served as deputy chairman of the U.S. delegation for negotiations on arms transfers and as head of the agency's policy planning and coordinating staff. After leaving the government in 1979, Blechman became a senior associate of the Carnegie Endowment for International Peace, where he directed a study of the role of military forces in contemporary international politics.

Blechman's published works on defense issues include the widely respected study of politico-military operations, *Force Without War,* as well as *Strategic Forces, The Changing Soviet Navy, A Guide to Far Eastern Navies,* and numerous articles in newspapers and magazines. He has served as a consultant to the Department of Defense, the Rockefeller and Ford Foundations, several Congressional committees, the National Academy of Sciences, and private firms. He has taught at The Johns Hopkins University, Georgetown University, and the University of Michigan.

ABOUT THE
CONTRIBUTORS

Christoph Bertram has been director of the International Institute for Strategic Studies in London since 1975. In the fall he will assume responsibilities as foreign editor of *Die Zeit*.

William G. Hyland is a senior associate of the Carnegie Endowment for International Peace. During 1975–6, he was deputy assistant to the president for national security affairs.

Michael May is associate director at large and former director of Lawrence Livermore National Laboratory. In 1974 he was the Atomic Energy Commission's technical representative on the Threshold Test Ban Treaty negotiating team in Moscow. May has also been a member of the U.S. delegation to the Strategic Arms Limitation Talks and senior personal adviser to the secretary of defense for SALT.

Michael Nacht has been associated with Harvard University since 1973. He is presently an associate professor of public policy and associate director of the Center for Science and International Affairs. Nacht's degrees include a B.S. from New York University, M.S. from Case Western Reserve University, and a Ph.D. from Columbia University.

Joseph Nye is a professor of government at Harvard University. From 1977 to 1979 he served as deputy under secretary of state for security assistance, science, and technology. His degrees include a B.A. from Princeton and a Ph.D. from Harvard University. He is also co-editor of *Energy and Security* (Ballinger, 1981).

William J. Perry is currently managing partner of Hambrecht and Quist, an investment banking firm in San Francisco. He was under secretary of defense for research and engineering during the Carter administration. Perry has B.S. and M.S. degrees from Stanford University, and a Ph.D. from Pennsylvania State University, all in mathematics.

Alan Platt is a senior associate at the RAND Corporation. While preparing his chapter, he was a national fellow at the Hoover Institution of Stanford University. Platt has a B.A. from Princeton, a M.S. from the Johns Hopkins School of Advanced International Studies, and a Ph.D. from Columbia University.

Marshall D. Shulman is Adlai E. Stevenson Professor of International Relations and director of the Russian Institute at Columbia University. He served as special advisor on Soviet affairs to the secretary of state, with the rank of ambassador, from 1977 through 1980.

Walter B. Slocombe is a member of the Washington D.C. law firm of Caplin and Drysdale, Chartered. He served during the Carter administration as deputy under secretary of defense for policy planning (1979-81), and as principal deputy assistant secretary of defense (international security affairs) from 1977 to 1979. A graduate of Princeton, Slocombe studied law at Harvard and Soviet politics at Oxford.